FORCE AND FOLLY
*Essays on Foreign Affairs
and the History of Ideas*

M.I.T. Studies in Comparative Politics

Under the general editorship of Harold D. Lasswell, Daniel Lerner, and Ithiel de Sola Pool.

Personality and Culture in Eastern European Politics, Dinko Tomasic, 1964.

The Emerging Elite: A Study of Political Leadership in Ceylon, Marshall Singer, 1964.

The Turkish Political Elite, Frederick W. Frey, 1965.

World Revolutionary Elites: Studies in Coercive Ideological Movements, Harold D. Lasswell and Daniel Lerner, editors, 1965.

Language of Politics: Studies in Quantitative Semantics, Harold D. Lasswell, Nathan Leites, and Associates, 1965 (reissue).

The General Inquirer: A Computer Approach to Content Analysis, Philip J. Stone, Dexter C. Dunphy, Marshall S. Smith, Daniel M. Ogilvie, 1967.

Political Elites: A Selected Bibliography, Carl Beck and J. Thomas McKechnie, 1968.

Force and Folly: Essays on Foreign Affairs and the History of Ideas, Hans Speier, 1969.

Social Order and the Risks of War, Hans Speier, 1969.

FORCE AND FOLLY

Essays on Foreign Affairs and the History of Ideas

Hans Speier

The M.I.T. Press
Massachusetts Institute of Technology
Cambridge, Massachusetts, and London, England

Preface

MOST OF the papers presented here were written in the last ten years, so that this book may be regarded as a sequel to *Social Order and the Risks of War*, a collection of essays first published in 1952.

While the earlier volume reflected my interests as a student and teacher of sociology — including the sociology of war and of literature — and my experiences in government service, the present book bears the marks of more recent preoccupations. All but one of the essays in Part I were written either in discharging professional responsibilities at the RAND Corporation, or in response to intellectual stimulation by colleagues in an atmosphere unusually conducive to research on policy issues affecting national security. Part II contains papers in the fields of the history of ideas and of literature which have been of continuous interest to me.

The Introduction to Part II sets forth in some detail the reasons for including in the same volume essays on literary subjects, in particular certain portrayals of human folly, along with papers on the role of force in international affairs assembled in Part I.

At this point the reader need merely be warned against a possible misunderstanding which the title of this book unfortunately does not preclude. I neither subscribe to the general thesis that the use of force in national or international affairs is foolish, nor have I attempted to examine the specific circumstances in which the resort to force is indeed a sign of folly. As the first essay on "War and Peace in the Nuclear Age" indicates, I do not expect war to be abolished in the future. It is to be hoped, however, that future wars will be limited wars, since limited war is a more civilized form of conflict than is total war. While man may lack the intellectual power and moral strength to restrict violence in the future, it seems to me more reasonable to entertain the modest hope that he will manage to do so than to expect all war to be avoided. Thus, the title of this book is not meant to be understood as "The Folly of Force," and to the extent that the discussions in Part II deal with human foolishness, they treat this subject as a phenomenon in its own right.

All but one of the papers are reprinted here as originally written or published, the only exception being Chapter 3, in which I have revised the last section. The Introductions to Parts I and II as well as the introductory remarks to be found at the beginning of some of the chapters were written upon the suggestion of Harold D. Lasswell and Daniel Lerner, the editors of the series in which this book is included. I wish to thank them for the active interest they have taken in my writings and for encouraging me to prepare this volume for publication.

Five of the papers (Chapters 3, 4, 9, 11, and 12) have not been published before, and one of them (Chapter 7) has been available only in German. The other material is reprinted here from American and British books and journals. I am grateful to the following publishers and magazines for permission to republish from the original sources cited at the beginning of each chapter: Columbia University Press, New York, New York; Princeton University Press, Princeton, New Jersey; Prentice-Hall, Inc., Englewood Cliffs, New Jersey; Basic Books, Inc., New York, New York; *World Politics*, Princeton, New Jersey; *Survey*, London; *Social Research*, New York, New York; *Wehrkunde*, Munich; and the RAND Corporation, Santa Monica, California.

Herbert Goldhamer is co-author of one essay. I am indebted to him for allowing me to include Chapter 10 in this book. I also want to acknowledge with special thanks the cheerful and competent help of my secretary, Mrs. Richard Brown, in preparing the manuscript for the printer.

H. S.

Santa Monica, California
March 1968

Contents

I

Force

Introduction

In the period following World War II many students of national security have tried to divine the nature and outcome of a World War III, and some analysts at the RAND Corporation have made pioneering contributions to this endeavor. Work of this nature draws heavily on mathematics, physics, and on technological projections. To the analyst of World War III — a synthetic phenomenon — man comes into view, as it were, only as homo bellicosus, *rationally applying the means of destruction that are assumed to be available, in such a manner as to prevail at the least cost — however prevalence and cost be measured — much as in classical economics* homo economicus *was supposed to behave rationally in perfect competition for productive ends.*

Different from analyses of a World War III, past wars and the contemporary struggles for power below the threshold of total nuclear war are open to empirical study. So are the behavior of leaders and followers, of the fighting and working parts of the population, and the interrelations between political, economic, and military actions in such conflicts. Most of the essays in the first part of this book are empirical studies. They deal with conflicts of lesser intensity — political crises and wars limited in various ways: objectives, number of belligerents, area of conflict, and destructiveness of the weapons employed.

Two essays in Part I deal with methods of simulating conflict for the purpose of focusing attention on contingencies that might arise in the future.

The reader may disagree with the author not only on specific points in the following discussions but also with their underlying tenets. They had perhaps better be stated explicitly in this Introduction.

1. Thus far the nuclear age has been an age of political crises and nonnuclear wars. The exploitation of nuclear weapons has been confined to warnings and threats and to the creation of beliefs in the efficacy of nuclear deterrents.

2. *Since the early postwar years when the Soviet Union failed to take advantage of the demobilization of American forces and of the weakness of Western Europe, the Soviet government has not embarked upon further military conquests. Both the United States and the Soviet Union have avoided fighting, if not confronting, one another. This pattern of international behavior has stood the test of severe crises: the first Berlin crisis in 1948, the Soviet effort to crush the rebellion in East Germany in 1953, the Suez crisis and the Soviet intervention in Hungary in 1956, the second Berlin crisis lasting from 1958 to 1962, the Cuban missile crisis in 1962, and the Arab-Israeli war in June 1967.*

3. *This is not to say that the Soviet Union has no expansionist objectives. Nor is it meant to argue that the Soviet government has accepted U.S. superiority in nuclear power as an unalterable fact. Rather, the aims of Soviet security policy have been to defend against, to reach equality with, and if possible, to surpass U.S. nuclear power. Should this strenuous effort, the end of which is not in sight, ever be successful, it might not be necessary for the Soviet Union to wage war in order to reach its political objectives. It could "win" by creating and exploiting the fear of nuclear war in a far more effective manner than it has done in the past.*

4. *Although nuclear war has been avoided and the period of peace among the great powers following World War II has now been longer than that separating the two world wars, it cannot be concluded that nuclear weapons will not be used in the future. If the balance of power were upset by a unilateral technological breakthrough, there might be less talk about successful "crisis management" than there is now. Recklessness may replace prudence at any time in high places. Nor have passion and error been eliminated from human affairs merely because man can afford less than ever not to be reasonable and prudent.*

5. *For various reasons — strategic, economic, and political — the focal point of American security interests lies in Europe rather than in Asia. The Soviet Union, and not Communist China, has been and in the foreseeable future will continue to be America's most formidable adversary. This is assuming that the two most powerful Communist states will continue to be rivals rather than allies. As to Communist China, her foreign policy has been distinguished by caution. Given China's weakness in relation to Soviet strength and to the power of the United States, this is not surprising. Of course, the Chinese nuclear capability must be expected to grow (while*

that of the other present nuclear powers is unlikely to diminish). The main danger attending this development does not appear to be a military attack on the United States but the political exploitation of this capability for "blackmail" in Asia, principally India and Japan. In addition, it will be important for the Soviet Union and the United States in the 1970's to guard against the proliferation of Chinese and French nuclear weapons to other lands.

 6. The confrontation of the United States and the Soviet Union in Berlin and Germany continues to deserve the primary attention of American foreign policy. Even the maintenance of a regional balance of power in the Middle East — precarious as it will continue to be — is of greater importance to U.S. power and influence in the world than is the future of Vietnam, excluding the possibility that the United States will be humbled by North Vietnam. This seems to follow, since Communist domination of the Middle East would seriously jeopardize American security interests in Europe. By the same token, DeGaulle's stance on NATO, Vietnam, and the Arab-Israeli war in 1967 is detrimental to American interests not because of his theatrical defiance of the "Anglo-Saxons" but because of the effect his policy has had in Western Europe and Great Britain. The erosion of NATO, for which the United States is co-responsible, is the major unearned success of Soviet postwar foreign policy. No substitute for the American commitment to the security of Europe guaranteeing peace on that continent is in sight. Certainly, the power of France is no such substitute. The French need for protection is greater than the ability of France to guard the security of other middle and small powers. Furthermore, the effects of Bonn's disappointment with Washington may in time be aggravated by disenchantment with Paris, in which case it is conceivable that hapless Germans may yet wish to travel the road to Moscow.

 7. Although the focal point of American security interests abroad is central Europe, the danger of a global war does not reside exclusively in that area. In the tightly knit net of international relations global war may develop from a local conflict anywhere in the world, if either the Soviet or the U.S. government believe that vital interests are at stake.

CHAPTER ONE

War and Peace in the Nuclear Age

WHEN WE CONSIDER the relation between war and civilization, we face the disheartening fact that peace is no measure of civilized life. Wars have occurred throughout history, and in no civilization has peace been secure for a very long time.

Ours is a progressive civilization, and yet we have not conquered war. In past ages, which we sometimes call dark and unenlightened, large parts of the population lived in misery; the rich as well as the poor were exposed to pestilence; and famines took their toll among the masses of the people. In the modern era, scientific ingenuity has gradually eliminated or greatly reduced these hazards, at least in the West. Medicine has learned to cope with many of the natural risks to which man is exposed from infancy to old age. The average span of life has been doubled since the eighteenth century. We have even succeeded in greatly reducing the casualties among the wounded and in curtailing death from infectious diseases in wartime. Until the second half of the nineteenth century, the number of soldiers who fell victim to these causes of death exceeded the number of those killed in battle. At the same time, our peacetime comforts have multiplied. Science and technology have reduced the hardships of everyday life and lightened

From *Man's Right to Knowledge,* An International Symposium Presented in Honor of the Two-Hundredth Anniversary of Columbia University, 1754–1954, Second Series (New York: Columbia University Press, 1955).

the burdens that in earlier times pressed down upon the many, sparing only the privileged few.

In this age of progress, however, the conduct of war as well has changed: warfare has been industrialized. For every new labor-saving device we have developed, a more ingenious weapon has been put in the hands of man. Every machine to cheapen peaceful production has been matched by an instrument of violence more efficient than the cruder implements of the past. Thus the unprecedented progress of science and engineering has served Western society in peace and war alike; it has not promoted peace itself. As progress has enabled man to live more securely and more comfortably in peacetime, it has also lifted him to a higher plane of destructiveness in the wars which he has not been able to conquer. Enlightened as we are, can we really claim that ours is a more civilized age than the barbarous, dark times preceding gunpowder and the printing press, the steam engine and the harnessing of atomic energy to human designs?

The newest weapons which industrialized civilization has placed at the disposal of man reach far behind the lines of battle. Today, the airplane and the rocket threaten civilians as well as soldiers with violent death. Modern war has become a struggle between besieged nations in which both combatants and noncombatants participate. In certain phases of the second World War, the civilian casualties even exceeded those among soldiers — this was true during the Battle of Britain — and there is indeed no assurance that this perversion of civilized warfare may not become the pattern for the next war as a whole.

In previous ages, war was usually waged with the weapons available in arsenals at the outbreak of armed conflict or captured from the enemy in battle. In modern civilization, the instruments of war are produced and reproduced while the struggle lasts. Large parts of the civilian population, therefore, contribute to the war economy in all its phases, as producers, distributors, organizers, and propagandists. No longer are civilians exposed merely to the risks of foreign rule after a military defeat, but they must fear death from the sky and the destruction of their factories and homes while the battle rages. Such mutually inflicted death and destruction may well be the decisive event in a future war. For air power as well as atomic and thermonuclear weapons have become such that civilization as we know it may not be able to survive another world war.

No matter how much we may shrink from the lessons of history, the outstanding truth about the relation between civilization and war is that there have been civilized wars and uncivilized wars. A similar observation, I submit, can be made with regard to peace. Peace itself is no token of civilization. Whether or not a society at peace with its neighbors may be called civilized depends altogether upon the way of life which the people of that society lead. Man can be coarse and cruel in peacetime, and in certain circumstances he has been capable of conducting war in a civilized manner.

Second, we learn from history that the height of civilization which a society has reached cannot be gauged by the frequency with which it resorts to arms. Ancient Greece at the time of its glory lit the beacons of civilization which still shine in our time, however dimly; but Greece was not blessed with peace. The time of Louis XIV was called by Voltaire "the most enlightened age the world has ever seen," but during the reign of that king France embarked upon many wars against her neighbors.

The recurrence of war throughout history does not of course mean that man has always resorted to the sword for aggressive ends. Many countries have been embroiled in armed conflict in order to defend their way of life, their possessions, or their faith against aggressors. Sometimes wars have been waged for the maintenance of a prevailing balance of power. In general, power in international affairs has been attained and preserved through war, and in modern history the powerful nations have been at war more frequently than the small countries. During the last five hundred years, France, for example, has been engaged in about ten times as many battles as Sweden; and Austria, once a great nation, in eight times as many. The United States was free from major foreign wars from 1776 until 1917. History sounds the warning, however, that her new status as a world power is no guarantee of a peaceful future.

I have said that wars can be civilized. You might ask in what sense this statement can possibly be true. Men are killed in war, property is destroyed, and ruthlessness often rewarded. Since the productive capacity of society is used for destructive ends in war, how can war ever do anything but arrest or retard civilization? The answer is simply that civilized war is limited in nature: it is waged under certain constraints and restrictions. By contrast, uncivilized war is what we have become accustomed to calling "total war." In total war, no bounds are set to violence and treachery, except by the limitations inherent in the technical means of destruction that happen to be at man's disposal, whether they be swords, machine guns, or atomic bombs.

The conduct of war can be restricted in many ways. To begin with, the area of active warfare can be limited by tacit consent or explicit agreement among the belligerents. I am not thinking so much of respect for neutrality as of the more severe constraint manifest in sparing certain places in the enemy country the ravages of war. Such places may be sacred shrines or inhabited cities.

There is a moving letter which Totila, King of the Ostrogoths, received in the year 546, when he was about to turn the city of Rome "into a sheep-run." In it his opponent Belisarius, the general in command of Emperor Justinian's forces, reminded his barbarous enemy that Rome was the greatest and most glorious city under the sun. "If you should prove to be the conqueror," Belisarius wrote, "how great will be your delight in having preserved the most precious jewel in your crown. If yours should turn out to be the losing side, great will be the thanks due from the conqueror for your preservation of Rome, while its destruction will make every plea for mercy and humanity on your behalf inadmissible." Totila, the barbarian, did not destroy the city of Rome.

Certain time periods also may be considered unsuitable for warfare. In some civilizations, for example, the belligerents shrink from fighting at night. This constraint may be rooted in superstitious fear, or it may be caused by mere prudence, as was the case with the armies of Frederick the Great. Since his forces, like most of the harshly disciplined armies in the eighteenth century, were full of lowly men pressed into service, desertion was frequent, and night marches would have provided too many opportunities for escape.

The climate, of course, may rule out the winter season for warfare, particularly when supply of the armies with food and shelter is precarious. More interesting, however, than these constraints, imposed by fear, prudence, or the vicissitudes of nature, are limitations on the time of fighting for religious or moral reasons. Beginning in the eleventh century, the Church forbade private wars from Thursday evening until Monday morning and on religious holidays. The penalty for the infraction of this rule was excommunication. This so-called Truce of God contributed much to the internal pacification of France, Flanders, Germany, and Italy until the absolute state asserted its centralized authority.

Other constraints in war have been observed with respect to persons, such as women and children or, more generally, noncombatants. Violence against heralds and ambassadors has almost always been regarded as base treachery. If we assume that man's natural inclination is to abuse his power, we cannot be surprised that prisoners of war have been tortured and killed in many wars. Achilles dragged Hector triumphantly through the dust. The Babylonians cut off the heads of their slain enemies and piled them up in heaps, claiming thus "to augment their death."

Perhaps mercy has had little to do with changing such barbarous customs; it is certain, however, that the self-interest of the victor in obtaining ransom has entailed leniency toward prisoners. The interest in economic gain, however crude its manifestation, is a more civilized human trait than the unbridled enjoyment of power. For this reason, we find that interest in the enslavement of conquered peoples has exerted a civilizing influence upon warfare. When the victor wants labor or tribute from those he subjugates, lives must be spared, whereas conquerors who want the soil itself deal ruthlessly with the settlers that fall into their hands.

Constraints placed upon violence extend to weapons as well. In the Korean war, the atomic bomb, though available, was not used. As to the second World War, we know from Churchill's history that the employment of poison gas by the Germans was feared and that retaliation would have been both possible and swift. In contrast to the first World War, gas was not used. We must remember, however, that other customs of war were freely violated at the time, and other weapons, more effective than gas, were used in abundance and without scruples. Perhaps it was as much the conviction of the relative ineffectiveness and the mutual fear of retaliation as the Geneva Protocol of 1925 which caused the belligerents to abstain from gas warfare. Be that as it may, it remains true that in the last war with its scorched earth policy, its partisan warfare, its carpet bombing, its concentration camps, and its Katyn murders, one weapon dreaded by all was not used. By contrast, the Italians in the Ethiopian war, only a few years earlier, employed gas against the helpless natives in Africa.

Throughout history we find that man has refrained from using certain weapons at his disposal, or from using the same weapons against all enemies. In earlier periods of our civilization, for example, weapons that were not used in wars among Christians were employed against infidels.

If the technology of war alone were to determine the character of warfare, we should see the constraints of war disappear as science and technology progress. All wars of the past would have been more civilized than the conflicts of more recent times. This is evidently not the case. Genghis Khan was a more terrible war lord than Napoleon, if only because the latter did not raze the cities he conquered and slaughter the people he subjugated, but the barbaric horsemen would have been no match for Napoleon's artillery.

Every major technical advance in armament has led some people to bewail the depravity of man or to predict the doom of mankind. For instance, the invention of gunpowder appeared to many contemporary observers as an invention of the devil, because it did away with chivalrous combat and enabled the knave to slay his master from a safe distance. It seemed to destroy the virtues and shake the social foundations of an older society in which social class distinctions were strict and severe.

Or consider air power. It was first put to military use at the turn of the eighteenth century for the purpose of observing from captive balloons the dispositions of enemy forces in battle. This innovation was regarded as an outrage, and the men engaged in such unheard-of reconnaissance were threatened with execution as spies upon capture. Every major new and unconventional weapon has caused moral shock and indignation. In order to determine the complex nature of total war, however, we must look beyond the technology of fighting and indeed beyond the aims of war. We must look at the image man has of his enemy and his designs for the peace he hopes to establish. We must also take into account the social and economic structure of the belligerent societies.

Every war is waged for victory. But what constitutes victory? Winning a battle? A campaign? The occupation of a province or of the enemy's whole territory? The establishment of military superiority? The suppression of all organized resistance? The destruction of inhabited places? The enslavement or decimation of the enemy population? The conversion to another faith of the survivors on the enemy side? All these are possible war aims, and man has fought for the one or the other of them with crude and refined weapons. The nature of war depends not only on its technology or on the economic resources of the belligerents, but to a large extent also upon the notions of victory which the belligerents entertain. These notions in turn reflect the character of their society, their image of the enemy, and, above all, the kind of peace they seek.

Unrestrained violence and treachery are characteristic of civil wars and partisan warfare, of wars of religion and their modern equivalent, which we may call with Jomini, the military historian, "ideological wars"; they occur also in some colonial wars, when violence is not curbed by fear of retaliation and the savage strangeness of the enemy inspires horror. All these conflicts have one feature in common. The enemy is fought with intense hatred and with religious or moral indignation. His way of life, and indeed his very existence, is deemed offensive and atrocious — a denial of the true destiny of man. Such wars can have no end other than total subjugation of the vanquished by the victor and the subsequent attempt to undo and reform his way of life.

By contrast, limited wars are waged for limited objectives, the winning of a campaign or the occupation of a province. They are political instruments rather than struggles for survival or crusades to impose a superior order or form of life upon the vanquished. The peace following limited war leaves the enemy society intact and, as a rule, does not entail revolution or political upheaval, which has been the lot of the vanquished in major wars ever since the days of Napoleon.

Certain conditions are conducive to civilized, limited warfare. One of them is a division of international power which permits shifting alliances and therefore a shifting balance of power; another is the existence of common religious or moral bonds among the leading groups in the societies at war. When international power is balanced, wars are not abolished, but the belligerence and expansionism of any one power are checked by the self-interest of others striving to prevent permanent imbalance among all. Such conditions prevailed during the *Pax Britannica* which reached its peak in the nineteenth century; it was based on British sea power and the division of land power among many national states. When a common faith unites the belligerents despite their conflict, or when certain notions of honor and baseness in human conduct are shared by the ruling few on both sides, limits are set to violence and treachery in war. Such conditions existed in the period of the Truce of God and were absent in the Thirty Years War. They reappeared in the dynastic wars of the eighteenth century, although some of the restrictions of war at that time were imposed by economic necessity.

By contrast, the current international scene is darkened not only by the fearful progress in the technology of war but above all by the division of the world into two irreconcilably hostile systems of political belief. The intensity of this conflict has prevented the peaceful conclusion of the second World War.

In the past, military power could be measured by the armies a country was able to put into the field or by its naval forces. The power of Sparta, Rome, or Prussia was based upon armies, while Athens, Spain, and Great Britain owed their greatness to naval strength, colonies, and seaborne trade. Protected by the oceans and by their fleets against the peril of sudden invasion from the sea, naval powers have been able to extend their realms far beyond the borders of their homelands. Reliance upon naval power has extraordinary advantages for the structure of society. Imperiled or ambitious land powers do not easily escape a pull toward militarism in times of peace; naval powers, which need not maintain large armies, do. By militarism, in this context, I mean not so much the propensity to wage war as the organization of the civilian sector of society after the model of a military establishment. A society is militaristic if its civilian members behave like soldiers, value discipline above freedom, and pay more respect to valor than to work. Naval powers are less militaristic, not only because they are less in danger of invasion, but also because in war they can often afford not to commit large parts of their people to fighting on land. Unlike states which maintain large armies, naval powers can rely to some extent on the ground forces of their allies, making their contribution to victory in strategic defense of the sea lanes on which the coalition depends, and in wealth rather than blood. As Francis Bacon put it in his essay "On the

True Greatness of Kingdoms": "Thus much is certain, that he who commands the sea is at great liberty, and may take as much and as little of the war as he will."

While in some measure Bacon's observation still holds, the advent of air power has reduced the importance which in the past attached to the command of the sea. Air power not only supports those who fight the ground battle but can be employed over long distances in devastating attacks upon many targets, including the war economy of the enemy. Like naval strength, superior air power is a guardian of peace as well as a bulwark against the militarization of society. Like the development of naval power, but unlike that of land armies, the evolution of air power is closely linked to the peaceful extension of travel and trade.

There are important differences, however, between naval and air power. While the rise of naval power is contingent upon access to the sea, air power can be developed against the natural obstacles of geography by any great country possessing large economic resources and sufficient technical skill. It is easier for a great land power to attain supremacy in the air than it is for it to seize command of the seas. Furthermore, we cannot afford to regard air power only as a deterrent from war, but must recognize the fearful temptation it may present: under modern conditions of technology, surprise attack may amount to surprise devastation, if not to victory.

Thus, modern civilization is faced with a task of fatal urgency. Unless man can find ways of limiting war, modern civilization itself may perish. The difficulties of civilizing warfare are today far greater than the capacity of the major powers to wage total war with ever fewer restrictions and ever fewer survivors. Today, it is no longer a common belief in the dignity and destiny of man, but only prudence and fear, that can prevent total war. And yet, in the light of reason the efforts to avert total war hold more promise of success than the hope for freedom from all war. It still is easier, as it has always been, for man to restrict war than to establish peace on earth.

CHAPTER TWO

International Political Communication: Elite vs. Mass

The following essay was written at a time when some distinguished Americans believed that massive doses of information and political enlightenment administered to foreign nations could defeat world communism and insure peace. The essay takes issue with this optimistic view for three main reasons.

First, international political propaganda is not a stream of words freely flowing from one geographical area to another. It is directed at foreigners living under foreign law. The political authorities in the "target" country control the access to foreign propaganda. They can impede such access by jamming foreign broadcasts, by licensing receiving equipment, by censoring and confiscating printed and written materials, and by imposing fines, imprisonment, or death upon citizens who disseminate foreign propaganda. The authorities may, of course, pursue instead a liberal policy permitting the citizens free access to foreign communications or actually safeguarding and facilitating it. Which policy will be adopted depends on the nature of the foreign political system, which may be headed by a dictator or a democratically elected man, on the stability and legitimacy of the government, on the confidence it has in the loyalty and judgment of the people it governs, on the nature of its relations with the country from which the propaganda emanates, and on the "content" of that propaganda. In any event, the power of the "receiver" to control access to foreign

From *World Politics*, Vol. 4 (April 1952).

communications exceeds the power of the "sender" to insure the reception of his messages.

Second, the ultimate aim of international propaganda is not to change opinions, affect attitudes, or create moods. It is something more tangible, namely political action. In a free country, people who change their political opinions sometimes change their actions accordingly, for example by withdrawing their "support" of one officeholder in favor of his opponent, by criticizing the former in public so as to convert others to their critical view, or in other ways. Illiberal political regimes not only prevent the conversion of popular doubt and criticism into action against them, but also suppress doubts and disseminate approved news and opinions. In order to be effective, propagandists must know what they can possibly accomplish. The most important limits of their accomplishments are set by the political conditions under which their audiences live. It is therefore important for propagandists to know precisely what their audience can do.

A few illustrations may be in order. In a dictatorship, it is not possible for the masses to vote their government personnel out of office; the ruling elite itself preserves or changes its own composition. In war, a foreign population cannot surrender, regardless of the character of the government; only the government or the fighting forces can do so. Elements of the civilian population cannot "desert" like soldiers, provided the latter know or are told how to desert and do not fear mistreatment after capture. In the face of police terror, workers risk violent death when they embark upon a political strike, although they may be able to engage in malingering with impunity.

Third, if actions, and not changes in attitude, are the ultimate aim of international propaganda, it is erroneous to believe that all people in the "target" country are equally important political actors. As regards foreign policy, the foreign government, i.e., the governing "elite," usually is more important than are the "masses" of the population, but an incipient "counter-elite," formed by leaders of secret or open oppositional elements of the population, may vie for the loyalty of the masses. Such oppositional elements may be disloyal to their government for ethnic, religious, racial, economic, or "political" reasons. If they are organized as a "resistance movement" opposed to their government, they occupy a position between the ruling elite and the masses, and foreign propagandists may use them as "social relay points" for reaching larger masses by a circuitous route, as it were.

My interest in political propaganda dates back to the last years in the Weimar Republic where both right and left wing extremists tried to undermine law and order. I noticed that their fierce mutual enmity did not prevent exchanges of terroristic personnel or occasional close cooperation between the Communists and the National Socialists, as in the 1932 strike that paralyzed public transportation in Berlin.

In the early years of World War II, prior to Pearl Harbor, I was co-director of the Research Project on Totalitarian Communications in New York, analyzing closely the content and techniques of German radio broadcasting, both domestic and foreign. The work was summed up in a book on this subject published in 1944, of which I was co-editor (with the late Ernst Kris) and one of the authors. While learning in these years a great deal about Goebbels and his activities, I helped to train younger social scientists in the techniques of content analysis, a field in which Harold D. Lasswell had made the pioneering effort in the 1930's. In 1942, many of my colleagues and students rejoined me at the Foreign Broadcast Intelligence Service of the Federal Communications Commission, where I was in charge of analyzing German wartime propaganda. Later during the war I became Propaganda Policy Advisor at the Overseas Branch of the Office of War Information. Beginning in 1944 I witnessed the transition of U.S. postwar policy from its early punitive stance — disarming, de-Nazifying, deindustrializing Germany — to its anticommunist phase involving West Germany's imposed democratization and rearmament, and her reindustrialization with Marshall Plan aid. In those years I was Associate Chief of the Occupied Areas Division in the Department of State.

Thus, for a period of more than ten years I had good opportunities in two countries to observe and participate in international political propaganda or, as the British used to say during the war, "political warfare." I was at a vantage point permitting me to study both clandestine and regular communications, Nazi as well as American propaganda, the making no less than the execution of communications policy, the problem of cooperation between British and American agencies as well as that of settling intragovernmental conflicts in the United States during and after the war. All this time, social scientists along with journalists, poets, movie directors, and military officers struggled not only with the enemy but also with civilian officials of their own government who were horrified by an

invasion of unprecedented patriotism and naiveté into their do-
main of traditionalism and bureaucratic calm. In those years, I
learned about the effects of speech in relation to the impact of
terror and military force in international life.
The present paper is a by-product of other studies of public
opinion and international communication that I undertook
during and after World War II. Chapters 5 and 6 in this vol-
ume deal with atomic blackmail, a salient feature of interna-
tional communication in the nuclear age; they draw upon my
understanding — such as it is — of the relation between force
and persuasion that I had first gained in observing Paul Joseph
Goebbels and Elmer Davis in a context of operations con-
ducted by para-military and military forces.

IN THE SECOND HALF of the seventeenth century, European philosophers began to regard the enlightenment of ignorant and
prejudiced people as a means of reducing persecution and of
promoting just and reasonable government. In international
affairs, the first dramatic application of this doctrine occurred
during the wars of the French Revolution when diplomacy, the
traditional form of elite communication, was supplemented by
missionary appeals to the common man on the enemy side.
Since that time, the technology of communication has greatly
improved; ever larger literate masses of the population participate in politics and war; the social homogeneity of the political
elites in various nations has been lost, and in the West the ideas
of liberty and equality have been drained of their revolutionary
power.

In the United States, the notion that international understanding and peace can be promoted by enlightenment across
national frontiers survived the First World War and the establishment of the post-democratic, Communist and Fascist, regimes. During the Second World War, the American foreign
propaganda effort was ostensibly conducted according to a
"strategy" of truth — the manipulative twentieth-century equivalent of enlightenment. Soon afterwards, the old belief in the
affinity of international harmony and enlightenment was incorporated in a burst of remarkable optimism in the Constitu-

tion of UNESCO.[1] The notion that wars can be prevented if only a large enough number of ordinary, good, and reasonable people dislike the evil designs of the men whom power has corrupted, survives in the opinion that social psychologists can relieve international "tension" because they know how to measure ignorance and study prejudice in their home towns. In the meantime, the conflict between the Soviet bloc and the Western alliance has nonetheless sharpened, but the belief in the benefits to be derived from the political enlightenment of large foreign masses continues to be proclaimed with force and conviction, albeit in language which confirms the distance between our enlightened age and the age of Enlightenment. Senator William Benton has advocated a "Marshall plan of ideas," General Eisenhower has spoken of the need for a "truth bomb," Paul G. Hoffman has put forth proposals to "wage the peace" "on the information front."

Other voices have been less sanguine about the beneficial effects of international mass communication. Thus, George Kennan wrote:

> It is a shallow view of the workings of history which looks to such things as foreign propaganda and agitation to bring about fundamental changes in the lives of a great nation. . . .

> Any attempt at direct talking by one nation to another about the latter's political affairs is a questionable procedure, replete with possibilities for misunderstanding and resentment. That is particularly true where spirit and tradition differ and the political terminology is not really translatable. This appreciation in no way weakens the importance of the "Voice of America," the function of which, with respect to Russia, is to reflect as faithfully as possible the atmosphere and attitudes of this country. . . .[2]

There are many conflicting reasons for such skepticism concerning the political worth of international mass propaganda.

---

[1] For a critical discussion of the opinion that the origins of war can be found in the minds of the masses of men, see Frederick S. Dunn, *War and the Minds of Men* (New York: Harper and Row, 1950).

[2] George Kennan, "America and the Russian Future," *Foreign Affairs,* Vol. 29 (April 1951), pp. 368–369.

Apart from the opinion widespread in Protestant middle-class civilization that "propaganda" is a form of deceit and therefore immoral, specialists often regard other instruments of policy — e.g., diplomacy, armaments, economic measures — as both more respectable and more effective in the pursuit of foreign policy than the activities of journalists and radio script writers, or of the producers and distributors of motion pictures. Moreover, the technicians of the modern mass media are separated from the Foreign Service personnel by differences in their respective professional codes of behavior — differences which give rise to reserve, impatience, irritation, misunderstanding, and sometimes distrust. By tradition and experience, the Foreign Service personnel is inclined to observe time-honored ways of communicating with their peers in other capitals and to view communications to peoples at large as either wasteful or dangerous. Their preference is consequently for negotiation with their foreign colleagues and is linked with a deeply rooted aversion to techniques and procedures which interfere with the sovereignty of foreign states. And indeed, no degree of righteousness and veracity in mass propaganda directed at another state can alter the fact that the propaganda aims often are subversive. Traditionally in foreign affairs, communications between political elites are persuasive efforts which do not attack directly the power position of other elites in their home countries, i.e., their relations with the masses they govern. Mass propaganda, which does not support allied and friendly governments in their fight against domestic opposition and counterelites, does precisely that by promoting strife and actions which restrict the freedom and, in extreme cases, the security of a hostile elite. For, ultimately, propaganda does not aim at changes in popular "attitudes" and "public opinion" abroad but at politically relevant actions.

Thus no less than sovereignty is at stake in international mass communication. This fact has been realized with particular clarity and of course without pain in antidemocratic regimes. The Soviets, in fact, regard peace as a continuation of war by other means and hold that foreign subversive propaganda without concomitant organizational efforts (which are even more sharply focused on subversion) cannot possibly be an effective instrument of policy. Basically, the Soviets use international mass communication like the more radical forms of subversion and like all other policy instruments, in order to *win* the international struggle for power, whereas in the West it is still widely believed that enlightenment across national frontiers may *abolish* that struggle. It is therefore easily felt that the interference with sovereignty which mass communication involves must be pardoned in view of its lofty goal, and the unwillingness of the experienced skeptics to do so is readily traced by the enthusiasts to the intimate involvement of the skeptics in the continuing struggle for power.

There is no adequate evidence to support the opinion that free international mass communications reduce conflict in foreign affairs. Given the lack of adequate data, there is little point in reiterating that they have or do not have this political value. It may be useful, however, to consider briefly a few *specific political conditions* without which international communications cannot possibly result in desirable actions. The main point of reference in this discussion will be the measure of control that can be exercised over politically relevant actions by the communicating and the receiving powers respectively. Clearly, international communication can be the more effective as an instrument of foreign policy the less stringently the power against which this policy instrument is used controls the responses of its citizens. Correspondingly, the communicating power having no direct control over these actions and trying to influence the motivations of people it does not govern has a better chance of being successful if it can or does employ other instruments of policy in conjunction with "communications." The most radical case in point is of course the use of violence in times of war, either in order to eliminate the enemy government or to create a situation which induces that government to yield to persuasion backed up by preponderance of force.

The following discussion will disregard many ramifications of the processes under review, especially the so-called "cultural"

predispositions of the target population, e.g., literacy, superstitions, "good will" toward the communicating power; the moral
restraints or the considerations of expediency which may limit
the exploitation of existing favorable conditions and the efforts
at their creation, e.g., the employment of assassins; and, finally,
the skills and arrangements needed for exploiting favorable
conditions, e.g., proper combination of *all* available instruments
of policy by the communicating power.

The effectiveness of mass communication with foreign audiences depends on the extent to which these audiences can be
reached. The communicating power can attempt to increase
the accessibility of the communications by technological improvements — say, by installing more powerful transmitters for
broadcasting — but the receiving power can counteract such
measures by jamming, confiscation of printed matter, and by
severe punishment of political curiosity among its citizens.
Whether or not it does act in this way depends, of course, on
the form of government and on the political relations of the
powers concerned. Democratic governments do not restrict accessibility, dictatorships do; access to communications from
allied and friendly powers is less likely to be barred than access
to enemy communications. In time of war, the struggle for accessibility becomes more intense; it is impossible to say to what
extent the offensive power succeeds in recouping through
grapevine communications what it loses because of tightened
control of the defensive power.

In general, the optimum offensive strategy in the wartime
struggle for accessibility does not seem to be that of increasing
the output of mass communications, but rather that of feeding
information to organized resistance groups in the receiving
country which can function as social relay stations. This may
be called *group communication* as distinguished from mass or
elite communications [see below].

The communicating rather than the receiving power has
monopolistic control in peace as well as war over the status
and prestige of the communicator. The communicating power
can maximize the attention which its output receives by per-

sonalizing its source and in particular by letting it originate with persons of high authority.

During World War II, certain commentators in all major belligerent countries, like Lord Haw Haw, Tokyo Rose, General Dittmar, succeeded in building up audiences which were theirs in much the same way in which domestic commentators or columnists have a personal following. Even more important perhaps is the intermittent participation of highly placed persons in international mass and group communication. An interview Stalin gives is a more powerful communication to the Western world than an opinion expressed by a battery of unknown Stalinists. Goebbels' wartime articles and broadcasts were carried on the front page of the *New York Times*. The United States made no corresponding efforts to increase the effectiveness of its communications by utilizing the prestige of a government spokesman. Elmer Davis ceased broadcasting when he became Goebbels' official counterpart.

Similarly under monopolistic control of the communicating power are those communications which do not depend on uncontrollable events or on actions taken by other powers, but which arise from the political, military, or economic initiative of the communicating power. Clearly, such initiative is, above all, a consequence of power, but foresight, imagination, willingness to take calculated risks, and coordination in the use of all policy instruments can compensate for inferior power. Witness the Soviet peace campaign or Soviet propaganda activities in Iran during World War II. No professional skill in communications can compensate for lack of power, planning, and coordination.

Since the ultimate aim of international communication is response in the form of politically relevant action, its efficacy varies with the freedom of political action which the receiving power permits its citizens. In democracies this freedom is relatively great; under dictatorships it is small. It is therefore a democratic fallacy to assume that the masses of the population can always act according to their political preferences. In dictatorships political preferences are shaped by the government and made public; if they remain private they are either hidden and inconsequential or betrayed and disastrous to the dissenters. This is true in peace as well as in wartime. Civilian dissenters cannot desert like soldiers; if they engage in deviant political behavior they run severe political risks in addition to the hazards of life under tyranny. In wartime they increase the military risks which they suffer anyhow in modern battle. The importance of this consideration cannot be overestimated: the control of the most crucial condition of effective mass communication, namely, freedom of responsive deviant behavior, is exercised not by the communicating but by the receiving power. Disregard of this condition — the power structure in the target area — makes for callousness among the propagandists and inefficacy of their output.

The political constraints imposed upon deviant political behavior have gained increased importance with the improvements in the techniques and organization of violence which have strengthened the power of dictatorial elites. The modern state disposes of streamlined instruments of intelligence, domestic communication, and repression of dissent, while the corresponding instruments of the opposition are technically obsolete. The technological differences between civil wars in the preindustrial age and in modern times are as great as those between a sermon in a church and a broadcast over a national hook-up. Barring defeat in a major war, the primary condition of the fall of a totalitarian regime is not "tension" or dissatisfaction among its masses, but organized defection among the armed forces and the police, who have access to the modern means of violence. Propaganda planners who disregard this rule of thumb transact their vernacular business in a dead language.

Even in totalitarian regimes, however, the means of domestic intelligence, communication, and control are not invariably in a state of top efficiency. In fact, they may become less reliable through infiltration, sabotage, defection, and kidnaping, or they may be disrupted by force. To the extent that this occurs, opportunities for mass action against the regime re-emerge. In war, the communicating power can enhance the efficacy of its mass communication by weakening the means of domestic control at the disposal of the receiving power. Unfortunately, long-range weapons are socially not highly selective. They cannot easily be so used as to spare the mass of the people and rid it of its police. Disorganization resulting from weapons of mass destruction disrupts life in general rather than merely the political control apparatus. It is difficult to predict which of the following responses among the survivors of mass attacks will be predominant: transitory panic, apathy, localized revolts against the authorities, increased dependence of the population upon the authorities for the immediate alleviation of acute misery, and so forth. Purposeful revolutionary activities can in no case be expected to result naturally from large-scale destruction and carnage, whether preceded or followed by international mass appeals to rise among the ruins. Rather, the essential prerequisite of such activities is a revolutionary organization that accepts politically and survives physically the attacks of the enemy.

Socially selective means of violence, such as assassinations, may lead to severe repressive measures and thus be inopportune, viz. the extermination of Lidice after the killing of Heydrich — a risk which the British perhaps miscalculated prior to the event. Plausible *threats* against Germans in high authority were of considerable effectiveness in occupied Poland.

Generally speaking, the basic task of the offensive power is not to break the morale of the people who live under a dictatorial regime, but to create both the morale conditions and the material prerequisites of effective action against that regime. The disruption of social relationships in general is likely to be an ineffective means toward this end unless supplemented by positive measures. Some of these measures can be adopted by the communicating power only in time of war, since overt resort to them in time of peace would almost certainly constitute a *casus belli*. Others can be taken by the communicating power in time of peace, if its political elite is willing and able to face the inevitable risks involved in their adoption, to estimate their consequences, and to reconcile the domestic interests favoring or tolerating their use with those opposing them.

To be specific, in order to increase the effectiveness of mass communications, the communicating power must take account of, and facilitate, the rise of organizations in the target society which it can enlist as operating allies. It appears that in dictatorial target societies the emphasis will have to be on organization rather than on interests at large, which was sufficient in nineteenth-century practice. By addressing such organizations a double gain ensues. Diffused and unfocused communications directed at anonymous audiences with an unknown capacity for action are replaced by focused communications with known activist elements of the population. In addition, the recipients themselves can serve as brokers in the further processing and spreading of communications. The knowledge of local political conditions and opportunities which can guide them in the performance of that function exceed those of the distant communicating power. The process can be compared with establishing operating bases in foreign territory.

During World War II, such opportunities of group communication were exploited almost exclusively in countries occupied by the enemy. Recently, General Bor-Komorowski has given an impressive account of the propaganda activities in which the Polish underground engaged when Poland was occupied by the Germans. The Polish underground press, periodicals, and other publications, as well as leaflets and pamphlets — no less than 200,000 copies of various printed items per day — relied to a large extent on British overt broadcasting for its main supply of news.[3] No mass communication from abroad could possibly have achieved comparable results by a direct and unfocused effort, i.e., without the aid of organizations in the target area. If it is true that a major prerequisite of mass communication to a country under hostile and stern political and military control is the utilization of social relay points within that country, accessibility is not only a problem of the

[3] T. Komorowski, *The Secret Army* (New York: The Macmillan Company, 1951), pp. 164 ff.

technology of communication, as mentioned above, but of the political relationship between governments and of the utilization of organized groups in the target area.

If the relations between the communicating power and the government in the target area are friendly, organizational efforts in support of group communication can be made by nongovernmental associations and organizations with international ties.

Since dictatorial elites do not tolerate such ties and the organization of legal opposition, the communicating power must decide how far it is prepared to violate the sovereignty of hostile dictatorial powers by supporting illegal organizations through funds, weapons, intelligence, liaison personnel, and in other ways. In time of war, this problem is faced with less inhibition than in time of peace, particularly by powers forced to look for allies because of military weakness, or anxious to trade political commitments to foreign resistance groups for sacrifices in native blood, or overreacting in war to the futile utopianism of a preceding period of peace. Political elites with a conspiratorial past and doctrine have no qualms about applying radically subversive techniques in peacetime, if expedience favors their employment.

The formation or support by the communicating power of puppet governments and governments-in-exile for the target society is another political measure which affects the influence of international mass communications on that society. It is a measure that can be used either sincerely or for purposes of deception and that demonstrates dramatically the political intent which the communicating power must convey to the masses it wants to act in its favor. In addition, organized and recognized counter-elites may facilitate the organization and more efficient action of any group or mass opposition to the hostile elite. Finally, such counter-elites can speak in their own name against the elites whose legitimacy is contested.

In time of peace the support of counter-elites, not to mention their diplomatic recognition, is usually a matter of refusing recognition of a revolutionary change of government, viz. current relations of the United States with the two Chinese governments. Wartime conquests offer many more opportunities for establishing counter-elites as "puppets," particularly in countries occupied only in part. Correspondingly, the loss of whole countries in consequence of military defeat can be politically softened by holding on, through governments-in-exile, to the fiction that the sovereignty of allied states is not injured. The advantage which the communicating power gains by such political maneuvers must ultimately be secured by force, i.e., by the consolidation and territorial expansion of power in the case of puppet governments or by reconquest of territory in the case of governments-in-exile.

In either case, some elements of the target population that had supported, or accommodated themselves to, the actually ruling elite will have secretly waited and hoped for the day of "liberation." To the extent that the communicating power was able to sustain such hopes and to turn them into realistic expectations, it will have added greatly to the credibility of *all* its communications and thus to their effectiveness. The emphasis is on "realistic." The arousal of premature expectations or of unjustified hopes damages the influence which the communicating power may otherwise exert. By the same token, expectations of liberation can be more readily aroused if the main military instruments of the communicating power are ground forces, which are poised to strike and advance, rather than air or naval forces.

These observations on the importance of outside relief of inside opposition to the ruling elite apply not only to situations in which puppet governments or governments-in-exile compete with the ruling elite for the loyalties and support of the target population, but also to situations in which no counter-elites are diplomatically recognized by the comunicating power. For example, the threat to noncommunists, and the hopeful expectations on the part of the communists, that the Red Army may be near and powerful enough to "liberate" Western Europe, increases the impact of all Soviet communications to Western Europe today, including Soviet peace propaganda.

The communicating power controls, of course, the content of its communications. It can turn this control to maximum advantage by appreciating the risks and feasibility of all actions which it wishes the target population to undertake. During World War II, all belligerents repeatedly violated this principle by rhetorical demands from a safe distance that the impossible be done by those to whom doing the possible held much danger. For example, after August 1941 Soviet propaganda attempted for years to incite the Poles to act precipitously against the Germans, but the Soviet armed forces facing Warsaw did not come to the support of the insurgent Poles when many thousands of them died battling the common enemy.

Concern of the communicating power with the risks which deviant political behavior abroad involves is only a specific way through which the communicating power can demonstrate its general intention to respect the interests of those whose actions it tries to influence. The communicating power increases the effectiveness of its international information and propaganda, as it generalizes this concern so as to find in all its endeavors the point where its own interests can be reconciled with those of its allies, whether they be sovereign states or an organized opposition in the enemy camp.

In time of war, inevitable difficulties arise in reconciling the interest in the most efficient use of violence with that of sparing allies in the enemy camp, i.e., friendly populations in territory occupied by the enemy or opposition in the territory ruled by the enemy elite. As Mr. Churchill and others have related, Allied bombing of targets in German-occupied Western Europe during the last war created conflicts with the governments-in-exile and there was apprehension in Allied councils of unfavorable repercussions among the affected populations. Nevertheless, by means of discretion in the selection of targets and by forewarnings, an alienation of the organized resistance was avoided. It is more difficult to say whether popular resentment as well was reduced, since its possible cause was superseded by successful liberation. Focused and well-timed communications attempted at any rate to minimize the undesired material and psychological effects of the bombing of Western Europe.

It is of major importance to the issue under review that while the technical means of communicating ideas, particularly to anonymous masses of recipients, have greatly improved and will undoubtedly improve further, the faith which great ideas used to inspire — or at least the fervor with which they were spread — seems to have notably lessened. In addition to the pertinent observations to that effect which Kris and Leites have made,[4] it may be pointed out that the easy counterfeit use of great words like liberation, democracy, peace, and justice aggravates the weariness, distrust, and privatization with which all official inspirational or conversion propaganda has to contend. The trend toward greater factualness seems irresistible, at least in the West. Behind the Iron Curtain, liberation may still be an idea which the controlling authorities have to fear and combat, particularly in satellite areas, while they can use it to their own benefit in Asia.

If there is indeed such a trend toward greater factualness in saying things, it would be conceivable that there is also a trend toward greater violence in doing things; and the future of propaganda to foreign masses may belong to threats and speechless horror rather than to ideologies in an epoch in which at moments of greatest turbulence the masses do not act but merely suffer.

[4] Ernst Kris and Nathan Leites, "Trends in Twentieth Century Propaganda," in *Psychoanalysis and the Social Sciences*, Vol. 1 (New York: International Universities Press, 1947).

CHAPTER THREE

The Political Value of Arms

The popular preoccupation with military deterrence in the nuclear age has grown from two roots — the unprecedented destructiveness of nuclear arms and the concern over Soviet expansionism after World War II, when Russian mobilized manpower had no match on the continent of Europe; in the late 1940's the second strongest conventional force-in-being in Europe was that of — Yugoslavia. Those were the years when Churchill — and not only he — believed that peace in Europe was safeguarded only by the atomic capabilities of the United States. Not much later Russia acquired atomic and nuclear arms of her own. Attention then turned to "mutual deterrence," as though American aggression as well could be checked only by fear of nuclear retaliation.

Deterring military aggression is not a novelty of the nuclear age. It is as old as is international conflict, and below that level it is as universal as is the respect of the weak for the strong or the fear of the weak when the strong confront them. Basically, deterrence is as old and as universal as are threats and counter-threats, the defiance of threats or the yielding to threats, the expectations of threats and efforts to be better prepared to meet them.

Understanding the nature of "deterrence" is simple as long as one eschews simplifying precision in talking about it and as long as one realizes that only men, not weapons, can be deterred. Both the adherence to inapplicable standards of pre-

Based on a paper presented at the annual meeting of the American Sociological Society, Seattle, Washington, August 1958. The last section was revised in 1967.

*cision and the reification of the phenomenon are bound to lead
the analysis of deterrence astray.*

*Beginning in World War II and especially after its end, a
new type of civilian expert made his appearance in government councils and in research organizations serving the
governments of nuclear powers. Among advisors, professional
competence in mathematics, nuclear physics, other natural
sciences, and various branches of technology was added to
competence in geography, law, and economics, which had
traditionally been valued most highly in government. The new
advisory elite was accustomed to regard political and moral
studies as "unscientific," because inevitably only few results of
such studies can be presented in quantitative terms and many
of them are controversial. Nor had education and training
prepared this elite to deal with problems that do not stay
solved once a solution has been found. Unfortunately, in international life few problems are ever solved permanently.*

*Deterrence cannot be studied without estimates of the bal-
ance of forces, without assessments of their performance, and
without calculations of damage and losses presumed to be inflicted or suffered in war. In an age of the most rapid technological change, these and related aspects of deterrence can
indeed be analyzed only with the help of the new advisory elite.
But deterrence remains nevertheless a political problem. It involves the passions and interests of politicians and statesmen
in commanding positions, who are more or less well informed,
estimate the power of their foreign adversaries more or less
correctly, and are not infallible in calculating the costs, hazards,
and gains of war. Thus, inevitably, in the analysis of deterrence
there remain uncertainties. And when a modern scientist faces
uncertainty that appears to be irreducible, he is perhaps more
deeply disturbed than the professional student of political life.
It is my impression that the new advisory elite, no less than
ordinary men subject to bias — whether it stems from feelings
of guilt, vengefulness, righteousness, or pride — do not excel
historians or professional students of contemporary politics in
the ability to control bias. In "scientific" analyses of deterrence
it seems to me that a specifically "scientific" bias consists in
imprudently belittling the weight of uncertainty.*

*Deterrence, like diplomacy, works on decisions before they
are made, i.e., on uncertainty. But diplomacy, which presupposes direct contact and the exchange of words between persons, permits the exploration of uncertainty, whereas deterrence
acts upon the mind in an uncertain manner. The following*

*essay attempts to call attention to some of the uncertainties
involved in deterrence. It sets forth some of the general conditions on which the political value of nuclear weapons depends.
The last section consists of ten propositions on the peacetime
exploitation of the political value of arms in the nuclear age.
Chapters 5 and 6 deal with related subjects.*

Military Worth and Political Value of Arms

ON ALL LEVELS of technology — primitive or advanced, nonnuclear or nuclear — arms have political value as well as military worth. Their military worth is established through use in
war. In peacetime, it can be estimated with varying degrees of
accuracy, from past wartime performance and from the result
of tests, maneuvers, and war games. The political value of
arms is more elusive than their military worth, since it is constituted in the minds of men.

The effect of weapons that have been used in war can be
gauged by the casualties they have caused, the destruction and
disorganization they have inflicted upon the enemy or the territory they have denied him through occupation, blockade, devastation, or in other ways. As a rule, any of these effects involve
certain losses incurred in meeting enemy resistance and coun-
terattack. Military worth is therefore the measure of a balance
of gains and losses established by the use of weapons in earnest.
This balance may be struck for weapon components, one or
several weapon systems, or for the way any or all of them were
employed. Similarly, the military worth of weapons may vary
with the unit of time on which analytical attention is focused
— a battle, a campaign, a phase of the war, the war as a whole,
as the case may be. The military worth of weapons should not
be confused with the balance of military power, which is a
balance of weapons or weapon systems that have *not* been
used, either because of the absence of violent conflict in peacetime or because the war has not yet run its course.

The political value of weapons in war depends not only on
their use, but also on their nonuse. In addition to the physical
harm that employed weapons do and to the political *faits ac-*

complis they may create, for example by seizure of territory, their use demonstrates the user's determination to pursue his interests at the possible risk of employing violence on an even larger scale. In other words, the use of some weapons increases the probability that more or all weapons in the available arsenals will be used. Before that stage is reached even a restricted use of weapons may have high political value if the decision-makers on the enemy's side are thereby killed and cannot be quickly replaced, or if the means of command and control necessary for effective enemy action are destroyed or disrupted; or finally, if the persons who must obey the orders given by the opposing decision makers no longer are able or willing to do so. In any of these extreme contingencies, "the enemy" is *politically* paralyzed at a relatively low military cost and is at his opponent's mercy. In less extreme cases, when the enemy retains his ability to govern and to conduct the war, the political values of the weapons that have been used by both sides reside in large part, though not exclusively, in the new balance of power established in battle. The enemy must estimate the outcome of continued fighting on that new basis. In particular, he is obliged to estimate the military effect of those weapons which have been withheld but may be used before the war reaches its end. The enemy may seek peace or an armistice. He may decide to keep the war restricted or to expand it in the expectation thereby to attain a balance of power either more favorable to him than to his adversary or at least less unfavorable to himself after the last battle than it is after the first. The definite political value of the arms that have been used or withheld in the war as a whole emerges only when peace is established. Disregarding the diplomatic skills that are brought to bear in the peace negotiations, the power of bargaining on each side varies with the new balance of military power.

Before considering the constituent elements of the political value of weapons in peacetime more closely, it should be noted that in war their military worth may be high, although their employment may prove politically fatal to the user. For example, it is conceivable that a small power succeeds in inflicting higher losses on a vastly superior enemy than it suffers itself in a struggle with him, but exhausts itself in the process and at the end of the war is worse off in relation to the enemy than it was at the outset.

In peacetime arms have political value only because they may be used. The possibility of their employment may be remote or close at hand, depending on the degree of international "tension" that prevails at a given time, but even when war appears to be remote, weapons do not lose their political value. This value is always related to the ultimate risk incurred by an adversary that they may be used against him, offensively or defensively, and to the comforting expectation of an ally that he will receive military help when he is imperiled, or — in offensive alliances — when he imperils others.

Different from this military worth, the political value of weapons cannot be directly controlled by the owner. Within the constraints of its resources any government can freely increase the military worth of its arms by improving its defense posture relative to that of its adversaries, but the political value of its defenses can be enhanced only by measures which affect the opponent's estimate of the balance of military power, his expectation regarding military aggression and defense, and his calculation of the outcome of war. Let us now discuss these three aspects of the political value of arms in somewhat greater detail.

Information

Information on the defenses of foreign powers, which affects the estimate of the military balance of power, is seldom complete and reliable, and incomplete information may lead to various conflicting estimates. Arms on which the estimating foreign government has no information whatever are politically worthless to the owner, but if the adversary is fully informed of the owner's armament its political worth is thereby not necessarily established. Complete information does not always result in correct estimates of the opponent's strength, since the reliability of the information usually remains in doubt; in peacetime reliable estimates of the military worth of the opponent's weapons are strictly speaking impossible since this worth can be accurately established only in combat. Furthermore, estimates of the military worth of foreign weapons are based on information which is often incomplete, even if judged to be reliable. It is the more nearly complete the more freely the opponent discloses information on his military might, or else the less effectively he guards his secrets against espionage. Information on the efficiency of weapons is subject to additional uncertainty when the weapons which the opponent is known to possess have never been used in war and when he has a monopoly on such weapons, and therefore on weapons tests. Despite espionage or defection of weapons experts, the owner in these circumstances is likely to have more reliable information than his interested adversaries.

In any event, the estimating government may credit its opponent with a higher, rather than a lower, capability than he actually possesses. In order to avoid the danger of optimistically low estimates, it may err on the side of pessimism. Or it may commit errors in the opposite direction: it may regard very good intelligence as unreliable, discount the opponent's truthful disclosures, underrate his progress in weapons development, etc. In short, the political value of weapons may be paradoxically high when little information on them is available to the estimating government, or low when that government lacks good judgment although it has good information.

It follows that there is no foolproof way for the owner of weapons to increase their political value by disclosure. Under certain conditions he may reduce that value by his disclosures; under other circumstances he may enhance it. Similarly, successful efforts to withhold information from the adversary will keep him guessing, but do not necessarily increase, and may possibly depreciate, the political value of secret weapons.

Instead of disclosing that it possesses specific arms in certain numbers capable of doing a specified amount of damage, a government may merely make it known that it has or will soon have at its disposal a novel weapon. If we distinguish the latter claim as *"intimation"* from the former as "information," intimation may be said to be a disclosure that fails to give information, although it is more appropriate to regard "intimation" as information of low specificity. (Vague information may, of course, be highly reliable, just as very detailed information may be judged to be quite unreliable.) Through "intimation" the owner of weapons often attempts to minimize two different risks, that of reducing the military worth of his weapons through disclosure, on the basis of which the adversary can take protective countermeasures, and that of eliminating their political value through complete secrecy. In addition, unlike information such "intimation" may cause anxiety in the enemy camp by suggesting shapeless, ominous danger. Frequently specific information on weapons is shrouded in jealously guarded secrecy, while at the same time some disclosures are made by verbal intimation or actual demonstration of samples, e.g., in parades. In this way, both the interest in maintaining military secrecy and that in manipulating the political value of weapons are satisfied at the same time in the hope of influencing the decisions of foreign governments in a desired direction.

The only weapons about which "intimation" as well as more specific information is often withheld are arms that are outlawed or widely regarded as fiendish. The attribution of barbaric lack of restraint to the use of certain weapons is subject to change over time, but as long as "conventionality" is not yet accorded to such weapons, any disclosure about their existence and possible use is tantamount to an admission of unscrupulousness. If such a disclosure is made, it reduces the credibility of the owner's claims to peacefulness and moral excellence: he appears to be capable of "anything." Hence "fiendish" claims are made only in order to strike terror in the heart of an enemy when the claimant is either in a state of morally unbridled belligerency or in despair. To put it differently, powers so strong that they need not fear the moral indignation of others and its political consequences may indulge their own disregard of morality; conversely, powers so desperate that resort to fiendishness appears as the only alternative to extinction may discard the humane fetters of civilized warfare.

Expectations

Decisions about war and peace depend not only upon information, imperfect as it may be in completeness, specificity, and reliability, concerning the opponent's armament, but also upon certain expectations regarding the circumstances in which the opponent will resort to war. Such expectations arise from a variety of considerations: observations of the opponent's past international behavior, judgments as to which of his interests are vital to him and which he will be ready to compromise; views of the nature of his long-range aspirations, the credibility of his policy declarations; and, to no small extent, the estimate of the prevailing balance of power which the *opponent* is believed to entertain. The political value of weapons vanishes if the owner is not credited by allies and adversaries with the resolution to use them in certain circumstances. This is particularly true if he has solemnly declared that he will resort to arms should such circumstances arise, and if his actions belie his words.

Declarations of this kind may be said to stipulate explicitly or to intimate the negative or positive conditions under which peace will be preserved. The other powers may meet the conditions either by abstaining from certain acts, e.g., aggression, or by committing certain acts, e.g., evacuation. The most solemn form in which the conditions can be stated is that of an *ultimatum*. Less momentous declarations merely warn the adversary of the "serious consequences" which his actions have had or will have, should he venture to take them. Warnings can themselves be more or less formal and differ in seriousness according to the language that is used, the position and authority of the official who issues them, and according to the media of transmission. A deliberate indiscretion committed at a diplomatic gathering may be more effective than a formal communication, if only because it is taken as a disclosure of "true" intention that was held to be obscure in formal communications. Conversely, the impact of clear and strong formal warnings may be softened by deliberate indiscretions. The opponent's complete failure to heed warnings discredits the power which issues them. If the warning power does not apply the military sanctions which it has threatened to apply in the event of defiance, its bluff is called and international respect for its political commitments impaired or lost.

Declarations of political intent, including warnings and reassurances, threats and promises regarding the use of force, can be effective only under two conditions. First, the foreign government must regard military sanctions threatened against it as undesirable (or welcome the promise of military help). If a government wants to go to war anyhow (or does not seek military help), its decision cannot be altered by a threat of war (or a promise of aid). Second, declarations of intent must be credible, so that the threats inspire fear and caution, and the promised favors are appreciated and rewarded. A notorious aggressor declaring his peaceful intent is likely to be distrusted, even as a weak, pacifistic, or vacillating government that warns others of its resolution to resort to arms in certain contingencies may be held to be merely bluffing. Governments never form their expectations of an opponent's behavior by the letter of his policy declarations but in the light of whatever credibility they attach to them. In evaluating such declarations, the foreign government must try to take account not only of the possibility of deliberate deception, but also of objection and subjective factors which in time may modify the declared intent and invalidate the declaration. For example, the balance of power may change or the warning power may have second thoughts on the implications and consequences of the sanctions it contemplated and announced.

In peacetime, a warning that force will be used is the less credible, the fewer measures are taken by the warning power to adopt a military posture enabling it to meet its commitments. In order to remove all doubt about the seriousness of a warning, the verbal threat of force must be backed up not only by military capabilities but by their mobilization, i.e., by steps toward war. The political significance of the difference between military potential and forces-in-being in a state of alert and the nature of the measures that are required to get from one state to the other vary with the level of military and logistical technology and organization.

Generally speaking, the more time it takes to assemble, equip, and train military forces for war and to deploy them in places from which they can strike at an opponent, the less serious is the merely verbal threat that they will be ordered to attack, should the opponent fail to comply with the terms of continued peace. Conversely, the less time is needed for mobilizing and deploying striking forces, the more ominous are mere intimations that a crisis may develop into war. On any level of technology the threatening character of measures toward mobilization, of "alerting" forces for use and protecting civilians against enemy action, is graver than that of diplomatic or other verbal warnings. So grave indeed are such measures that often special care is taken to deny their true purpose in public in order to give the opponent a chance to comply with the political demands of the mobilizing power without forcing him to assume the humiliating appearance of yielding to force. Even in a nuclear age, conventional deployment of troops near an opponent's frontier or naval demonstrations have frequently been presented as routine maneuvers or operations, rather than as preparations for violent conflict.

Calculations

Estimates of the opponent's relative military strength and expectations concerning his intent to resort to arms are only two of the three principal considerations which enter into comparatively rational decisions on the resolution of serious international conflict. The third consideration consists of calculations concerning the outcome of the war, which involve, among other things, estimates of one's own future conduct. Such calculations are unimportant only when the opponent is either overwhelmingly strong or very weak. In the first instance, information on his military strength and expectations of his aggression are sufficient grounds for reaching a decision to yield to him in a serious conflict, unless defiance is likely to gain allies in a cause otherwise lost or unless a sense of honor commands that a lost cause be pursued to the bitter end. Conversely, in the second instance, use or unscrupulous political exploitation of one's own military superiority will be checked, if not by any moral restraint of the elite, only by fear that a counter-elite may come to power, i.e., for domestic political reasons, and by apprehension that lack of restraint might now or sometime in the future lead other powers to align themselves against the aggressor.

If clashes of interest between, say, the United States and Egypt, or the Soviet Union and Israel were purely bilateral conflicts without repercussions on other powers, the parties immediately involved would not need to calculate the outcome of a possible war between them before deciding what step to take next. To put it differently, in such conflicts the political value of weapons under the control of the interested parties would be outweighed by their military worth.

It is different in the more realistic case of conflicts occurring either in a larger arena or directly between powers whose military strength is more nearly equal. In the latter case the way in which the weapons are employed by the potential belligerents may tip the balance so that even the most accurate, previous, estimates of the quantity and destructiveness of the adversary's weapons appear inconclusive. Indeed, estimates of their military worth may be poor merely because intelligence on strategic and tactical plans is defective. And even if complete information on arms is combined with perfect knowledge of strategy and tactics and is confidently held to be fully reliable, there still remains some irremovable uncertainty about "the fortunes of war." Pragmatically, today's information on the opponent's plans is a prediction of his future behavior, but unforeseeable events may intervene to invalidate the prediction. Similarly, "the fortunes of war" are uncertain if only because predictions of one's own performance in war may be invalidated in the heat of battle.

The fact that the outcome of a war cannot be calculated in advance without lingering doubt does not mean that such calculations are futile, but it does mean that the confidence in their reliability is subject to some political manipulation by the opponent. For example, in an effort to enhance the political value of his defenses, the opponent may intimate or declare that he confidently expects to win the war, if peace be broken. He may give specific reasons for his expectation, for example, by stressing the vulnerability of his adversary, dwelling on the advantage of surprise or preemptive attack, intimating that he is ready to fight to the bitter end, boasting of his morale, etc.

Political Value of Nuclear Arms

In the nuclear age, the peacetime exploitation of the political value of weapons has assumed some novel forms. This is partly a consequence of the fact that the opportunities for such exploitation have increased greatly, and partly a result of the increased risks that are associated with these opportunities. In addition, the impact of nuclear weapons upon peacetime diplomacy has some purely political components that cannot be derived from technology.

The destructiveness of nuclear weapons is of unprecedented magnitude. Their military worth in total war has not been tested, but it is generally known that their effect upon life and property would exceed anything ever experienced in past wars. In past phases of industrialization the risk of violent death in war was gradually extended from the front lines to the rear of the combat forces, the home centers of war production, and to the noncombatant population at large, including useless people who do not work. In an all-out nuclear war, the risk of violent death would be ubiquitous. Life and property in whole regions rather than merely at strong points or in cities might perish.

Death might not respect the frontiers of war and engulf neutral populations; even the health of future generations might be impaired.

The destructive power of atomic and thermonuclear warheads is combined with the availability of delivery systems against which distance no longer offers protection. Insularity of countries and continents has lost much of its strategic defensive value, since long-range bombers and missiles can reach their targets within hours or minutes.

Large-scale nuclear war would be waged with the trained combat forces, delivery systems, stockpiles of weapons, and the defensive arrangements available at the beginning of the conflict. In the event of attack there would be little or no time to convert war potential into forces-in-being. The mobilization of the war potential, which was a characteristic trait of the past wars of industrialized societies enabling them to accept initial defeats and yet win in the end, is in the present, and will be in the future, important only in *limited* wars.

The power and range of advanced modern weapons and delivery systems and the fact that they can be alerted for use in a short time augments the strategic significance of surprise. In the 1950's Soviet military doctrine took account of this fact by revising the deprecatory evaluation of surprise in Stalin's theory of war. Soviet military leaders declared that an attempted surprise attack must be countered by pre-emptive action. Stripped of its euphemistic form, this doctrine suggested that Soviet forces had to be expected to try to secure as many of the aggressive and defensive advantages of surprise as possible. It still is true that taking a victim by surprise might attain decisive strategic gains and not merely great initial advantages, but only by a surprise attack on the victim's striking forces that is successful can the aggressor insure the survival of his own life and political institutions, let alone his military power.

A nuclear surprise attack in which a relatively small portion of the victim's retaliatory forces were able to survive might still have disastrous consequences for the aggressor. The fact that in the nuclear age surprise has become easier to accomplish

must not obscure the fact that the penalty of unsuccessful surprise has also increased momentously. In the past, failure of
strategic surprise evened the chances of victory by the victim,
if the struggle lasted long enough; in the future, a ragged
surprise attack may be tantamount to defeat through retaliatory
annihilation, and even a successful attack may have that result.
The feasibility of attempting strategic surprise and the risks of
doing so have risen simultaneously. The extremely grave penalties of failure provide a check on the unprecedented opportunities which modern technology offers. It has become a matter
of providence and a task of diplomacy not to let the feasibility
of surprise obscure its risk and the penalty of failure. As long
as no international arrangement eliminating the danger of surprise attack has been agreed upon, the diplomats of the nuclear
powers insist that surprise will be unsuccessful and that its
risks and penalties are forbiddingly high. This is one of the
reasons why the strategy and diplomacy of the big powers in
the postwar era has been much preoccupied with threat and
counter-threat, and with claims and denials that in nuclear war
there can be no victor.

In all countries in which opinions can be freely expressed,
the fear of nuclear war and of fallout from tests of nuclear
weapons has increased ever since the end of World War II.
This is evident from public opinion surveys, parliamentary
debates, governmental declarations, protests and warnings by
political parties opposing the defense policies of their governments, particularly in Europe, warnings by church groups,
scientists, students, and journalists. In the absence of freedom
of speech in the communist orbit, it is not reliably known
how far this anxiety is shared by people behind the Iron Curtain. Except for a period of a few weeks after Stalin's death,
the Soviet rulers were slow to subscribe to the view expressed
in the West by President Eisenhower and others since 1953,
that all-out nuclear war would mean the end of civilization;
nor did they share the official British view that their country
could not be defended against nuclear attack. Instead, Khrushchev and other prominent Soviet leaders until the end of the

1950's stated that communism would emerge victorious from
nuclear war. Only Tito and Gomulka agreed earlier with President Eisenhower's thesis. Khrushchev first came close to it,
without endorsing it, when he dwelt in ominous detail on the
dangers of fallout, shortly before the Soviet government announced its unilateral, temporary suspension of nuclear tests
on March 31, 1958. At that time the Soviet government had in
fact underwritten Eisenhower's assertion, whereas the Chinese
communists have continued to this day to adhere to the earlier
defiant position of the Soviet leaders. This is also true in respect
to the doctrine of the inevitability of war, which Mao still
espouses, whereas the Soviet leaders revised it at the Twentieth
Party Congress in 1956 and abandoned it altogether at the
Twenty-first Congress three years later.

The destructive character of nuclear war has affected the
perception and resolution of international conflict. To begin
with, wars between nonnuclear powers — even though poison
gas may be used, as in Yemen — appear less terrible than they
are, because they no longer constitute the worst kind of war
that is technologically possible. Perhaps the decision to go to
war is made even more lightly by nonnuclear powers than was
true in the prenuclear era, because now the biggest powers
fearing escalation of the conflict to the nuclear stage are not
expected to throw their full weight into such struggle, but to
confine themselves to giving military aid and political support
and to expressing moral praise or blame. Thus, the existence
of nuclear arsenals may both facilitate armed conflict between
nonnuclear states in "third areas" and keep such conflict from
setting the world afire.

Even in the many wars involving the active participation of a
nuclear power that have occurred since 1945 no nuclear power
has ever used its nuclear arms against its nonnuclear enemy.
This fact has given rise to the somewhat optimistic expectation
that no nuclear power will ever use its most effective weapons
against an enemy that cannot retaliate in kind. It is not self-
evident, however, that the decision not to attempt the annihilation of the enemy is more likely to be made on grounds of

generosity than because of fear that annihilators may provoke their own doom by retaliatory action.

As to strife between the two big nuclear powers, two contradictory expectations have decisively influenced international affairs since the end of World War II. On the one hand, it is widely believed that serious political conflict between the United States and the Soviet Union places peace in particular danger, because conventional war between nuclear powers is more likely to turn nuclear than war between a nuclear and a nonnuclear power. On the other hand, since nuclear war has been avoided despite serious conflict and since neither power has embarked upon a policy of military conquest, increasing credence has been given to the irrational, self-congratulatory belief that a growing nuclear stockpile strengthens international responsibility and entails a growing reluctance to use nuclear weapons in earnest. It is absurd to believe that France is more likely to commit suicide, as it were, than is Russia, although it is true that France can die more easily than can Russia. Nor is it at all plausible to assume that Communist China will become more peaceable as it grows more powerful. Nor, finally, is it true that the Soviet Union has become more peaceful because it has learned of the fatal dangers of nuclear war from its ample experience in the research, development, and production of nuclear weapons. Instead, the Soviet Union has changed its method of exploiting the political value of the nuclear arms at its disposal. Broadly speaking, it has turned from intimidating by nuclear threats the nuclear have-not powers allied with the United States to permitting the alliance to disintegrate in consequence of the divisive forces within it.

In the 1950's and early 1960's, the allies of the United States were subjected to ominous Soviet warnings that safety from the devastating effects of nuclear war lay only in dissociation from the United States. The Soviet government carefully refrained from issuing overt threats of aggression, but under Bulganin and Khrushchev it evoked the specter of nuclear devastation of the nuclear have-not powers in the free world — and even of Great Britain — if war should break out. It tried to turn the fear of Soviet aggression into a fear of the weapons that might be employed in a war with Russia. It used propaganda and epistolary diplomacy for the purpose of preventing improvements of the defense posture of the West, and of disrupting the Western system of alliances.

The last Soviet effort to use nuclear weapons for purposes of political intimidation was both audacious and abortive. In 1962, Khrushchev, the champion of coexistence, attempted to place offensive nuclear weapons on Cuban soil, in order to humble U.S. power and defeat American policy, presumably to begin with in Europe. Had Khrushchev succeeded, all of Berlin might now be under Communist influence and NATO might have crumbled without DeGaulle's help. Khrushchev did not succeed in the face of American resistance after his attempt at surprise had failed. Subsequently, the Berlin crisis was terminated, and the era of Soviet nuclear blackmail seemed to have come to an end. It would be rash to assume, however, that in no circumstances will any Soviet government ever again resort to nuclear threats. In fact, the nuclear circumstances favorable to communist political aggressiveness can be predicted at least in general terms. They will exist whenever Western fear of nuclear war is intensified by the belief that the enemy's relative nuclear strength is great enough to be politically activated by his resolution to risk its use. Admittedly, uncertainties, judgment, and willingness to take risks are part of such circumstances, but the absence of objective factors — such as a "missile gap" may be compensated by subjective factors — for example by the belief that a "missile gap" exists.

And the possibility that *objective* conditions may at some time in the future be inducive to a renewed policy of Soviet pressure and blackmail cannot be dismissed out of hand. Any strategic asymmetry in nuclear forces favoring the Soviet Union would present such conditions. They could conceivably result from the future unilateral development of a Soviet antiballistic missile defense.

The ensuing danger to the United States and to the countries depending on U.S. protection of their security interests would not be primarily that of nuclear war but that of political defeat brought on by the dramatically rekindled fear of such war.

In the years following the Cuban missile crisis the Soviet Union no longer resorted to nuclear warnings and threats against the Western nuclear have-not powers. It relied instead on the divisive interests in NATO to serve the Soviet cause of disintegrating the Western alliance. These divisive interests were spearheaded by France, partly in response to the American policy of opposing the formation of national nuclear arsenals outside the "nuclear club." For a while, the United States promoted the idea of a multilateral nuclear force (MLF) in order to solve the political problems stemming from the virtual American nuclear weapons monopoly in NATO. The Soviet government strenuously objected to this plan, as it had resisted all improvements of Western defense since the formation of NATO. This time, however, it was successful partly because the objections against an MLF were shared by France and other NATO countries, which like the Soviet Union and France, feared that through multilateral nuclear arrangements Germany would regain too much power.

Furthermore, given the intense American interest in a global treaty designed to arrest the further spread of nuclear weapons, the Soviet government found itself in a position where it would promote schism in NATO without nuclear intimidation. It simply refused to agree to the draft treaty on nonproliferation unless certain of its wishes concerning the defense arrangements for the NATO area were taken into consideration and the non-nuclear status of Germany remained assured.

Thus in the years following the Cuban missile crisis the Soviet government discontinued to exploit the political value of its nuclear arms for diplomatic ends. It watched instead the disintegration of NATO and turned to the political exploitation of the American desire for reaching international agreement on a policy of nonproliferation.

CHAPTER FOUR

Revolutionary War

During the administration of President John F. Kennedy, the term "counterinsurgency" became fashionable to denote efforts to prevent or thwart the success of such armed coups d'états, insurrections, and revolutionary movements abroad as were deemed undesirable from the viewpoint of the U.S. Government. The following paper outlines the conflicting notions of revolutionary war held in the West on the one hand and by Russian Communists on the other. In the West, and particularly in the United States, many people believe that economic misery is the cause of "insurgency" and consequently that economic aid can prevent political disorder abroad. This simplistic view was most succinctly put forth by Secretary of Defense Robert McNamara in his speech at Montreal early in 1966.

The communist notion of revolutionary wars — its current term being "wars of (national) liberation" — can be traced back from Khrushchev to Friedrich Engels. If a tendency toward "vulgar Marxism" may be detected in the Western belief that economic improvements generate political stability, Marx's and Engels' original doctrine of "popular" or guerrilla warfare eulogized the uncivilized, i.e., unrestricted use of violence in war. The founders of communism were enthusiastic about "total war" in economically advanced countries. By contrast,

This paper was written in 1962 as a section of a Memorandum for the RAND Corporation.

Any views expressed in this paper are those of the author. They should not be interpreted as reflecting the views of the RAND Corporation or the official opinion or policy of any of its governmental or private research sponsors.

it is the function of Khrushchev's doctrine to persuade non-communists that all but communist intervention in the violent struggles for power in other states is futile and "unjust." Khrushchev's doctrine has been fitted to serve communist aspirations in economically backward countries in the age of decolonization.

Confusion of Terms

THE COMMUNIST term denoting insurrection in former colonial areas is "war of national liberation" or "revolutionary war." In it the insurgents are said to be fighting for "the right of self-determination, for their social and independent national development." Khrushchev has declared that such wars are "justified": they are "just wars," "sacred wars." He has predicted that there is "the likelihood of such wars recurring": they are "inevitable." Finally he has proclaimed that "the communists support just wars of this kind wholeheartedly and without reservations."[1] The term "wars of national liberation" has strong political connotations. Like "people's democracy," "peace movement," and "coexistence," it serves to promote, and at the same time to conceal, the aggressive purposes of communist foreign policy and propaganda.

In the West it is realized that the communists often justify sabotage and terror, subversion and anarchy born of civil violence in Asia, Africa, and Latin America, by calling such conflicts "wars of national liberation." Western writers have avoided mixing analysis with propaganda and have treated this type of conflict under such headings as "sublimited war,"[2] "the

[1] Nikita Khrushchev before a meeting of Communist Party organizations of the Soviet Union, January 6, 1961. For the text, see *The World Marxist Review*, London, January 1961. For a comparison of this speech with the statement issued from a meeting of communist leaders of eighty-one countries held in Moscow in November 1960, see *Two Communist Manifestoes* with introduction and brief commentary by Charles Bruce Marshall, The Washington Center of Foreign Policy Research, Washington, D.C., 1961.

[2] The term "sublimited war" was employed by President Kennedy in an address to Congress in May 1961 (see *The New York Times*, May 26, 1961) and by Secretary McNamara in his testimony to the Armed

twilight zone between political subversion and quasi-military action,"[3] "internal war,"[4] "intrastate war," "domestic war," "anti-governmental war,"[5] "intra-societal war,"[6] "guerrilla warfare,"[7]

Services Committee on January 19, 1962; McNamara used "sublimited war" synonymously with "insurrection, subversion and covert armed aggression." Subsequently he abandoned the term.

[3] Secretary McNamara in his address to the Fellows of the American Bar Association in Chicago on February 17, 1962; see *Army Navy Air Force Journal*, Vol. 99 (February 24, 1962), p. 701.

[4] The Center of International Studies at Princeton University initiated an Internal War Project in the fall of 1960 which has already produced a number of studies, including: Peter Paret, *Internal War and Pacification. The Vendée, 1789–1796* (Princeton University: June 1, 1961); George Modelski, *The International Relations of Internal War* (Princeton University: May 24, 1961), and the book by Paret and Shy cited in footnote 7.

[5] The terms "intrastate war," "domestic war," and "antigovernmental war" are used interchangeably in Samuel P. Huntington's interesting essay, "Patterns of Violence in World Politics," in *Changing Patterns of Military Politics*, cited in footnote 8.

[6] "Intra-societal war" is a term used by J. K. Zawodny in his paper "Guerrilla and Sabotage," *The Annals of the American Academy of Political and Social Science*, Vol. 341 (May 1962), pp. 8–18.

[7] The old term "guerrilla warfare" derives from the operations of Spanish peasants against the Napoleonic armies in 1808–1813 following the general insurrection in Spain of which Jomini wrote that "at no period of the French revolution was France so near ruin." (Baron Jomini, *Life of Napoleon*, translated by H. W. Halleck, Vol. 1 (Kansas City: 1897), p. 583.) Jomini said, "I seek the causes of an extraordinary event" in a "nation which three centuries of political nullity and apathy had so degenerated under the yoke of the monks," "but I confess myself unable to find them." (*op. cit.*, p. 584.)
Modern Western literature on guerrilla warfare and partisan warfare is so vast that any selection of references is arbitrary: F. O. Miksche, *Secret Forces. The Techniques of Underground Movements* (London: Faber and Faber, 1950); Alexander Papagos, "Guerrilla Warfare," *Foreign Affairs*, Vol. 30 (January 1952), pp. 215–230; Lucien Pye, *Guerrilla, Communism in Malaya* (Princeton: Princeton University Press, 1952); K. M. Hammer, "Huks in the Philippines," *Military Review*, Vol. 36 (April 1956); Richard Miers, *Shoot to Kill* (London: Faber and Faber, 1959); Ian Henderson and Philip Goodhart, *The Hunt for Kimathi* (London: Hamilton, 1958); Brian Crozier, *The Rebels: A Study of Post-War Insurrections* (Boston: Beacon Press, 1960); Bernard B. Fall, *Street Without Joy. Indochina at War, 1946–1954* (Harrisburg, Pa.: Stackpole, 1961); George K. Tanham, *Communist Revolutionary Warfare. The Vietminh in Indochina* (New York: Frederick A. Praeger, 1961); Peter Paret and John W. Shy, *Guerrillas in the 1960's* (New York: Frederick

etc. United States Army manuals on "unconventional warfare" deal with some types of military operations against insurgents, but not with all, for Army doctrine was developed primarily with a view to guerrilla or partisan activities that support regular forces. The British use the term "anti-terrorist operations" in referring to their counterinsurgency operations in Malaya. The French prefer to speak of "revolutionary war."[8] "Underground movements," "small wars," "brushfire wars," and still other terms are to be found in the literature. The time-honored term in political theory is, of course, civil war.

The "official" U.S. term for the tasks of the U.S. government and other allied and friendly governments in such revolutionary or civil wars is counterinsurgency. Unfortunately this term has a somewhat synthetic flavor. It barely avoids association with the word "counterrevolution"; it connotes neither dedication to justice, nor faith in liberty, nor approval of aspirations to

---

A. Praeger, 1962); *Marine Corps Gazette* (January 1961) and *Army* (March 1962).

On the partisan movements of World War II, see Edward M. Howell, *The Soviet Partisan Movement 1941–1944*, Department of the Army Pamphlet No. 20–244, August 1956; *German Antiguerrilla Operations in the Balkans (1941–1944)*, Department of the Army Pamphlet No. 20–243, August 1956; C. Aubrey Dixon and Otto Heilbrunn, *Communist Guerrilla Warfare* (New York: Frederick A. Praeger, 1954); Stefanos Sarafis, *Greek Resistance Army* (London: Birch Books Limited, 1951); Fitzroy Maclean, *Eastern Approaches* (London: Jonathan Cape, 1949); Lothar Rendulic, "Der Partisanen Kreig," in *Bilanz des Zweiten Weltkrieges* (Oldenburg-Hamburg: Gerhard Stalling Verlag, 1953), pp. 99–114; Lothar Rendulic, *Gekämpft-Gesiegt-Geschlagen* (Heidelberg: Wels, Welsermuhl, 1952), pp. 151–232; Roberto Battaglia, *The Story of the Italian Resistance* (London: Odhams, 1958).

[8] There is a vast literature in French on "revolutionary war"; see especially Claude Delmas, *La Guerre Révolutionnaire* (Paris: Presses Universitaires de France, 1959); Gabriel Bonnet, *Les Guerres Insurrectionelles et Révolutionnaires* (Paris: Payot, 1958), and almost every issue since 1956 of *Revue de Défense Nationale, Revue Militaire d'Information,* and *Revue Militaire Générale;* see also Raoul Girardet, "Civil and Military Power in the Fourth Republic," in *Changing Patterns of Military Politics,* Samuel P. Huntington, editor (Glencoe, Ill.: The Free Press, 1962), pp. 121–149, and Peter J. Paret, "The French Army and La Guerre Révolutionnaire," *Journal of the Royal United Service Institution,* Vol. 104 (February 1959), pp. 59–69.

political self-determination and national independence; and it invites the misunderstanding that the United States would oppose insurgency under all circumstances so as to preserve the *status quo* (which would include opposing insurgency against communist regimes and against oppressive or corrupt noncommunist governments). Surely, none of this was intended in the choice of the term. But none of the undesirable connotations of "counterinsurgency" can be easily avoided, and the intended meaning of the term is not self-evident.[9]

Counterinsurgency requires both civic and military action. Civic action encompasses measures in various fields — sanitatation, agriculture, transportation, education, local administration, etc. — all designed to better the conditions of life of the civil population. Military action may consist of the training of antiguerrilla activities on a larger scale; and of fighting rebel forces in open battle.

Civic action is important in deterring insurgency as well as controlling it. All modern civil wars have as their object political power or, to put it differently, "popular support." Guerrillas need such support to exist and operate. When their popular support (whether extorted or freely given) dwindles, the insurgents' prospects of gaining power fade. Civic action wins support for the legitimate government.

The emphasis on civic action in dealing with insurgency is not only indicated by recent experiences in successful antiguerrilla operations (as in Malaya and the Philippines), it also follows directly from firmly held American beliefs about the underlying social and economic causes of insurrection.

---

[9] At a symposium on limited war held in April 1962, a U.S. Army officer pointed out that the meaning of the term counterinsurgency was obscure to American military personnel and special indoctrination (by means of lectures and films!) was needed to clarify the meaning. It is difficult to imagine Chinese or Soviet military officers having corresponding difficulties in understanding the meaning of "war of national liberation."

Communist Doctrines

Let us consider the communist view of insurgency. Insurrections ("wars of national liberation") are distinguished by Khrushchev from two other types of war, namely, "world wars" and "local wars." The communist attitude toward these three kinds of war is schematically described in the following table, which is derived from Khrushchev's speech of January 6, 1961. The communists' general doctrine of war is based upon the distinctions among these three kinds of war. For various reasons, both world wars and local wars are undesirable from Khrushchev's viewpoint. They endanger communist rule in countries where it has been established; they interfere with the economic progress of the communist bloc; and they jeopardize communist gains achievable by political and economic means in the cold war. By contrast, "wars of liberation" in the so-called third areas offer opportunities for the geographical extension of communist influence at the expense of the West without the hazards inherent in local wars or in world war as long as imperialist "intervention" is deterred by fear of reciprocal communist action.

According to Khrushchev, the specific forms of wars of national liberation vary from country to country. Of Indochina and Algeria, for example, he has remarked that, "these wars which *began* as uprisings of colonial peoples against their oppressors, *developed* into guerrilla wars." Other communist writers, such as Mao Tse-tung, Vo Nguyen Giap, and, most recently, Che Guevara, have put forth *ad hoc* "theories" of revolutionary war based on their own experiences in China, Indochina, and Cuba, respectively. In particular, Mao Tse-tung and Vo Nguyen Giap have emphasized that violent conflict in which revolutionary aims are at stake is protracted and goes through various stages. It culminates in regular war only when the initially weak insurgent forces have become strong enough to abandon guerrilla tactics (that is, sabotage, ambush, raid, and terror) and can face the weakened forces of the enemy in

Khrushchev's Description of Types of Wars

	Wars Between States		Liberation Wars
	World Wars	Local Wars	
Examples	World Wars I and II	Egypt, 1956	Indochina, Algeria, Cuba
Likelihood of future occurrence	not likely	dwindling	likely
Cause	(1) contradictions and antagonism between imperialist countries (2) wish to restore capitalist rule in socialist countries	imperialist aggression curtailed by imperialist fear of world war	popular opposition to tyranny and colonialism, people's wish for self-determination and national independence
Morality	immoral, unjust	immoral, unjust	moral, just, sacred
Imperialist purpose	conquest	conquest	maintaining colonial exploitation, social oppression, either directly or by "puppets"
Consequences	fatal to imperialists	may develop into world war by escalation	(1) weakens imperialist powers politically; (2) may develop into world war if imperialist "intervention" is not deterred by justified fear of reciprocal socialist armed assistance
Socialist task	(1) prevent (2) if necessary, "smash the aggressor"	(1) prevent (2) intervene in order to nip in the bud, as in Suez, 1956	(1) support insurgents (2) prevent imperialist "intervention" or counterinsurgency

open battle. In other words, guerrilla operations are a sign of military weakness rather than strength, and unless the opponent accepts political compromise or surrenders, the final test of insurgency occurs in regular, rather than irregular, operations. In Indochina the Vietminh succeeded in inflicting military defeats on the French in what approximated conventional battles; in Greece, the communists failed.

Modern communist doctrines of revolutionary war can be traced directly to the Marxian theory of history and the class struggle, and they retain the medieval schoolmen's distinction between just and unjust wars. The communists claim that right and justice reside in that particular class, party, or social movement which fights against capitalist exploitation and for progress toward socialism. In his assertions that wars of liberation are "just wars," Khrushchev merely repeats communist opinions of long standing. Lenin, for example, in 1918 characterized as "criminal war" any war waged with the object of strengthening the rule of the exploiting class, and as "legitimate and 'holy'" any war "waged with the object of strengthening and expanding socialism."[10] The *Short History of the CPSU* describes Lenin's distinction between these two kinds of war as follows:

> . . . the Bolsheviks held that there are two kinds of war:
>
> a) Just wars, wars that are not wars of conquest but wars of liberation, waged to defend the people from foreign attack and from attempts to enslave them, or to liberate the people from capitalist slavery, or lastly, to liberate colonies and dependent countries from the yoke of imperialism; and
>
> b) Unjust wars, wars of conquest waged to conquer and enslave foreign countries and foreign nations.[11]

It may, therefore, be said that there is basic continuity of agreement from the founders of Marxism to Khrushchev about

---

[10] Lenin, "Left-Wing Childishness and Petty-Bourgeois Mentality" (1918), in *Selected Works*, Vol. 7 (New York: International Publishers, 1943), p. 357.

[11] *Short History of the CPSU* (Moscow: Foreign Languages Publishing House, 1945), pp. 168–169.

the "moral" element in the communist doctrine of war. Moreover, some of the tactical "rules" for communist insurrection
given in contemporary communist writings were put forth
as early as 1852 by Friedrich Engels. He advised insurgents
that they should surprise their antagonists while their forces
were scattered, "prepare new successes, however small, but
daily," "rally those vacillating elements to your side which
always follow the strongest impulse," etc.

But the communist theory of "irregular" war has undergone
certain changes in the last hundred years. When Marx and
Engels spoke of irregular or partisan warfare they had in mind
the resistance by the people of a weaker state against the
regular forces of a stronger state through mass uprisings, revolutionary methods, guerrilla bands, etc., or the continuation
of the fight by irregular forces after the regular armed forces
had been defeated. In other words, they looked at partisan
warfare in the context of regular war between states and regarded irregular operations as an extension and intensification
of regular war in two respects: first, irregular war was waged
for revolutionary aims, and second, it lacked moral restrictions.

The founders of Marxism despised the "etiquette" that
restricted violence in the limited wars between governments
in the eighteenth and nineteenth centuries. In these centuries,
the conventions of regular war made it a more civilized institution than it had been in the past, but Marx and Engels considered these conventions to be obstacles to "real war." They
believed that the conventions of regular war had their origins
in the upper classes of society and served to safeguard the continuation of class rule despite the vicissitudes of war. In 1870,
Engels wrote,

> It seems that only the Barbarians have recognized and made use
> of the right to fight individually and that the civilized nations
> conform to a certain etiquette which precludes them from con-
> tinuing the struggle after the official capitulation.[12]

[12] Cited in F. O. Miksche, *Secret Forces. The Techniques of Underground Movements* (London: Faber and Faber, 1950), p. 23.

When franc-tireurs continued to fight the Prussian invaders of France after the surrender of the main French forces at Sedan in 1870, Marx applauded this unconventional form of resistance and was amused by British indignation at the countermeasures that the Prussians took in their effort to control the French "war to the knife." With approval Marx characterized these Prussian measures — requisitions, the burning of villages, the execution of franc-tireurs, the taking of hostages — as revivals of practices common in the Thirty Years War:

Of course, the English have done such things in India, Jamaica, etc., but the French are neither Hindu, Chinese, or Negro, nor are the Prussians heaven-born Englishmen. It is a typically Hohenzollern idea to believe that a nation commits a crime by continuing to defend itself after the destruction of its standing army.[13]

The ideas that Marx and Engels entertained of unlimited, total war, in disregard of the rules of civilized warfare, were inspired by admiration for the Spanish guerrillas who had helped Wellington to defeat Napoleon's armies and by other irregular operations in the nineteenth century undertaken for nationalist and revolutionary ends. The early theoretician of these operations was Carl von Clausewitz, who was an Hegelian just as Marx was, and who was studied closely by Lenin. Clausewitz was not so enthusiastic about irregular warfare — "people's war" in his terminology — as Marx and Engels were. Clausewitz was a soldier who knew war at first hand and was less bloodthirsty than civilian intellectuals sometimes are who, as protagonists of religious or political beliefs, make light of the price to be paid for the conversion or annihilation of nonbelievers or heretics. Clausewitz noted that "the people's war in civilized Europe is a phenomenon of the nineteenth century." Recognizing it as a heritage of the French Revolution and as the result of the politicalization of the

---

[13] Karl Marx, *Briefe an Kugelmann*, with an introduction by N. Lenin, 2nd ed. (Berlin: Vereinigung Internationaler Verlags-Anstalten G.m.b.H., 1927), p. 88.

people, he pointed out that the "people's war" had both adherents and opponents for political as well as military reasons. The political opponents disapproved of the arming of the people because it was a "revolutionary measure, a state of anarchy declared legitimate," while military opposition to this new form of armed strength was based on the conviction that success in a people's war was not commensurate with the considerable effort involved. Clausewitz himself raised the question whether "this new strengthening of the military element was beneficial to mankind or not," but he left the answer "to the philosophers," stating at the outset of his purely military analysis that he would not examine "the price that the people have to pay for the resistance of a whole nation in arms."[14] He knew that people did have to pay a price for it.

Marx and Engels, Lenin, Stalin, and other later communists were quick to answer Clausewitz's question differently: to them the price did not matter, their aims — revolution or liberation from invaders — were "sacred," "holy" causes. Any sacrifice seemed justified, and it was the "justice" of such war aims, the desire to wrest power from the ruling class or the invader, that led to their disdain for the rules of civilized warfare. To them, limited, conventional war was war between conservative governments.

To this strand of the communist theory of war Engels added the belief that modern mass armies would function as a democratic ferment and that universal military service would undermine the class basis of modern industrial society. Grossly underestimating the staying power of political institutions, Engels exclaimed in 1891:

> The real strength of German Social Democracy does not reside in the number of its voters but in its soldiers. . . . By 1900, this army, once the most Prussian, the most reactionary element of the country, will be socialist in its majority, as inescapably as fate.[15]

---

[14] Carl von Clausewitz, *Vom Kriege,* ed. by A. W. Bode (Leipzig: H. Schaufuss, 1935), Book VI, Ch. 26, "Volksbewaffnung," pp. 473–474.
[15] Cited in Sigmund Neumann, "Engels and Marx: Military Concepts

Later communist leaders, particularly Lenin and Trotsky, combined Engels' views of the mass army as an egalitarian social ferment with the militant theory of revolution as an off-spring of international war. To quote Khrushchev, "the finest representatives of the working class" — a communist euphemism for intellectuals leading communist parties — "advanced the slogan of turning an imperialist war into a civil war. . . . A situation of this kind set in during the First World War, and it was used in classical fashion by Lenin and the Bolshevik Party."[16]

Under present conditions this old theory of revolutionary war has been explicitly relegated by the Russian communists (though not by the Chinese) to geographically limited application in Asia, Africa, and Latin America. As has been pointed out, Khrushchev believes that the probability of war between capitalist countries is low, and that imperialist aggression against the Soviet Union and countries of the communist bloc is deterred by the power of the "socialist world camp." Instabilities in the global balance of power are most likely to occur in underdeveloped areas, and it is in these areas that the communist doctrine of revolutionary war now has primary application. From the standpoint of the U.S.S.R., "wars of national liberation" are desirable revolutionary wars if they shift the balance of power in favor of the communists; as long as the participation of major powers in such wars can be held to an acceptable minimum, they involve only low risks for the U.S.S.R. itself.

It follows that the communists oppose "wars of national liberation" in territory they already control, for example, in Eastern Europe. And while claiming the moral right to support "national liberation" in third areas, the communist governments try to inhibit Western support of counterinsurgency operations in such areas; and they are extremely sensitive to the possibility,

---

of the Social Revolutionaries," in *Makers of Modern Strategy*, E. M. Earle, editor (Princeton: Princeton University Press, 1943), p. 169.

[16] N. Khrushchev's speech of January 6, 1961.

however remote, of Western intervention in support of insurgency within the communist camp.

Partisan warfare against an invader, in support of operations by regular armed forces, occurred on a large scale in World War II. Both the Western powers and the Soviet government resorted to it. It was, if anything, even more fierce and ruthless than the "unconventional" operations of the Spanish guerrillas against Napoleon that had inspired Marx and Engels. It is likely that the partisan warfare in World War II has influenced the political and military thinking of the Soviet leaders on modern "wars of national liberation," although these are wars waged as revolutionary, violent struggles of low intensity against legitimate governments in third areas, rather than operations against invading armies in support of conventional operations on a world-wide scale. Khrushchev himself participated in partisan operations in the Ukraine during World War II, and he and other Soviet leaders may be influenced by this experience. Again, Tito and Mao Tse-tung may have taught the Soviet leaders a tantalizing lesson. Guerrilla leaders who take over their countries without large-scale help from the Soviet Union not only attain political power at home but also enjoy greater independence from Moscow than satellite leaders who owe their position mainly to Soviet arms.

The Western Views

In the West, two explanations are commonly given for the nature and frequency of the insurrections in third areas since World War II. Insurgency and political strife are attributed either to communist instigation or to economic distress and political oppression.

The first view offers a purely conspiratorial theory of political upheaval, the second an economic explanation of a political phenomenon.

While it is true that insurrection in former colonial areas is readily supported and exploited by communist regimes, primarily by the Soviet Union and Communist China, not every instance of violent political change that is unwelcome to the Western powers is the result of communist subversion. Certainly the subversion of legitimate political authority is not a communist invention. In the 1930's it was equally common — and equally fallacious — to consider "fifth-column" activities as an insidious subversive technique invented by Hitler. In fact, subversion and insurrection were common in the international struggle for power long before the birth of Khrushchev, Hitler, or Marx, and in the modern era democratic governments as well as totalitarian regimes have used subversion against the enemy in times of war. In peacetime and in a "cold war," communist governments find it easier to make use of subversion abroad than do democratic regimes, because the former command the services of disciplined international parties and other organizations; but subversion is not necessarily a monopoly of any particular form of government.

The second view, attributing insurrection in third areas to economic misery, has been given strong expression by President Kennedy in his speech of June 6, 1961:

> It is easy to dismiss as Communist-inspired every anti-government or anti-American riot, every overthrow of a corrupt regime or every mass protest against misery and despair.
> But these are not all Communist-inspired. The Communists move in to exploit them, to infiltrate their leadership, to ride their crest to victory. But the Communists did not create the conditions which caused them.
> In short, the hopes of freedom in these areas which see so much poverty and illiteracy, so many children who are sick, so many children who die in the first year, so many families without homes, so many families without hope — the future for freedom in these areas rests with the local peoples and their government.
> If they have the will to determine their own future, if their governments have the support of their own people, if their honest and progressive measures helping their people have inspired confidence and zeal, then no guerrilla or insurgent action can succeed.

According to this view, insurgency in economically backward countries with governments friendly to the United States can be deterred by *economic aid* and *military assistance*. In particular, such economic aid as helps to increase productivity and (in conjunction with economic planning and tax and land reforms) alleviates economic and social ills is held to be a strong deterrent to civil strife in such countries. Hunger and misery breed revolt, it is argued, and political stability can be purchased with wealth and generosity. This view avoids the pitfalls of a conspiratorial theory of history and calls attention to what are clearly very important aspects of the problem, but it suffers from the shortcomings of economic determinism. The high incidence of insurgency and other forms of civil strife in Asia, Africa, the Middle East, and Latin America cannot be explained in terms of communist conspiracy and human misery alone. To deter and take effective action against insurrection, we need a fuller understanding of its causes.

There is much evidence to suggest that, whatever the relative importance of communist subversion and economic distress in the creation of political instability, other factors have also been instrumental. Generally speaking, these factors are the unintended long-range consequences of earlier developments on the international scene. Specifically, they include:

1. the activation of partisan movements during World War II in the territory occupied by the Germans, Italians, and Japanese;
2. the decline of the former colonial powers, especially the United Kingdom and France, and the rise to unchallenged primacy of the United States and the Soviet Union;
3. the rapid modernization of life in colonial areas, together with the catalytic effects of the Atlantic Charter and similar political declarations;
4. the fact that the main struggle for power in the postwar era between the United States and the Soviet Union is constrained by fear of direct, nuclear confrontation, and finds its expression at a lower level of violence.

In the early phases of World War II, Axis military forces overran almost the whole of continental Europe, many countries in Asia, and certain parts of Africa. The Allied powers, while mobilizing their resources for reconquest, decided to encourage partisan and underground activities in the vast territories that had been lost and to support anti-Axis governments-in-exile. Thus, political subversion, sabotage, and guerrilla action against enemy authorities and enemy military forces reached a scale far larger than that of Western-organized subversion in World War I; in fact, subversion on this scale had no precedent in history. In various occupied countries, for example in Yugoslavia and Greece, various partisan organizations fought not only the enemy but also one another, since they differed in their political aims. After the war, some of these partisan organizations, even many that had been assisted by the Western Allies more generously than by the Soviet Union, turned to subversion and guerrilla action against the Western powers. This was true, for example, in Greece, Indochina, Malaya, and the Philippines. Often the postwar guerrillas used weapons given to them by the Western Allies during World War II. Their political aims were frequently, though not invariably, nationalistic. Often, but not in all cases, they received assistance from communist governments. In any event, postwar insurgency, particularly in the first decade after the war, owed much of its military and political skill and organizational strength to World War II experience.

It is important to note, however, that certain wartime partisan movements with strong anticommunist orientation, such as the Polish underground army and the Chetniks in Yugoslavia, became politically impotent with the rise of communist rule in their countries. Similarly, in countries such as France and Italy whose wartime partisan organizations included sizable communist elements, the legitimate authority of noncommunist postwar governments was strong enough not to be challenged by continued subversion. In these Western countries, as in Yugoslavia and the Soviet Union, wartime guerrilla actions were ancillary to the operations of the regular armed forces. When peace came, the guerrillas disappeared. It was only in outlying areas, less tightly controlled by either communist or Western Governments, that insurgency continued and prospered, for example in Greece, China, Malaya, Indochina, and the Philippines.

The loss of primary power status by the United Kingdom and France was another factor aiding insurgency in the dependent areas not voluntarily given their independence by the colonial powers. Examples are the insurgent movements and uprisings in Indochina, Cyprus, Morocco, and Algeria. The smaller colonial powers, such as Belgium, the Netherlands, and Portugal, were affected similarly in their own dependent areas.

Contact between certain parts of the indigenous population in former colonial areas and the economically advanced societies has led to the so-called "revolution of rising expectations" in Asia, Africa, and the Middle East. Such contacts with the West have multiplied in the fields of education, technology, sanitation, mass communication, etc. The aid programs of foreign governments and foundations have worked in the same direction. Progress in the Soviet Union (and Communist China) in achieving higher standards of living, in reducing illiteracy, and in challenging the political pre-eminence of the United States and allied colonial powers has aroused expectations of rapid political and economic advancement in the less developed countries. This is particularly true of the native, foreign-educated elites. Cold war conflicts between the Western powers and the communist bloc have offered opportunities to these elites to play the West against the East and vice versa. These elites have been encouraged in struggles for independence by communist anticolonial propaganda, but their expectations of political progress have also been aroused by Western support of progressive decolonialization.

As early as 1941, the Atlantic Charter affirmed that it was "the right of all people to choose the form of government under which they will live." While this right was disregarded in the European countries that fell under communist domination, it was seized upon by African nationalists. In 1943 Dr. Azikiwe in Nigeria demanded the immediate establishment of representative government in his book *The Atlantic Charter and British West Africa*. Three years later, the United Gold Coast Convention was established, the Kenya African Union held its first Congress, and the important Rassemblement Démocratique Africaine was born at a French West African Conference at Bamako in the French Sudan.[17]

The electrifying influence of the Atlantic Charter on nationalist movements in dependent areas merely illustrates the importance of westernization in the global postwar process of decolonization. There is much evidence to suggest that political instability and social turbulence are stimulated by steps toward modernity (such as the education of a native elite and the economic advances brought about by contact with the West) rather than by abject misery and ignorance. Even in Kenya, the Mau Mau, no matter how superstitious and even satanic a reaction to oppression, developed among the Kikuyu people, who of all the Africans in Kenya were the most advanced.[18]

Given the destructiveness of the weapons that could be used in general nuclear war and given the risk that a conventional, localized war involving forces of the major powers might develop into general war, the communists must be highly selective in their efforts to change the global balance of power. The postwar process of decolonization offers them opportunities for contesting Western influence in areas outside the most dangerous theaters of conflict. They like to believe and to make the noncommunist world believe that the rise of new, independent states in the former colonial areas is an irresistible historical trend favoring the communists by a gradual, global shift of the balance of power. But from the Western standpoint, the communist efforts to exploit insurgency can be regarded as proof that the more direct and violent forms of communist aggression are being effectively deterred. Nor is the West con-

[17] James Cameron, *The African Revolution* (New York: Random House, 1961), p. 22.

[18] The loyal members of the Kikuyu were mainly responsible for the defeat of the Mau Mau. In the first two and one-half years of the insurgency in Kenya, 7,811 members of the Mau Mau, 510 of the security forces, and 1,465 civilians lost their lives. Four hundred and seventy of the security men and 1,316 of the civilians were Africans. James Cameron, *op. cit.,* p. 84.

vinced that the new states will inevitably embrace or favor communism. According to Walt W. Rostow, "communism is best understood as a disease of the transition to modernization."[19]

The task of the United States in the underdeveloped areas is difficult because we are interested in deterring insurgency against friendly governments and like to assist those governments against the communist-aided insurrections that do occur, while at the same time we encourage fundamental social changes in these areas. Our primary means for deterring insurgency are suitable economic aid *plus* encouragement of the local authorities to undertake such reforms as will minimize the unsettling effects of modernization — reforms leading toward a better distribution of national income and "toward human freedom and political democracy."[20]

To quote Walt W. Rostow again:

> Thus our central task in the underdeveloped areas, as we see it, is to protect the independence of the revolutionary process now going forward. . . .
> Despite all the Communist talk of aiding the movements of national independence, they are driven in the end, by the nature of their system, to violate the independence of nations. Despite all the Communist talk of American imperialism, we are committed, by the nature of our system, to support the cause of national independence.[21]

The principal means of assistance to friendly governments in countering communist-supported insurgency is, of course, U.S. military aid.

Although many people believe that economic aid promotes political stability, democracy, and peace, it has been argued that the several doctrines by which foreign aid is justified "consist mainly of unverified and unverifiable assertions" and that "there is at least as much to be said against it as in favor

[19] Walt W. Rostow, "Countering Guerrilla Attack," *Army*, Vol. 12 (September 1961).
[20] *Ibid.*
[21] *Ibid.*

of it."[22] Economic aid may produce political instability rather than stability, and facilitate antidemocratic rather than democratic tendencies. Desirable political results of economic policy depend on the political conditions under which the policy is pursued and on other factors, e.g., population changes, many of which cannot be foreseen or manipulated by economic means. The same holds true of peace. This is not to argue against economic aid as an instrument of American security policy (let alone as a humanitarian measure), but it is to emphasize that deterrence of subversion by economic aid is more precarious than is deterrence by military means, and that the political effects of economic aid are as problematic as is the relation between economic misery and political insurgency.

[22] See the careful analysis by Edward C. Banfield, "American Foreign Aid Doctrines," in *Public Policy. A Yearbook of the Graduate School of Public Administration,* Harvard University, 1961, Carl J. Friedrich and Seymour E. Harris, editors (Cambridge, Mass.: Harvard University Press, 1961), pp. 44–95.

Soviet Atomic Blackmail and the North Atlantic Alliance

In the 1950's, the Soviet Government repeatedly warned the European NATO powers and other free countries associated with the United States that in the event of war a few Soviet bombs would turn these countries into so many graveyards. Such threats were not confined to journalistic writings or to speeches made by propagandists at party gatherings or ceremonial occasions, but became a standard feature of Soviet diplomacy. The threats were contained in official diplomatic notes and letters that Bulganin and Khrushchev sent to foreign heads of state. Aimed at the erosion of the Western alliance system these Soviet threats were to create and exploit fear of nuclear war among the governments and populations of the nuclear have-not powers, depending for their security on the United States, a nuclear superpower.

The following analysis of Soviet threats was written in 1954, before the term "nuclear blackmail" gained wide currency. The analysis contains a few predictions of the form such threats would take in the future; these forecasts seem to have stood the test of time.

By 1957 when the essay was published in two places — in World Politics *and as a chapter of my book,* German Rearmament and Atomic War — *the Suez crisis of 1956 had occurred. Chapter 6 in the present volume, originally published only in* World Politics *following the general analysis of atomic blackmail, examines the nuclear threats made by the Soviet*

From *World Politics,* Vol. 9 (April 1957).

government in that crisis against the United Kingdom and France.

To this day the unequal distribution of nuclear power in NATO has remained a main source of political weakness and dissent in the Western alliance. Although the Soviet government again resorted to nuclear blackmail during the second Berlin crisis, its main efforts in the 1960's to exploit the nuclear inequality among the NATO powers have centered around the American plan to establish a multilateral nuclear force in NATO and, after the U.S. government abandoned that plan, around the treaty to control the spread of nuclear weapons.

At the time I wrote this paper, it appeared to me that atomic blackmail would be used in the future with increasing caution. For example, I did not expect any nuclear power to issue an atomic ultimatum. I observed that "under conditions of parity of ever more destructive weapons . . . and with ever-increasing appreciation of that destructiveness among political leaders, it stands to reason that authoritative threats of unrestricted war will in the future become less rather than more explicit and final." In this connection it may now be noted that the joint Soviet–United States draft of a United Nations Security Council resolution of March 7, 1968, contained the following provision: The Security Council "recognizes that aggression with nuclear weapons or the threat of such aggression against a nonnuclear-weapon state [emphasis mine] would create a situation in which the Security Council, and above all its nuclear-weapon state permanent members, would have to act immediately in accordance with their obligations under the United Nations Charter."

Thus, in 1968 the two super-powers acted jointly to deter a conceivable effort of a minor nuclear power, such as Communist China, to use nuclear blackmail against a nonnuclear-weapon state, such as India. This joint Soviet-American draft may be read to signify both an understanding and an expression by the two super-powers of their common interest in deterring a conceivable military or political move of Communist China that involved the use of nuclear weapons or the threat of their use. In addition, the draft explicitly authorized a quick, unilateral or common, response by the super-powers to the use of nuclear weapons or nuclear threats by minor nuclear-weapon states. It also contributed to deterring such threats by any major nuclear-weapon state.

In the Suez crisis of 1956, the Soviet Union implicitly

threatened the use of atomic weapons against Britain and France in order to halt their intervention in Egypt. At that time, only Great Britain, not France, was a nuclear-weapon state. In a comparable future crisis the Security Council resolution of March 1968 would not oblige the Soviet Union to be more careful in directing nuclear threats at Britain and France, since now neither of these countries is a nonnuclear-weapon state. But, in the hypothetical case of another Middle East crisis, should the French resort to nuclear threats, say, against Israel — which, needless to say, is unlikely — the Soviet Union could take counteraction "immediately" without waiting for a resolution of the Security Council authorizing such action. So indeed could the United States or Great Britain. Generally speaking, the joint Soviet-American draft, if accepted by the United Nations Security Council, would make it more difficult for all nuclear-weapon states to expose any nonnuclear-weapon state to an explicit threat that nuclear weapons will be used against it.

The resolution is therefore a move toward civilizing diplomacy in the nuclear age. Unfortunately, it cannot prevent the subtler forms of nuclear blackmail — allusions, conditional warnings, generalized or implicit threats — which while not constituting open threats may closely resemble them. Their impact on the threatened country will depend not so much on the specific form of the threat as on the response to it by other nuclear-weapon states; and this response may, but need not, be an "immediate" one.

THE UNCERTAINTY about whether atomic weapons will be used in future war, whether local or general, lends itself to political exploitation in the cold war. The efficiency of nuclear weapons in wartime, and their resulting threat-value in either war- or peacetime, constitute their political-military worth. In peacetime, the threat-value of weapons can be exploited in many ways: by an ultimatum, by authoritative or inspired statements on capabilities or intentions, by studied disclosures of new weapons at ceremonial occasions, by means of maneuvers, redeployments of forces, or by so-called demonstrations.

In the preatomic age, naval demonstrations and partial mobilizations of ground forces were standard measures for bringing to bear military pressure on foreign governments in peacetime. In the present era, such pressure can be exerted also by using the threat potential of modern air power and of the weapons of mass destruction. Evidence of this is seen in official statements on deterrence, in threats of instant retaliation, in propaganda to foreign populations about the vulnerability to air or missile attack of their bases, industries, and cities, and in discussions of the vastly increased importance of surprise in war.

The political worth of modern military power does not reside merely in threats that certain weapons may be used or in promises that they will not be used. Political worth attaches also to technical and scientific accomplishments, for the power that is unlocked by such advances can, like all power, be used for military as well as for peaceful ends. Witness the political value of airlifts, of rescue missions and expeditions, of international exhibitions of advances in modern technology, of international congresses and "years" devoted to progress in the basic or applied sciences.

Yet, it cannot be said that all of the many possibilities of peacetime exploitation of the political value of military power are being realized. This is particularly true with respect to certain military activities, such as weapons tests or training missions. Here military purposes usually overshadow consideration of the political advantages that might be gained or disadvantages that might be avoided by changes in the timing of military activities, and in the public information practices accompanying them. For example, the atomic exercise CARTE BLANCHE, which was held in June 1955, largely in West Germany, took place just prior to a debate in the Bundestag on German rearmament, and it caused the Federal government no little trouble. Better timing or a more carefully considered policy of informing the public could have saved some political embarrassment in this instance.

There exists no doctrine of the peacetime exploitation of military power comparable to military doctrines on the employment of military forces in war. That gap remains to be filled. The present article discusses only "atomic blackmail," one of the many ways in which the political worth of military power can be exploited.

A government that is exposed to atomic threats in peacetime readily regards them as "blackmail," whereas the threatening power is likely to call them "deterrence." In order not to fall prey to this confusion of terms, it is useful to distinguish threats according to (1) their nature, (2) their conditions, and (3) their terms of compliance. First, what actions are threatened; i.e., what is the precise nature of the threat? Second, what actions does the threat seek to forestall; i.e., what are the conditions under which it will be carried out? Finally, what alternative actions is the threat meant to induce; i.e., what terms of compliance does it attempt to impose?

In the early years of the postwar period, Western statesmen used to speak of the deterrent power of the United States monopoly in atomic weapons. Churchill put it thus in Zurich on September 19, 1946: "In these present days we dwell strangely under the precarious shield and, I might even say, protection of the atomic bomb. The atomic bomb is still only in the hands of a state and nation which we know will never use it except in the cause of right and freedom. . . ." The deterrent value of all such statements lay in their implied warning to the Soviet Union. Leaving aside the degree of verbal explicitness or directness of such warnings, what gave them force was the threat that the United States would employ atomic weapons against the Soviet Union. The condition of the threat — what it sought to forestall — was an attack by the Soviet Union upon the United States or Western Europe. Compliance with the threat required only that the Soviet Union abstain from such an attack.

In Secretary Dulles' doctrine of instant and massive retaliation, the nature, conditions, and terms of compliance of this threat were changed.[1] The new threat implied the possibility

---

[1] John Foster Dulles, "Policy for Security and Peace," *Foreign Affairs*, Vol. 32 (April 1954), pp. 353–364. Cf. also Vice-President Nixon's radio and television address on March 13, 1954, published in *The New York Times*, March 14, 1954. For a useful discussion of the various forms and possible motives of Mr. Dulles' statements on the New Look, see E. Raymond Platig, "The 'New Look' Raises Old Problems," *Review of Politics*, Vol. 17 (January 1955), pp. 111–135.

that thermonuclear weapons would be used not only against the Soviet Union, but against any communist aggressor. It sought to forestall any communist attack (by Soviet forces or by proxy) anywhere (in Europe or elsewhere). Correspondingly, the compliance which the new threat hoped to enforce consisted in communist abstention from local aggression anywhere in the world.

This new threat was given its most radical expression by Vice-President Nixon: "We found that economically their [the Soviet] plan, apparently, was to force the United States to stay armed to the teeth, to be prepared to fight anywhere — anywhere in the world — that they, the men in the Kremlin, chose. Why? Because they knew that this would force us into bankruptcy; that we would destroy our freedom in attempting to defend it. Well, we decided we would not fall into these traps. And so we adopted a new principle. And the new principle summed up is this: Rather than let the communists nibble us to death all over the world in little wars we would rely in the future primarily on our massive mobile retaliatory power which we would use in our discretion against the major source of aggression at times and places we chose."[2]

Mr. Dulles was more cautious when he clarified the newly announced policy in his *Foreign Affairs* article. He said: ". . . obviously, the possession of that capacity to retaliate on a massive basis comprehends within it the capacity to retaliate on a less than global or massive basis." He continued, explicitly: ". . . I believe that it is disastrous for us to believe that the danger can be met by our concentrating merely upon one form of defense or one type of deterrent."[3]

This last statement came very close to subscribing to the doctrine of graduated deterrence, in which the British have shown much interest.[4] Graduated deterrence is an attempt to

[2] *The New York Times,* March 14, 1954.
[3] Dulles, *op. cit.,* pp. 5 and 22.
[4] See Rear Admiral Sir Anthony W. Buzzard, R.N., "Massive Retaliation and Graduated Deterrence," *World Politics,* Vol. 8 (January 1956), pp. 228–237; Sir John Slessor, "The Great Deterrent and Its Limitations,"

scale down the nature of the atomic threat so that it will match less exacting terms of compliance. While there is still a threat that all-out nuclear war would follow any thermonuclear attack on the United States (and/or Western Europe) by Soviet forces, restricted or local communist aggression could be met by less than total retaliation. In the words of Admiral Buzzard:

> The suggestion is that we work out and declare, without waiting for Communist agreement, distinctions of the following order. The *tactical* use of nuclear weapons, we might say, is to be confined to atomic weapons, and is to exclude even these from use against towns and cities. Their *strategic* use, we might further declare, is to include hydrogen weapons and the mass destruction of targets in towns and cities. We might also state generally that, in order to pursue the moral principle of never using more force than necessary, we would not resort to the strategic use of nuclear weapons unless their employment proved absolutely essential. Thus, without committing ourselves unalterably in advance, or showing our hand too clearly, we would have the option, when threatened with a limited aggression too great for our conventional forces to cope with, of saying to the prospective aggressor: "If you do attack, we will, if necessary, use atomic and perhaps chemical weapons against your armed forces. But we will not, on this issue, use hydrogen or bacteriological weapons at all, unless you do, and we will not use any mass destruction weapons against centers of population, unless you do deliberately." To this statement we might append certain exceptions, such as cities in the front line of the land fighting and those with airfields alongside.
>
> By an announcement of this character we would be modifying our present policy of massive retaliation to one aptly named "graduated deterrence."[5]

In the preatomic age, at the time of the *Pax Britannica*, for example, it was sometimes possible to exploit military capabilities in peacetime by threatening other powers with war and possible defeat. The development of atomic and thermonuclear weapons allows for threats of extinction. Such threats can demoralize a whole population, if it values life more than national

---

Bulletin of the Atomic Scientists, Vol. 12 (May 1956), pp. 140–146; and Hanson W. Baldwin, "The New Face of War," *ibid.*, pp. 153–158.
    5 Buzzard, *op. cit.*, p. 229.

interest. Threats of unrestricted war, therefore, may move the threatened government either to yield or to react aggressively, and may subject it to pressure for defiance or compliance from its own population; such threats could even provoke panic or rebellion in a threatened nation. To some extent, the possibility of such developments under threat has always existed, especially in literate societies — in which relatively large parts of the population take an interest in politics — even when war involved less than total destruction. Atomic threats, however, are likely to heighten the probability of such popular pressures; what is more, the probability increases with the degree to which the threat of extinction is understood, and in inverse proportion to the confidence enjoyed at home by the threatened government, and to its capability of effective defense.

It may be objected that the last of these three conditions does not apply, in view of the fact that often in history small countries have fought against hopeless odds rather than submit meekly to subjugation by a greatly superior enemy. It should be remembered, however, that in most such cases the weaker power was not threatened with physical extinction; in the few cases where it was, resistance sprang from a resolution to take a last toll of the conqueror. But, under conditions of thermonuclear warfare, it may not always be possible to exact such a last toll, for it is conceivable that a small country fighting alone might suffer total annihilation without inflicting a single casualty on the more powerful enemy. In such circumstances, resistance is considerably less likely. Any decision not to submit can then be based either on the chance that the threat is a bluff, and will not be carried out if the threatened country is staunch, or else on an extremely strong sense of honor that requires a nation to die rather than submit.

As atomic and thermonuclear parity replaces a situation of nuclear monopoly, the threat-value of these weapons diminishes. Threat can now be met by counter-threat, at least so long as the threatened power does not lose its nerve before the specter of reciprocal death and destruction. That is, bilateral threats will tend to neutralize one another. What is even more likely to happen when parity is achieved, however, is that the *explicitness and finality* of unrestricted threats will be avoided; threatening behavior as such is not likely to cease. When war can mean total annihilation, bluff among equals is too dangerous to be tried against a resolute adversary. It is difficult to believe that a country will ever issue an explicit atomic ultimatum to a power enjoying nuclear parity, for the only rational response to such an ultimatum is either compliance or a preventive attack; in the latter case, the ultimatum would defeat its own purpose by giving the enemy the advantage of the first strike. Under conditions of parity of ever more destructive weapons, therefore, and with ever-increasing appreciation of that destructiveness among political leaders, it stands to reason that authoritative threats of unrestricted war will in the future become less rather than more explicit and final.

This analysis requires two qualifications, however. First, a country facing invasion may reason that the aggressor has no desire for a nuclear war, and is about to attack in the belief that the war will not be nuclear. In such a situation, the threatened country might conceivably issue a defensive atomic ultimatum in the hope of avoiding both war and political extinction. Second, it does not seem impossible that certain extreme states of the world could lead to explicit and final authoritative threats of unrestricted war, even upon lesser provocation than a threat of extinction. For example, assuming a world in which everything except the Western Hemisphere has fallen under Soviet domination, a further step to force the submission of South America might be seen by the United States as tantamount to direct aggression against itself. In such a "back-against-the-wall" situation, it does not seem inconceivable that the United States might make final and explicit threats of unrestricted war in order to forestall what it judges to be its own political doom. It should be noted that, in contingencies such as these, the atomic ultimatum would be a measure of desperate defense rather than reckless aggression.

Since the end of World War II, nuclear weapons have increased in destructiveness and variety, and have decreased in cost. With the development of warheads of widely differing power, and delivery capabilities differing in range and kind, there has grown a tendency to regard the smaller atomic weapons as already so "conventional" in character as to be virtually indistinguishable in quality from "classical" weapons. Speaking of the development of atomic weapons since the end of World War II, President Eisenhower, in his address on "Atoms for Peace and Progress" before the General Assembly of the United Nations on December 8, 1953, declared that "the development has been such that atomic weapons have virtually achieved conventional status within our armed services."[6] Again, at his news conference on March 16, 1955, the President said that, if necessary, we could hit military targets with atomic warheads just as we would "hit them with a bullet."[7]

Such redefinition of conventionality affects the threat-value of nuclear weapons in two ways. On the one hand, references to tactical atomic weapons as conventional may be construed as restricted atomic threats; they imply that such weapons will be used in future local wars, just as "bullets" have been used in the past. The conditions and terms of compliance of such threats involve enemy abstention from local aggression, not merely from employment of nuclear weapons. Hence, in the present cold-war situation, such threats supplement, with respect to local war, the threat of unrestricted retaliation.

On the other hand, the very possibility of restricted threats implies a differentiation and gradation of threats. It remains possible, after a restricted atomic threat has been made, to specify different, more severe terms of compliance by threatening to use the bigger atomic and thermonuclear weapons. By reiteration, restricted threats may lose some of their effectiveness and become just as "conventional" as the weapons are supposed to be. In that event, bigger, less restricted threats may be needed to enforce terms of compliance that could originally be

[6] *The New York Times,* December 9, 1953.

[7] At his press conference on January 23, 1957, the President made a statement which implied that the United States might use small atomic weapons in opposing Communist armed aggression in the Middle East.

exacted by restricted threats, thus once more transcending an enlarged sphere of "conventional" weapons. It should be noted, however, that the calculations of a potential aggressor are not so much influenced by new definitions of the conventionality of weapons as by estimates of the effectiveness of weapons. Therefore, although calling tactical atomic weapons "conventional" may strengthen the belief that they will be used in defense, such renaming carries no assurance that bigger "unconventional" weapons will not be used.

Thus, any general announcement, prior to the actual outbreak of violence, about the conventionality of tactical atomic weapons can be read in two ways: either as a declaration of intent to extend the old boundaries of wars waged only with high-explosive weapons (i.e., as a threat), or as a declaration of intent not to extend the new boundaries of conventionality (i.e., as a promise). But the threat is stronger than the promise. The promise would become more credible if precedents supported the definition of conventionality, but no relevant precedents exist. Three conditions must be met before tactical atomic weapons can in fact be viewed as conventional: (1) they must be used in a war; (2) they must be the *only* atomic weapons used in that war; and (3) *the war must end either in a stalemate or in defeat of one of the combatants who did make tactical use of small atomic weapons.* The first and second requirements alone do not suffice to establish the conventionality of small atomic weapons, for victory resulting from their use in a local war would not preclude the possibility that, had the victor faced stalemate or defeat instead, he might have disregarded — or might disregard in the future — the weapons restrictions that, as victor, he had no sufficient reason to ignore.

Hence the third requirement. Prior to the end of a war, it is not certain whether it will end in victory, stalemate, or defeat. Any announcement that precedes its beginning, then, to the effect that *only* less than maximum atomic and thermonuclear power will be used, carries no more conviction than any other declaration of intent.

Since these conditions have not been met, there remains

uncertainty as to whether the use of "small" atomic weapons somewhere may not lead to the use of all available kinds of weapons anywhere. We do not know whether it is possible to control the transition from local to general war and from restricted ("conventional") atomic war to unrestricted violence. Several local wars have occurred since 1945 without leading to world war, but these have involved no atomic weapons whatever, so that they do not provide a precedent of control. For this reason, if for no other, the mere threat, not to mention the outbreak, of a restricted local atomic war is likely to arouse deeper apprehensions than would the outbreak of another local war similar to the one in Korea. It may also be predicted that, for the same reason, resistance among the atomic have-not powers to the *use* of tactical atomic weapons will increase as the power and number of atomic and thermonuclear weapons increase. This will occur so long as there are no wars serving to prove that atomic weapons can be controlled and local wars restricted.

Soviet exploitation of the threat-value of nuclear power in peacetime is enhanced by the fact that most of the powers in the Western alliance are atomically destitute. These have-not powers have no protection against a Soviet atomic attack except that which the retaliatory capability of the United States can provide. With the partial exception of Great Britain, that is at present [1957] the situation of all the nations with which the United States has common defense arrangements of one kind or another.[8] In fact, protection by the United States is their only safeguard against conventional as well as nuclear attack;

[8] In his report to Congress on foreign aid in May 1956, President Eisenhower announced his desire to hand over armaments with "atomic capability" to certain allies. If such a policy is approved, British troops stationed in Germany are likely to be offered "Honest John" rockets, "Corporal" guided missiles, and the 280-mm. cannon, all three of which are capable of firing atomic warheads. The sharing of such warheads, however, requires a modification of the Atomic Energy Act. It is possible that the British will be able to produce an atomic projectile for the "Corporal" guided missile before the Atomic Energy Act is amended by Congress.

for, given the relative inferiority of the West in conventional armaments, its only hope against a Soviet attack with such weapons in Europe lies in the defensive use of tactical atomic power.

This fact, that our European allies are protected by a coalition that is unable to meet conventional aggression by conventional means, gives the Soviet Union a political advantage in peacetime. For the Red forces could embark upon conventional aggression with good prospects of success, if they could be sure of not meeting with unconventional local defense or all-out retaliation. But the West has no such advantage in its own defense posture. That is why West Europeans tend to view the prospect of an atomic war in Europe as the terrible consequence of United States protection rather than of possible Soviet aggression. The Soviet Union may be threatening war, but it is the United States that seems bent on making it an atomic one either by insisting upon unconventional resistance to conventional attack, or, for precisely the same reason, by forcing the aggressor himself to resort to atomic attack. Thus, the fear of war in consequence of Soviet aggression turns into a fear of the weapons that will be employed in that war, and the responsibility for aggression becomes less important in European eyes than the responsibility for the nature of the war.

If NATO were politically of one will, this situation might be less serious than it is, but NATO enjoys less than perfect political unity of purpose, and suffers from a military inequality among its members that is accentuated by the virtual United States monopoly of atomic power among the Allies. The division of NATO into atomic haves and have-nots was less momentous than it later became so long as the United States enjoyed unquestioned predominance in nuclear weapons over the Soviet Union. With the world balance of atomic power clearly favoring the West, the have-nots in NATO could expect that an American ultimatum of unrestricted retaliation against the Soviet Union itself would effectively counter any Soviet threat of aggression in Europe. The Europeans could hope to be spared the horrors of war, atomic or otherwise; they needed only to assure themselves that the United States, in its own interest, would not permit the Russians to gain control of Western Europe.

Under conditions of nuclear parity, however, with the distribution of atomic capability among the NATO powers remaining unchanged, this reassurance becomes somewhat more labored and dubious, for it presupposes that the United States would be willing to defend Europe even at the risk of suffering nuclear devastation in its own zone of the interior. It is the dubiousness of this presupposition that generates the fear of our European allies that we have discussed.

Thus, Soviet achievement of a respectable nuclear capability offers communist leaders novel opportunities to threaten or cajole the atomic have-nots in NATO. Against a background of fulsome protestations of peaceableness and desire for coexistence, the Soviet Union can suggest that, in the event of war, America's European allies would suffer the horrors of atomic destruction, but that they would be spared that fate if they ended their military support of the United States. As Marshal Zhukov stated at the Twentieth Party Congress, "One cannot fail to note that the governments of states making available their territory for American military bases are playing with fire and sacrificing the national interests of their countries; they are placing their lives in jeopardy. By the logic of armed conflict, these bases must suffer retaliatory blows regardless of upon whose territories they are located."[9]

Threats of this kind have long been familiar in Soviet propaganda. Toward the end of 1954, for example, Soviet leaders countered Field Marshal Montgomery's statements that SHAPE would employ atomic and thermonuclear weapons in the event of a Soviet attack[10] by reminding the British that their islands were especially vulnerable to nuclear destruction. In an article published in *Pravda* and broadcast to the Soviet people on

[9] *Pravda,* February 20, 1956.
[10] Field Marshal Viscount Montgomery, "A Look Through a Window at World War III," *Journal of the Royal United Service Institution,* Vol. 99 (November 1954), pp. 507–523.

December 4, 1954, Marshal Vasilevsky warned that "the one who would dare to unleash a war would find himself in a most unenviable position." Addressing Field Marshal Montgomery directly, he said: "We both know very well that atomic and hydrogen bombs are weapons of mass destruction of peaceful populations, weapons of destruction of towns, which are particularly dangerous for countries with a small territory and a large population."

To the extent that unilateral strategic deterrence is replaced by a strategic stalemate, such threats and promises are likely to fall on more fertile ground than they did in the "American monopoly" phase of the nuclear age. Since the atomic have-nots in NATO lack any strategic deterrent capability of their own, they do not share directly whatever benefits accrue from a strategic stalemate; but they appear particularly exposed to the brunt of the greater destructiveness of war that is inherent in the emerging "conventionality" of tactical atomic weapons.

Of course, the Soviet leaders cannot risk an explicit and final atomic threat to any member of NATO unless they are prepared to risk total war, for they must reckon with the possibility that the United States will react to any such unambiguous ultimatum as if it had been addressed directly to itself. It is more likely that Soviet "atomic blackmail" will take forms that will allow for reversals of policy and withdrawals from commitments. Atomic blackmail must be noncommittal, subtle, informal, and casual, rather than binding, gross, authoritative, and solemn. The Russians, therefore, are likely to use indirection, and to address their threats to the small and middle powers of NATO.

But the Soviet leaders are likely to observe such precautions only so long as they believe that the United States is determined to come to the support of its allies when they are threatened. If they believed that the United States was prepared to abandon Europe, then it is probable that Soviet threats to the small and middle NATO powers would become more explicit, and perhaps final. Only a strategic nuclear capability of their own would render our European allies invulnerable to Soviet blackmail in such a case.

Under conditions of a strategic nuclear stalemate the United States cannot use strategic threats to counter subtle Soviet tactics against NATO, particularly if the Soviet warnings are accompanied by a smiling and flexible policy of strength and coexistence. Instead, so long as the United States is the only major atomic power in the Western alliance, it has no choice but to press for arrangements making possible an effective use of atomic weapons in the defense of Europe.

But it is unlikely that such plans will be able to provide a strong counterweight to Soviet atomic threats. In 1954, for example, the NATO governments agreed to give General Gruenther, the Allied Supreme Commander, permission to proceed with defense plans that included the use of atomic bombs, missiles, and artillery.[11] Yet, shortly before the communiqué announcing this agreement was issued, the press reported that it had become apparent in the meetings of the Military Committee that the Dutch, Belgian, and Danish governments would never agree to the actual use of atomic weapons. And the communiqué of December 18 did indeed state that the approval of planning for atomic defense "did not involve the delegation of the responsibility of governments to make decisions for putting plans into action in the event of hostilities." The views of German military experts likewise give little reason to believe that NATO's plans for the atomic defense of Europe would provide an adequate shield against atomic blackmail.[12]

Thus, while the trend toward nuclear equality between the United States and the Soviet Union has led to increasing caution in the exchange of threats between the two great powers, there is still room in which the Soviets can exploit the threat-

[11] Communiqué of the North Atlantic Council Meeting of December 18, 1954, published in *The New York Times,* December 19, 1954.

[12] For views of German military experts on atomic defense and atomic blackmail, cf. Hans Speier, *German Rearmament and Atomic War* (Evanston, Ill.: Row, Peterson and Company, 1957).

value of their atomic weapons against European members of NATO.[13] This situation will change when individual NATO members acquire an effective atomic capability of their own, at which point the new balance of atomic power will produce a more complex basis for the political exploitation of military strength.

---

[13] On January 23, 1957, the Tass news agency, quoting "leading circles of the Soviet Union," mentioned specifically Great Britain, France, West Germany, Italy, Iran, and Japan as nations which had placed themselves "under the threat of retaliatory atomic blows" by allowing themselves to be used by the United States "as bridgeheads for the preparation of atomic warfare" (*New York Herald Tribune,* January 24, 1957).

CHAPTER SIX

The Suez Crisis 1956

DURING THE CRISIS in the Middle East in the fall of 1956, the Soviet Union came closer than ever before to using atomic blackmail in furtherance of its policy.

On November 5, Bulganin sent messages to Eden, Mollet, Ben-Gurion, and Eisenhower seeking to compel the Anglo-French and Israeli forces to cease fire in Egypt and withdraw their troops. On the same day, Soviet Foreign Minister Shepilov addressed a letter of warning to the Security Council of the United Nations. The threats contained in these communications varied in kind and explicitness. Decreasing severity was coupled with increased explicitness.

In the order of severity, four threats can be distinguished: (1) unrestricted global war might develop from the crisis; (2) there could be provoked a Soviet attack upon Britain and France in which rockets and other modern weapons would be used; (3) there might be occasion for unilateral intervention by communist forces in the Middle East; (4) the Soviet Union would not cooperate with the United States policy favoring U.N. Assembly action, but would advocate joint Soviet-American intervention in Egypt on behalf of the United Nations.

Not all the threats were made in the same form to all the

Section II of paper entitled "Soviet Atomic Blackmail and the North Atlantic Alliance," from *World Politics,* Vol. 9 (April 1957).

recipients of the Soviet messages, so that, in addition to the gradation of the threats according to severity, a differentiation could be observed in intensity of the same threat. For example, Bulganin warned the three major powers that the fighting in Egypt could spread to other countries and develop into a third world war. Ben-Gurion, however, was told only that he had placed "the very existence of Israel as a state" in jeopardy by acting "as a tool of foreign imperialist powers" in his attack on Egypt.[1] Ben-Gurion was also informed that the Soviet ambassador to Israel was being recalled to Moscow. When a spokesman in the Soviet Foreign Ministry was asked whether the Soviet Union had broken relations with Israel, he replied that there was a difference between breaking off relations and withdrawing an ambassador.

The Soviet ambassadors were not recalled from London and Paris, but the messages to Eden and Mollet, couched in extraordinarily rude language, were menacing enough. In both of them, the threat of unilateral intervention was stated in this form: "The Soviet government is fully determined to apply force in order to crush the aggressors and restore peace in the East." This phrase appeared to be all the more menacing, coming as it did the day after the Soviet Union had failed to vote in favor of the organization of the United Nations Expeditionary Force, which had been formed in order to help restore peace in the Middle East. The letters to Eden and Mollet contained many parallel passages, but the main Soviet threat to Britain and France was elaborated only in the note to the British Prime Minister. In his note to Mollet, Bulganin asked merely: "What would be the position of France if she were attacked by other states having at their disposal modern and terrible means of destruction?" To Eden, however, he wrote: "In what position would Britain have found itself if she

[1] Unless otherwise indicated, all quotations are taken from the text of the messages as published in *The New York Times*, November 6, 1956. The texts of the notes to Eden, Mollet, and Ben-Gurion were supplied by Reuters; all others by the Associated Press.

herself had been attacked by *more powerful states* possessing *every kind of modern destructive weapon?* And there are countries now which need not have sent a navy or air force to the coast of Britain but could have used other means, such as *rocket technique. If rocket weapons had been used against Britain and France,* they would probably have called this a barbarous action. Yet in what way does the inhuman attack made by the armed forces of Britain and France on the nearly disarmed Egypt differ from this?" [Italics added.]

Note that the threat of using rockets against Britain and France — the second Soviet threat — fell short of mentioning atomic weapons explicitly. The only direct reference to atomic and hydrogen weapons made in any of the Soviet communications occurred in Bulganin's letter to Eisenhower. It was altogether factual and read simply: "The Soviet Union and the U.S.A. are permanent members of the Security Council and the two great powers which possess all modern types of arms, including the atomic and hydrogen weapons." The conjunction of this statement and the warning that the fighting in Egypt might develop into a third world war could be understood to imply — however tenuously — that the threatened global war might be unrestricted.

The letters to Eden and Mollet did not stipulate the time in which Bulganin expected the British and French to comply with his demand; technically, the notes were not ultimata. Moreover, the threat to use rockets against France and the British Isles was made in the noncommittal form of a conditional question, *viz.,* "In what position would Britain have found herself, if . . . ?"

In contrast with the vagueness of the first and second threats, the Soviet messages to the United Nations and to the United States were quite specific on timing, area, and means of the action which the Soviet government was proposing to take. Bulganin's message to Eisenhower and Shepilov's letter to the Security Council specified the proposed action. These specifications reduced considerably the severity of the Soviet warning that a global war might develop, or that Britain and France might be rocket-bombed. The Soviet leaders were thinking of military intervention *in Egypt.*

This third threat, too, was so cautiously phrased, and the proposed action so carefully justified, that the appearance of a threat was technically avoided. Bulganin said that measures should be taken against France and Britain at U.N. headquarters and in Egypt, not in Europe. He did not threaten bluntly that the Soviet Union would act unilaterally, but made a proposal, elaborated by Shepilov, to establish legal ground for massive intervention by the United Nations. He suggested that the Security Council pass a resolution, amounting to an ultimatum, demanding of the British, French, and Israelis that they cease fighting in Egypt within twelve hours after the Council decision, and that they withdraw their troops within three days. According to the Soviet draft resolution contained in Shepilov's letter, this proposed measure of the Council was explicitly justified with reference to the fact that ". . . the resolution of the extraordinary session of the General Assembly of November 2, 1956, which recommended that the governments of Britain, France, and Israel should immediately stop military operations against Egypt and withdraw their troops from the territory of Egypt, has not been carried out by the above state. . . ."

In the event that Britain, France, and Israel did not comply with the projected resolution of the Security Council, it was further proposed that *all* members of the United Nations give armed aid to Egypt in response to an appeal that was to be part of the Council resolution.

The Soviet government went one step further. It proposed that the Council urge the United States and the Soviet Union, as the two most powerful members of the United Nations, to take the lead in acting on behalf of the United Nations. Impatient with, and probably distrustful of, the action of the General Assembly that had not stopped the British and French, the Soviet leaders threatened to reverse the policy of the United States that favored Assembly action. It appeared that

Bulganin did not want to confine military actions against the Anglo-French and Israeli forces in Egypt to an intervention by the least powerful nations in NATO, excluding both Soviet and American contingents from this venture, but advocated instead that the most powerful nations act to help Nasser. He also made it clear, however, that he did not want to preclude participation of smaller nations in the intervention.

This fourth threat was the most explicit of all. It attempted, among other things, to confront the United States with a dilemma: the United States would either have to face the consequences of the policy it had adopted when introducing the Assembly resolution of November 2, 1956, against Britain, France, and Israel, or stand revealed as a power which did not act in accordance with its declared moral principles. The first alternative would have involved committing American forces to fight side by side with communists against the British and French, and would have given a truly fatal turn to the deep conflict that had arisen in the Western coalition over the Suez issue. The Soviet Union would have been able "to bury the West," to use a word from Khrushchev's political vocabulary. The second course would have "unmasked" the political intentions of the United States before the Arab world and the uncommitted nations. As Bulganin put it to Eisenhower, "We are convinced that if the Governments of the U.S.S.R. and the U.S.A. would firmly declare their will to insure peace and oppose aggression, the aggression will be ended and there will be no war."

What Bulganin meant by firmness was made clear in Shepilov's draft resolution. If the Anglo-French and Israeli forces failed to cease fighting and to withdraw, armed and other aid to Egypt should consist of "naval and air forces, military units, volunteers, instructors, military equipment, and other types of aid."

Despite the elaborate rehearsal of the moral and legal justification for collective military intervention in the Middle East, it appeared from the Soviet communications that Russia was trying to gain a military hold on the Middle East, an objective of which her foreign policy had not lost sight for two hundred years. If the Security Council had issued the proposed ultimatum, the Soviet Union might have gained a legal pretext for intervening even if the Anglo-French and Israeli governments had yielded, simply because it might have been technically impossible to withdraw all forces within three days, or because Nasser and the Soviet leaders could have claimed that not all forces had been withdrawn in due time.

The warning of global war and the second Soviet threat of an assault by rockets and other modern weapons against Britain and France were considerably softened by the proposal for United Nations intervention in the Middle East on the specified terms. But the language used in connection with the second threat, the proposal of new, massive, military action by the United Nations, and, finally, the blunt declaration that the Soviet Union was determined "to crush the aggressors," all seemed to suggest that the Soviet Union might be eager to go further than its specific proposal indicated. The first two threats heightened the apprehension that the Soviet proposal for joint American-Soviet intervention in the Middle East might have been made in order to derive from its rejection a political justification for *unilateral* intervention in Egypt. This third threat was in fact never allowed to be forgotten. The Security Council did not put the Soviet proposal on its agenda, the Anglo-French and Israeli governments did yield to the Soviet pressure for a cease-fire, and yet the Soviet Union and China proceeded to frighten the West with the threat to send communist volunteers and more arms to the Middle East.

The Soviet threats against the Western powers were intensified by skillful Soviet propaganda, which helped to turn the Suez crisis into a major diplomatic defeat for the West. The text of the Soviet diplomatic notes was made public in Moscow in a version based on a press conference by Leonid F. Ilyichev and reached the world capitals by cable and broadcast on the evening before the official messages were delivered through the usual diplomatic channels. At the press conference, Ilyichev either used a more menacing wording than that which occurred in the official note to Mollet, or based his statements on the most threatening note, that which was addressed to Eden. In any event, the text that reached the West first through these propaganda channels sounded most ominous. The striking differentiation of the threat in the notes to Eden and Mollet was eliminated. Furthermore, the initial effect of the whole Soviet move was increased by the simple device of soft-pedaling, in the earliest communications, the Soviet proposal for action by the Security Council. Only this proposal, which was spelled out in the actual notes, made it fully clear that the Soviet Union was not at that time overtly threatening to take unilateral action in Egypt, and was not contemplating the achievement of peace in the Middle East by rocket-bombing England and France. A speaker on Radio Moscow had quoted the following sentence from Bulganin's messages to Eden and Mollet: "We are fully determined to crush the aggressors and restore peace in the East through the use of force." Only later did Defense Minister Zhukov and Party Secretary Suslov explain that the "we" in the sentence meant Russia in concert with the United Nations.

It is important to note that they volunteered this explanation. The attempt to "clarify" the nature of the most severe first and second threats was akin to the distinction suggested by the recall of the Soviet ambassador from Israel and the insistence that the Soviet Union had not broken off diplomatic relations. The gradation of the threats and the differentiation of the second threat in the messages to Eden and Mollet are other cases in point. The less severe threats controlled the fantasies aroused by the more severe ones, while the more severe ones, in turn, increased the intensity of the less severe. In addition, the lashing verbal aggressiveness of the severe threats was accompanied or followed by cautious efforts to prevent undesirable reactions on the part of the threatened powers. The doctrine of this procedure may be stated as follows: in order to exact compliance with an effort at blackmail, the cost of failing to comply must appear disastrously high to the victim. But once fantasies of disaster are aroused, they must be controlled. When they are once aroused, the relatively lesser cost of compliance appears a blessing. This technique corresponds to that of a holdup man who brandishes a gun in front of an armed victim but who, for fear that the frightened man may fight for his life, quickly tells him that he only wants his money.

When the official version of Bulganin's letter arrived, the United States took three kinds of action. It answered Bulganin with unusual dispatch. It prevailed upon France, Britain, and Israel to yield. And on the next day, when new military intelligence became available from Turkey and certain West European governments, it took certain precautionary military measures.[2]

The White House issued a statement in which the second threat to Britain and France and the warning that global war might develop were ignored, the Soviet proposal for action by the Security Council was rejected, and the third Soviet threat of unilateral action in the Middle East was countered by a declaration of opposition.

Bulganin's letter was characterized as "an obvious attempt to divert world attention from the Hungarian tragedy." It was pointed out that the United Nations had already called for a cease-fire, for withdrawal of foreign armed forces, and for entry of a United Nations force to stabilize the situation, "pending a settlement." "In this connection," the White House statement said, "it is to be regretted that the Soviet Union did not vote last night in favor of the organization of this United Nations force." The Soviet proposal for action by the Security Council was called an "unthinkable suggestion."

Before the Suez crisis reached its climax on November 5, President Eisenhower had repeatedly declared that the United States would not become involved in the Middle East. Without overtly contradicting this declaration of intent, the White

[2] On the effect of this intelligence upon the government, see the detailed account by Charles J. V. Murphy, "Washington and the World," *Fortune,* Vol. 55 (January 1957), pp. 78ff.

House statement attempted to deter the Soviet Union from sending volunteers or other forces to Egypt: "The introduction of new forces [other than the United Nations force, which contained neither American nor Soviet contingents] . . . would violate the United Nations Charter, and it would be the duty of all United Nations members, *including the United States*, to oppose any such effort." [Italics added.][3]

The concern of the United States was evident not only from the speed with which the White House statement was issued, but also from the strong pressure exerted on Britain, France, and Israel for a cease-fire. The application of this pressure was consistent with the policy the United States had adopted ever since the French and British had decided to intervene in Egypt. Since the United Nations Assembly had, upon American initiative, recommended a cease-fire and withdrawal, the United States could apply renewed pressure on Britain, France, and Israel without formally underwriting any of the Soviet threats of November 5. The effectiveness of these threats upon Britain, France, and Israel was nevertheless increased by the action of the United States. It is not implausible to assume that the Soviet leaders would not have dared resort to their blackmail maneuver if American condemnation of France and Britain, and American action against France and Britain in the United Nations, had not preceded it.

The British and French complied in a few hours after receipt of Bulganin's message, sooner than they would have had to act if the Security Council had voted on Shepilov's proposal that an ultimatum be issued to them. The military objectives of the British and French intervention in Egypt, which were within reach according to the judgment of British officers on the scene, could not be attained. The intervention became a fiasco.

[3] Compare this warning with the one which the Department of State issued on November 29 (*The New York Times*, November 30, 1956). In the second warning, the Soviet government was told, *without* reference to the United Nations, that the United States would view any change in the territorial status of the Baghdad Pact countries "with the utmost gravity."

Next day, Ben-Gurion announced that Israel had reversed its position under the pressure of the United States, the United Nations, and the Soviet Union. On November 9, Nasser explained in Cairo that the United States and the Soviet Union were on his side. When Mollet justified the French cease-fire order in the National Assembly, he ventured to praise the reestablishment of Western solidarity in view of the American warning that had been issued in response to the third and fourth Soviet threats: "When the Soviet Union thought it saw a crack in the free world and wanted to threaten, we at once found the United States at our side."[4] In view of subsequent events, it is doubtful that Mollet did more than try to save face.

Like Mollet, Eden ordered a cease-fire, ostensibly not in response to the Soviet threat and to American appeals to yield to it, but to the Israeli-Egyptian cease-fire and in implementation of the United Nations resolution of November 2. In his reply to Bulganin, which Eden read in Commons on November 6, he referred to the Soviet note as follows: "The language which you [Bulganin] used . . . made me think at first I could only return [your note] as entirely unacceptable. But the moment is so grave that I feel I must try to answer you with the counsels of reason. . . ."[5]

The Soviet attempt at intimidation by the allusion to rocket-bombing was mentioned neither in the British and French replies to Bulganin nor in the White House statement. The only explicit answer to this piece of blackmail was given by General Gruenther at his final news conference before he retired as Supreme Allied Commander in Europe. On November 13, a week after the fighting in Egypt had ceased, he referred to the Soviet intimation that rockets might be launched against Britain and France and declared: "Whether or not such rockets exist, they will not destroy the capacity of NATO to retaliate."[6]

The United States took certain military measures in view of the Soviet threat. The Continental Air Defense Command, the

---

[4] *The New York Times,* November 8, 1956.
[5] *Ibid.,* November 7, 1956.
[6] *Ibid.,* November 14, 1956.

Sixth Fleet, the Atlantic Fleet, and the Strategic Air Command were alerted. A naval force, including the aircraft carriers *Forrestal* and *Franklin D. Roosevelt* and the heavy cruiser *Des Moines,* received orders to sail. The Navy was secretive about the mission of this force. Speculations appeared in the press to the effect that the order served the double purpose of having these ships ready at sea for action and of protecting them against the possibility of an atomic surprise attack on American harbors. Speculations that the force was to augment the American Sixth Fleet in the Mediterranean were silenced by a naval announcement that the force would remain part of the Atlantic Fleet under the command of Admiral Wright. In a reply to a German inquiry, Headquarters of the United States Air Forces in Europe said that its forces had not been put on an alert and that orders for such an alert were not expected.[7]

Despite their rude wording, then, the most severe Russian threats seem to have been the least serious. In particular, the conditional threat against Britain and France in no way resembled an ultimatum, and it was virtually neutralized by the specific proposal for Soviet intervention in the Middle East. The use of atomic weapons was never overtly threatened.

The effect of the threats was heightened by propaganda, and by the techniques of gradation and differentiation. The primary function of the severe threats seems to have been to increase the effect of the lesser threats, but care was taken by

[7] *Frankfurter Allgemeine Zeitung,* November 9, 1956. Mr. Murphy's account (*op. cit.*), which seems to be based on inside information, suggests that the main concern of the government was not aroused by Bulganin's letters of November 5 but by later intelligence of Soviet military moves. It would appear from this account that without the additional military intelligence that became available on November 6, the government would not have taken the military countermeasures on which it decided that afternoon, but would have confined itself to issuing the White House statement and to urging Eden and Mollet to order a cease-fire. Mr. Murphy writes that the United States took military countermeasures despite the fact that CIA, in revising its estimate of Soviet intentions twice on November 6, had by 12:15 moved back from its alarmist mid-morning position toward the calmer estimate that it had held early that day; the government did so "just in case."

the Soviet leaders to control any possible undesirable reaction to the severe ones. Thus, while the Soviet maneuver was conducted in exceedingly rude language, it cannot be said to have been reckless. The Soviet leaders combined extreme rudeness with noticeable caution in threatening Britain and France. They exploited the conflicts among the Western allies at a time when they were themselves having unprecedented difficulties in keeping control over their own empire. But it does not appear that Russia was prepared to risk global war, or even that she expected to run such a risk by the form in which the blackmail maneuver was conducted. Rather were conditions such as to encourage the Soviet leaders to pursue, by means of carefully measured threats, any or all of the following long-known objectives of their policy: (1) to thwart British and French military plans in the Middle East and to ensure Nasser's victory over Britain and France; (2) to extend Soviet influence in the Middle East as far as Western lack of resistance would permit; (3) to destroy NATO while it was torn.

From the Soviet point of view, the basic conditions conducive to the blackmail maneuver, that is, to lowering its risks and heightening the probability of its success, may well have appeared to be the following: (1) the nuclear stalemate between the United States and the Soviet Union; (2) the prevailing paralysis of the Western coalition owing to the conflict of national interests among its chief members; (3) the slow pace of the British-French intervention in Egypt and its failure to establish quickly a *fait accompli*; (4) the previous authoritative American declarations that the United States would shun military involvement in the Middle East; (5) the United States policy of condemning France, Britain, and Israel on moral grounds, and of opposing the attainment of their military objectives in Egypt; (6) opposition in Britain to Eden's policy. In these circumstances, the Soviet leaders had to consider whether the blackmail maneuver would cement the crumbling alliance of the West, or whether the unprecedented rudeness of the first three threats would induce the United States to add its persuasion to their threats and ensure Soviet success. Apparently they decided that the probability of success was high if they could control the threats in a way such as not to drive the United States to reverse its policy and to repair the fences of NATO.[8]

In two important respects, the Soviet maneuver of November 5 differed from the cases of atomic blackmail considered in Chapter 5. First, the blackmail pressure on November 5 was not exerted in order to *create* a split in NATO; such a split existed before that date. Secondly, the attempt at intimidation was aimed not only at the lesser members of NATO, but, indirectly, at the United States itself, although the overt appearance of such intimidation was carefully avoided.

Soviet leaders often protest their dedication to the principle of minimizing violence in the world, but it can be argued that their devotion to this principle is an element of their propaganda rather than of their policy. Their policy is predicated on the principle that every opportunity for maximizing Soviet control over world events must be recognized and exploited, if only in order to avoid harming Soviet interests by inaction. The Soviet leaders recognized that the breach in NATO that had developed prior to November 5 was such an opportunity. In some measure, American fear of war was aroused by the direct threats against Britain and France. The American dedication to the principle of minimizing the use of violence in foreign affairs was turned to the advantage of the Soviet Union. But every appearance of Soviet pressure upon the United States was avoided. The United States could yield to the pressure without having to admit that it was in fact yielding to it. It could believe that it was merely continuing its own moral condemnation of British and French action, particularly since it could rightly claim that it had opposed the lesser Soviet threats in the process.

[8] On previous instances of Soviet rudeness and the function of such rudeness in the political behavior of Bolsheviks, see Nathan Leites, "It Pays to be Rude," in *A Study of Bolshevism* (Glencoe, Ill.: The Free Press, 1953), pp. 34–42.

CHAPTER SEVEN

Germany in American Foreign Policy

*The following paper was presented at an international confer-
ence in Munich, held in January 1966. Since that time at least
four major events have affected the political relations between
the United States and Europe in general and between the
United States and the Federal Republic in particular.*

*First, the United States has become ever more deeply in-
volved in the Vietnamese war. The number of American forces
committed to this struggle has risen. The use of violence in it
has mounted. Human losses and financial costs have increased.
At the same time, Soviet pressure on Western Europe has been
dormant ever since the resolution of the Cuban missile crisis.
To many Europeans it could, therefore, appear that the main
focus of American security interests had been shifting from
Europe to Asia. To the extent that West Germans have adopted
this view — fearfully or reluctantly or even hopefully — they
can point to the attenuation of American military manpower
stationed in Germany and to pressure on the Federal Republic to ease the American balance of payments problem.*

*Second, mainly if not exclusively in consequence of De-
Gaulle's defection, NATO is weaker in 1968 than it was two
years ago. In his letter to President Johnson of March 7, 1966,
the General predicted the casus foederis which would obligate
France to fight on the side of her Allies no longer on "armed
aggression," in accordance with Art. V of the North Atlantic
Treaty of April 4, 1949, but on "unprovoked aggression." Thus,
he unilaterally substituted for a condition to be established in*

Presented at the International Wehrkunde Conference, Munich, in
January 1966, and published in German in *Wehrkunde*, Munich, Vol.
15 (February 1966).

fact a condition to be fulfilled only by his interpretation of the facts. In addition, he cut long-established organizational ties between France and NATO. While all West European countries are exposed to a communist military threat to their security, the Federal Republic borders on communist territory. Any weakening of NATO, therefore, is of most immediate concern to the Germans.

Third, in December 1966, a Grand Coalition Government of Christian Democrats and Social Democrats under Chancellor Georg Kiesinger superseded the weak and troubled regime of Ludwig Erhard. While West Germany's dependence on the United States for protection of her security interests has in fact been increased by DeGaulle's defection, Kiesinger's government has continued a policy of trying to balance the "Continental" and "Atlantic" interests of the Federal Republic. In its first year in office, the new Federal Government was in fact more pro-French and more anti-American than Erhard's regime had been, because it believed that one could not risk losing DeGaulle's rhetorical support of reunification by resisting the General's anti-British and anti-American policies in Europe and by being as responsive to Washington's demands as Erhard's government had been.

Fourth, in January 1968, the United States and the Soviet Union finally reached full agreement on a draft treaty to arrest the spread of nuclear weapons to countries not yet possessing such arms. While it cannot be predicted whether or not the treaty will be ratified at all or which powers in addition to Red China and France will abstain from ratification, it is certain that West German ratification of the treaty would be most desirable to the Soviet Union and to France. If it should come to ratification by some major powers, the Germans will hardly be able to abstain from following suit, but they will not do so without resentment. It will appear to them that they were obligated to serve Soviet and French interests by the United States, their most powerful ally. They will notice that NATO was formed in opposition to the Soviet Union, whereas the treaty on nonproliferation is based on cooperation between the two superpowers trying to fix the nuclear status quo among the nations.

The Nature of the Alliance

THE UNITED STATES and the Federal Republic of Germany are allies in NATO because the governments of these two countries consider the Western alliance to be of value in the pursuit of their respective political interests. The alliance is not based on popular sentiment, cultural affinity, or historical tradition.

Many Americans "like" the Germans, admire certain outstanding writers, composers, or scientists of German nationality, and hold certain German political leaders in high regard. There are other Americans, however, who are attracted rather to Englishmen or Frenchmen or Poles. Furthermore, for every German who deplores the absence of nightingales in the United States or is bewildered by the American ability to temper the moralistic with the pragmatic in politics, you can find an American who dislikes what he takes to be the German propensity to march rather than walk or to love obedience as well as music. But neither such Germans nor such Americans bear witness against the worth of the alliance. Foreign policy cannot be shaped by sentiment or resentment.

NATO is not sustained by expectations or expressions of gratitude for American assistance rendered in the early postwar years to Western Europe at large and West Germany in particular. Nor is the functioning of NATO necessarily impeded by resentments of alleged hegemonic aspirations that some people even outside the communist camp attribute to the United States, others to France, and still others to a new generation of Germans. Such resentment becomes politically relevant only if it reinforces a government's decision to leave or weaken an alliance, judging it no longer to serve the purpose for which it was formed. In the case of NATO this purpose has been the protection of common security interests against hegemonic designs of the Soviet Union. Who is bold enough to act on the assumption that these designs have vanished?

As to cultural affinity, American bonds with Europe at large and Germany in particular are, of course, closer than they are with Asian or African nations, because in DeGaulle's words, America is "the daughter" of Europe, but by no means all Americans believe that they owe a greater cultural debt to Germany than to France, and if they read the Bible, it is in the

King James version and not in Luther's translation.[1] But cultural affinity between allies is no essential source of political solidarity — in art, if not in baseball, the Japanese are closer to the Chinese than to the Americans — and no alliance can be built on similarities of "national character," say, love for children or the capacity for inflicting unintentional, and hence ungentlemanly, insults on foreigners.

Finally, "fate" or "history" — favorite German entities — do not predestine any nation to be the ally of another nation. Today, neither Franco-German "friendship" nor the still rather cold climate in Russian-American relations follows a historical precedent. The United States has never been at war with Russia, while Frenchmen have often met Germans in battle. Alliances change with the changing constellation of national interests and appear to be fairly independent of similarities in the forms of government or in the ideologies to which the people in the countries concerned are accustomed. Just as in the alignment during the Thirty Years War, the Protestant-Catholic schism was superseded by the political interests of states and

[1] Similarly, the West Germans feel "culturally" closer to France than to the United States, but the majority of Germans consider cooperation with the United States on political, economic, and military matters to be more important than they regard such cooperation with France. An Allensbach survey taken in June 1965 found the following distribution of preferences:

Who Is More Important to Germany?
(With whom should Germany cooperate more closely?)

With regard to:	U.S.	France	Unde-cided	Total
1. Culture (education and art)	26	37	37	100
2. Reunification	64	8	28	100
3. Economics	58	20	22	100
4. Armament and Defense	63	11	26	100

Cf. Erich Peter Neumann, "Probleme unseres Frankreich-Bildes," *Die politische Meinung,* September 1965, p. 28.

It should be added, however, that such figures provide no guidelines for policy, but are in large part volatile public reactions to the prevailing policies of the three powers involved.

principalities, so in World War II the conflict between communism and capitalism receded in the face of Hitler's initial military victories, and in the postwar world, victors and vanquished in the West formed an alliance to guard against the communist peril.

Since political interests are the root of the defensive alliance, it follows that the coalition is likely to break up if one or more of the following estimates of the international situation come to prevail in government councils: (1) the rationale of the alliance has disappeared, i.e., the common danger of aggression is judged to have passed; (2) the means and arrangements for meeting such aggression are judged to be inadequate and no agreement on repair or reform can be reached; (3) as circumstances change, one or more members of the alliance conclude, or come to be persuaded, say by foreign governments or by the domestic opposition, that the alliance invites rather than deters aggression and harms rather than serves national interests; (4) the burdens of the alliance are judged to be inequitably distributed among the members of the alliance; (5) the European allies develop a capability to defend themselves without U.S. aid. To these five conditions must be added a sixth. The alliance will falter if the national policy of one or more of its members is judged by the others to conflict with the common purpose of the alliance. The seriousness of such intra-alliance conflict decreases with the power of the member state that causes it, and it increases with the power of the member state that is annoyed by the conflict. For example, if the United States became critically dissatisfied with its allies this would almost certainly spell the doom of NATO, while the dissatisfaction of France need not necessarily be disastrous, no matter how disturbing it is. Were NATO judged to be no longer serviceable to the common interests of its member states, each government would eventually face the question as to whether reform and repair are desirable and feasible — what specific compromise is acceptable? — whether selective bilateral arrangements should be substituted for those institutions and organizational features of the alliance which no longer command common support, or whether the complete restoration of freedom from the entangling alliance is the preferred course of action.

In examining the viability of a coalition one should not search for identity of national interests, but for compatibility. The national interests of the Federal Republic and of the United States are neither identical in scope nor equal in weight, nor do all of them point to the same objective; but for almost twenty years, Germany's interests and some American interests in foreign affairs have nevertheless been such as to help to create and sustain an alliance between the two countries — thus far mainly within the framework of NATO.

In the following observations on the place of Germany in current U.S. foreign policy,[2] I shall leave aside economic considerations and refer only to three points: (1) the American orientation toward political order in Europe; (2) the global character of American interests; (3) American nuclear policy. In all three regards German interests differ in varying degrees from American interests; this is to be expected. Unlike the United States, the Federal Republic is neither a global power nor a nuclear power. Moreover, despite its swift political and social resurrection from the ashes of World War II — a performance more impressive than the development of the West German economy — the Federal Republic lacks the fullness of sovereignty which all other member states of NATO enjoy. This fact is closely associated with the outcome of World War II and the division of the country into two parts, each with a regime hostile to the other.

Apart from being a continental European power like France, and not a power with global interests like the United States or Great Britain, and apart from being a nonnuclear power, like Italy, the Federal Republic has certain other political characteristics that bear upon its position within the alliance. Its borders are more vulnerable to communist encroachment than are those of the other West European NATO powers. Second,

[2] These observations are part of a larger study that I am undertaking for the Council on Foreign Relations in New York.

it is interested in the reunification of Germany and thus in a change of the territorial *status quo* in Europe; this interest is appreciated by its allies, but for evident reasons it is of greater importance to Germany than to her allies. In addition, her biggest industrial city, West Berlin, is isolated from both West Germany and East Berlin, a walled-up torso of a Western capital surrounded by communist territory. Third, of all NATO powers the Federal Republic contributes the largest contingent to the conventional defenses of the alliance. Finally, as a vanquished nation now allied with some of its victors, the Federal Republic still lives with some constraints on its sovereignty and cannot yet afford to forget that its predecessor was Hitler's Reich. In order to realize that the past still burdens the present, one needs only to recall the crisis in the Near East early in 1965 or the more recent international debates on halting the spread of nuclear weapons and on a joint nuclear force. In spite of the economic strength of the Federal Republic and its considerable military contribution to NATO, few tactical and strategic options are open to the foreign policy of West Germany. This is true whether one looks at German foreign policy in relation to other powers in Eastern Europe or the Near East, in Western Europe or North America, in Africa or Asia. And it is true whether one looks at the initiative German foreign policy might take or the way in which it can respond to the initiatives of other powers.

The American Interest in NATO

United States postwar foreign policy still bears the marks of the grand strategy of World War II. The last World War was fought in both the Atlantic and Pacific areas with the two theaters competing for primary attention and preferential allocation of American and British resources in arms and men. The most important decision concerning the grand strategy of the war was that determining the priority of the European theater. This decision influenced the course and phasing of World

War II to Churchill's satisfaction, and, occasionally, to McArthur's chagrin.

After the war, Europe remained the primary theater of the political, economic, and military engagement of the United States, although none of the fighting in which Americans have participated since the end of World War II has occurred in Europe.

The American postwar policy of containment in Europe has served the same interests that prompted the United States to participate in two world wars: for strategic and economic reasons the United States cannot allow Europe to fall under the domination of any single power, whether this power be Germany or Russia. In my view, the United States would also have to oppose a domination of Europe by a combination of powers, say a Russo-French or a Russo-German alignment, although in 1940 the United States would almost certainly not have objected if the French government had accepted Churchill's bid to join undefeated Great Britain with moribund France. Farsighted Germans, like Chancellor Adenauer, have always been concerned about the consequences which another "Kronstadt" or a German movement toward another "Rapallo" might have for the international position of the Federal Republic.

At Yalta, President Roosevelt told Stalin that American troops would be withdrawn from Europe within two years after the termination of fighting, but when the American hope for continued Soviet-American collaboration after the end of the war turned out to be ill-founded, the United States made the most radical break in the history of its foreign policy. It decided to abandon its time-honored tradition of avoiding entangling alliances in peacetime. It assisted Western Europe economically; it helped to form NATO; it stationed large forces in Europe, and it encouraged European unification.

The United States interest in the formation of NATO was four-fold: (1) It wanted to prevent an expansion of the communist domain into the noncommunist part of Europe in order to deny these territories to communist political domination and economic and military exploitation. (2) It wanted the powers whose vital security interests were at stake to share the burden of defense so that the United States would not carry this burden alone for allies that would apply their resources to increasing their comfort at American expense. (3) It wanted to organize the defense of free Europe in such a way that this relatively small part of the continent could be held at the beginning of the war and would not have to be reconquered at the end, as had been necessary in World War II. (4) It wanted to prevent a German *Drang nach Osten.*

Moreover, the task of defending Western Europe in the nuclear age impressed upon military planners the need to take account of the shrinkage of distance and time brought about by the development of long-range vehicles capable of delivering nuclear warheads on military targets and cities, on ports and beachheads. In the two world wars, the United States had mobilized for war after the outbreak of hostilities: America was protected by oceans and friendly powers. In the initial years of these wars — until 1917 and 1941, respectively — the brunt of the battle was borne by these powers friendly to the United States. In World War II even the decision to exact the unconditional surrender of the enemy was made long before a single American soldier set foot on European soil.

In a future world war the United States would have no time to mobilize its strength after the opening of hostilities in Europe. Nor would the West European powers of NATO be in a position to absorb a massive military onslaught in the hope that in the end the United States would join the battle to turn the tide. By that time, little would be left of what we now know as Western Europe. Khrushchev once remarked that not even the Acropolis would be spared. The Soviet leaders, in turn, cannot risk making war in stages against the West if they must count on U.S. resistance from the very beginning. Regardless of the musings of some Europeans about the "incredibility" of the U.S. deterrent, the Soviet leaders cannot afford to discount the hazard of having to contend in a war against Europe with the overwhelming might of the United States as well.

To be serviceable in the nuclear age as a deterrent, the alliance cannot rely on concepts and schedules of mobilization that were sufficient in the prenuclear age. It must have *in peacetime* integrated forces, a command structure that is not rendered ineffective by time-consuming political consultations during battle; it needs adequate logistical and warning systems. Its forces must be so deployed, so armed, and so instructed as to be capable of timely, concerted, defensive action.

West German forces were integrated into NATO not only for reasons of creating a more effective defense against the East, but also in order to safeguard against the resurgence of German national military power. West Germany's integration into the alliance has been of considerable benefit to her. NATO has assured her of a considerable measure of security, and NATO membership has made possible her political rebirth as one of the democratic states of Western Europe. In addition, West Germany has received assurances from her allies that they consider the Federal Republic as the only legitimate German government and seek Germany's reunification by peaceful means, that is, by negotiations with the leaders of the Soviet Union, the four-power responsibility for German reunification never having been abandoned. The Federal Republic, in its turn, obligated itself to its allies not to produce any atomic, biological and chemical (ABC) weapons and certain other types of arms; nor can it withdraw any of its contingents from NATO, as other members of the alliance have done on several occasions. It is unlikely that West Germany would today enjoy allied support for reunification had it not been for the German decisions to participate in the common defense and in West European institutions such as the Coal and Steel Community, Euratom, and the Common Market.

NATO has been an effective deterrent to Soviet expansion in Europe. When we speak of the deterrents having been successful, we generally think of success in keeping the peace. We should, in fact, be thinking more specifically of the success in controlling the escalation of political conflict. The use of military power is not confined to war, and the peacetime, political worth of deterrent power needs to be appreciated in operational terms. Such power is an instrument in conditions of acute conflict or in "crisis management" — if one prefers the new, inept term of political analysts. In U.S. postwar history the militarily significant operations in the resolution of European crises have included augmentations of deployed military power and sudden expansions of the military budget (during the second Berlin crisis in 1961), improvisations like the airlift and the redeployment of strategic bombers from the United States to Great Britain (in the first Berlin crisis); further, they have included putting certain naval forces and SAC on alert status on several occasions; they have also included efforts to persuade Western allies to agree on contingency plans for the defense of Berlin. All this has taken resources, resilience, and resolution, as well as restraint. It is worthwhile reflecting on what might have happened had a smaller power, or even a combination of smaller powers, been faced with the task of deterring the intensification of political crises.

The Unification of Europe

American policy has not only helped to form NATO but has also favored the political unification of Western Europe. Clearly, the United States is interested in preventing another war arising from intra-European conflicts: a united Europe would be pacified. Furthermore, American experience sustains the belief that a large politically integrated area, rather than a divided one, offers the best prospects of economic growth. Although American concern with the viability of the West European economy has not been entirely altruistic — what policy ever is? — this concern stemmed originally from the desire to strengthen common Western resistance to communist subversion and aggression. More recently, the United States has also wished that Europe assume a share of "the global responsibility" which the United States discharges through military and economic assistance in decolonized areas of the world.

Many Americans are aware of the fact that the United States spends a higher percentage of her GNP for national security than does West Europe, which spends relatively more than the United States on social security. But not all Americans take due account of the fact that burden-sharing outside the NATO area presupposes a unity of political purpose among the allies which has never been strong — witness Suez 1956; and it has progressively dwindled even within the alliance organization, as Europe has recovered her economic strength. Nor have all Americans given due consideration to the fact that in the process of decolonization some of the powers that are now expected to support U.S. policy outside Europe and engage themselves economically in Asia and Africa were not discouraged by the United States from divesting themselves of political responsibilities in these parts of the world.

Finally, the many American arguments in favor of European unity include one advanced on grounds of administrative convenience. It found expression in President Kennedy's yearning for "an opposite number" in Europe so that he would be spared troublesome multilateral negotiations with many European statesmen, none of whom could claim to be speaking for Europe. He said,

> There is no "Europe." I understand their objection to my speaking for them on nuclear matters, but who's to be my opposite number? I can't share this decision with a whole lot of differently motivated and differently responsible people. What one man is it to be shared with — DeGaulle, Adenauer, MacMillan? None of them can speak for Europe.[3]

In my view, which is not shared by many Americans, it is puzzling that U.S. policy has hardly ever been troubled by doubt that a united West Europe would be in the American interest. The U.S. government has not been deeply concerned

---

[3] Theodore Sorensen, *Kennedy* (New York: Harper & Row, 1965), p. 509.

with conceivable contingencies in which it would be more difficult for the United States to reconcile its national interests with those of a federal European state than it has been to reach such reconciliation with several sovereign states in a divided Europe. Instead, Americans believe that once Europe were united, American-European relations would be blessed with pre-established harmony. This admirable faith springs from a variety of national experiences, certain deeply rooted convictions about the moral nature of friends and the immoral nature of adversaries, and from unwillingness to suffer from history in the belief that one can make the future. In a skeptical mind this faith may invoke memories of the American dream about One World: as long as the peace of One World is unattainable, perhaps One Europe recommends itself, among other things, as a step toward that distant goal. It may be recalled that President Kennedy once solemnly stated that he was not seeking a *Pax Americana*.[4] Although there are considerably worse forms of peace he thought about a better one.

Whatever the reason for U.S. policy in support of European unification, attributing hegemonic intention to the American Grand Design is the result of misunderstandings. I do not think that any Grand Design — whether Kennedy's or DeGaulle's — is likely to be established in the foreseeable future, but if Kennedy's were realized, it would not be in execution of American hegemonic intent, nor could it fail to reduce American influence in European affairs.

Although not inspired by hegemonic aspirations, American policy toward Europe reflects, of course, the preponderance of American military power in the alliance. Moreover, while Washington in its support for the political unification of Europe has been farsighted, it has shown more enthusiasm than discretion. Encouraging the European governments to abandon or restrict their sovereignty in order to form a European super-state, Washington has misjudged the strength of national consciousness and pride in Europe. It has misjudged the offense

<hr />

[4] Speech at American University in Washington, June 10, 1963, *The New York Times*, June 11, 1963.

that even the strong who are benevolent give to the weak, when the latter rightly believe that they themselves are growing stronger and rightly or wrongly judge the need for protection by the strongest to be waning. As a nation that is fond of engineering, America may have been blinded to the sensibilities of Europeans by the vision of a future in which centuries of history were swept away like clutter on a drawing board.

American policy toward Europe after World War II learned from the mistakes it made after World War I, but it gave President DeGaulle above all others many opportunities for reminding Americans that their interest in continental unification encounters in Europe the re-established pre-eminence of nation states. Only in Germany the nation state was shattered by defeat, truncation, and division. Besides, like Italy, Germany had existed as a unified state only for a rather short time prior to World War II. Following defeat, even German nationalists like Ernst Jünger advocated the absorption of the country into a promising New Europe, about twenty years after the Social Democrats who had favored the unification of Europe as early as 1925, in their Heidelberg Program. For the Federal Republic there has been only gain in a united Europe: it is not by chance that the unification of Europe as well as the reunification of Germany are signposts of the future solemnly mentioned in the Preamble to the Basic Law of the land.

But political order in Western Europe, if not to be based either on balance of power or on hegemony, presupposes political cooperation of Great Britain, France, and the Federal Republic, and neither Great Britain nor France have been eager to become parts of a federal European state. Even proposals for less radical changes that in time might lead to a confederation of sovereign states have encountered strenuous opposition in several medium and small European states. Thus, it is only realistic not to entertain high hopes that the unification of Europe will soon be attained. Economic integration does not automatically lead to political integration. Organizational contrivances for purposes of common defense, like the multilateral nuclear force (MLF), rather than promoting unity either obscure or exacerbate the political problems they are designed to solve. And nationalism does not seem to be a spent force in Europe any more than it is in other parts of the world. Americans tend to regard national self-assertion as a natural, as well as a desirable, development, provided it occurs in Eastern Europe, because there it aims at liberty rather than aggrandizement. Instances of national self-assertion in Western Europe are often judged to be undesirable since they are suspected of being aimed at aggrandizement rather than liberty. European claims that national self-assertion serves liberty, i.e., freedom from American predominance, render such nationalism not only undesirable, but also "unnatural," since everyone is presumed to understand that history has relegated nationalism to the museum of obsolete passions and no one of good will is presumed to confuse the objective predominance of the United States in NATO with an intent to rule over Europe.

The Federal Republic is caught in a dilemma. Both its vital security interests and its interests in reunification force Germany to seek the closest possible relations with the United States in NATO. If NATO were to disintegrate, the Federal Republic would still have to try everything to keep the United States her closest ally. But a bilateral relationship with the United States might alienate West Germany from the rest of Europe, in the West as well as the East. Clearly, this would be tantamount to a peaceful Soviet victory over NATO.

DeGaulle

The American case against a radical change in the structure of the Western alliance has recently been restated by Secretary Rusk in response to French criticism of NATO. President DeGaulle has opposed the integration of NATO for a long time, because he believes, in the words he used on September 5, 1960 — "that the defense of a country must have a national character." His views on the Western alliance had been known well before 1960. In his celebrated memorandum to President Eisenhower, of September 17, 1958, he urged Franco-American-

British agreement on a common policy outside the North Atlantic area, in Asia, Africa, and elsewhere, with each of the three powers having a veto on the other. In the same memorandum he also sought control over the U.S. nuclear deterrent, suggesting that the United States should use nuclear weapons at its own discretion only if the U.S. were attacked directly, but that in all other situations French and British concurrence should be required. As to NATO, the memorandum of 1958 concluded that in the future French cooperation with its allies would be withheld unless France's global demands were met.[5]

Eisenhower, in his reply of October 20, 1958, accepted the idea of broader consultation on world problems but insisted that such consultation be held with all members of NATO. Some such technical consultations were arranged. Consultations among the three Western powers for the purpose of preparing a common position on such problems as Laos and Berlin were agreed upon between DeGaulle and Kennedy after their meeting on June 2, 1961, but the French failed to respond when they were later requested to name a military representative for this purpose. Since DeGaulle did not attain his original objective of restricting U.S. sovereignty outside the NATO area by a French veto, he proceeded step by step to contract his cooperation in NATO.

September 9, 1965, was the last occasion to date at which the President of France again distinguished the Atlantic alliance from NATO itself. In his view, the former serves the common security interest of European powers and the United States vis à vis the Soviet Union; the latter represents an unacceptable subordination of French sovereignty to U.S. domination. Since this press conference, French plans for the reform of NATO have not been further elucidated by DeGaulle in public, but the Paris edition of *The New York Herald Tribune* reported on

[5] The contents of DeGaulle's memorandum, subsequent consultation, and communication from 1958 to 1963 were described succinctly in two articles by James Reston in *The New York Times* of May 1 and 3, 1964; see also C. L. Sulzberger's commentary in *The New York Times* of March 18, 1963.

September 21, 1965, quite specific wishes that DeGaulle had expressed to Under Secretary Ball in Paris. According to this source, the French President wants (1) to put the twenty-seven U.S. base installations in France under French commanders; these installations, which are vital for the functioning of the U.S. forces stationed in Germany, were established by bilateral agreement outside the NATO treaty; (2) to replace the integrated NATO installations and command arrangements by bilateral agreement; and (3) to abolish both the American command over NATO forces and the integration of the relatively small French contingent in NATO. Despite official French denials of this report, rumors persisted that it was substantially correct; besides, it contained nothing that conflicted with DeGaulle's previously known views.

Shortly thereafter, in the Autumn issue of *Politique Etrangère*, an anonymous article titled *"Faut-il réformer l'alliance atlantique?"* advanced specific suggestions for the reform of NATO. The international press reported, this time without a French denial, that DeGaulle had read and approved this informal policy paper. The proposals for changes of NATO as well as the analysis of the current world balance of power again were highly critical of the principle of integration in NATO. The authors of the study assigned a merely symbolic value to the presence of U.S. troops in Europe. In a style of reasoning reminiscent of certain American intellectuals who write about war as though they were discussing traffic accidents, the authors asked the rhetorical question as to whether the U.S. government would not rather sacrifice the American troops stationed in Europe than expose the United States to nuclear destruction. At the same time the authors expressed confidence in U.S. willingness to protect American security interests in Europe.

Two systems, they said, should take the place of NATO, an old-fashioned western alliance that would include the United States, without integrated command, but with continuous coordination of the allied strategies of deterrence on a global scale; and a narrower, integrated, European defense system without the United States. In this latter system, until the day of reunification, the Federal Republic would have no voice in nuclear decisions, but would be given a nuclear guarantee by — France. Evidently, the authors of this study felt that a French nuclear capability and its credibility would be regarded by both Germans and other Europeans as well as by the Soviet leaders with the respect that they were believed or invited to deny to American nuclear capabilities and commitments. In any event, the Federal Republic, correctly regarded as a purely European country, would be strictly subordinated to France, which, despite the emaciation of her power outside the metropolitan area, claims global status. A flippant satirist may think that the proposals provide the setting for a fable in which a rooster tries to outdo the dog in fighting the cat. Perhaps these proposals are but an opening gambit in negotiations about the future of NATO.

Be that as it may, in a press conference on November 5, Mr. Rusk said that he would not deal with the French position until President DeGaulle himself had made specific proposals. Then addressing himself to the question of integration in NATO he remarked:

> We have a very substantial force in the heart of Europe — if my friends in Europe would forgive me — *surrounded in a sea of foreigners.*
>
> Now integration is imposed upon us by the de facto situation. Our responsibility for the effectiveness and the security and the future of those forces in Europe is such that we need to know who is going to do what, when, and where, if there is trouble.
>
> So that whatever one says in theory, we are integrated. Our forces are there in the heart of Europe. So people must forgive us if we have a rather strong view on the subject of integration. . . . [emphasis supplied][6]

Not all American students of NATO would fully understand and agree with Mr. Rusk. Prominent Americans, like Senator Douglas from Illinois, have advocated that the U.S. punish DeGaulle for his anti-American policy, but neither President

[6] *The New York Times,* November 6, 1965.

Kennedy nor President Johnson has ever considered it prudent to trade insults with the General. There are other Americans who point to the need for correcting existing inequities in NATO. For example, Paul Findley, Republican Congressman from Illinois and Chairman of a Republican Study Group on NATO, as late as October 14, 1965, spoke of "the unnecessary predominance of the United States in NATO," and of the need to abolish the nuclear "caste system" in the Western alliance. Observing that of the 17 main commands in NATO seven are held by the United States (including SACEUR), eight by Great Britain, and one each by France and Belgium, he advocated a more equitable distribution of commands among the member states of the North Atlantic Alliance. And, observing that the French command of Central Europe is limited by SACEUR's prerogative to decide on the use of tactical nuclear weapons, he advocated that the United States renounce its veto over the use of such weapons.

It is not possible to predict the future of NATO, but it is necessary to be aware of the dangers that a reform of the Western alliance must try to avoid. As I have indicated it would be neither in the American interest nor in that of the Germans to replace the current structure of NATO by bilateral German-American security arrangements. Such arrangements would fortify opposition to West Germany, not only in the Soviet Union and Eastern Europe, but also in Western and Northern Europe, Great Britain, and Canada. Moreover, the United States, rather than France, would appear as the architect of Western discord, who destroyed the house he had helped to build. In addition, the United States would be left in the end with a defense arrangement that would not be viable, for West Germany isolated in Europe could not serve as the mainstay of U.S. security interests on the continent.

Similarly, the continuation of NATO without France is most undesirable for all members of NATO, including France herself, since French political influence in the world, as well as her political influence on the development of the Common Market, would atrophy once isolated from NATO. For such policy to be viable France would need more than a Soviet support on which she could place no reliance. For example, could the Soviet Union be counted on to insure the French presence in West Berlin?

Europe and Asia

NATO is an alliance for the NATO area, but some of its member states — today primarily the United States and Great Britain — have vital security interests also outside that area. The United States has such interests in Latin America, Asia, the Middle East, and Africa, as well as Europe. By contrast, West Germany's main *political* interests outside Europe are limited to relations with the so-called nonaligned countries, since it is important to the Federal Republic that they do not recognize Ulbricht's regime. In addition, West Germany has an indirect, ambivalent interest in military conflicts outside the NATO area, primarily those in which the United States is involved.

On the one hand, the Germans, like other NATO allies, expect the United States to meet communist challenges wherever they may occur. The war in Korea testified in German eyes to the seriousness of the anticommunist commitment of the United States in Europe. So does today the American stand in Vietnam. And it would certainly take a strange twist of the imagination to deny that a failure to meet Khrushchev's challenge in Cuba would have caused dismay in Western Europe.

On the other hand, American participation in military conflicts outside the NATO area inevitably produces apprehensions in Europe. There is concern that war in Asia or Africa may dilute the U.S. commitment to Europe, that it may divert American military resources from Europe, or worse, that it may spread and engulf Europe in nuclear war.

Until about the middle 1950's, as long as a Soviet attack on Europe was a matter of intense concern and all hope was placed in American nuclear weapons to equalize Soviet superiority in conventional arms, the fear of war in consequence of Soviet aggression easily turned into a fear of the weapon that would be employed in that war.[7] It could happen that in the eyes of some Europeans the responsibility for aggression appeared less important than the responsibility for the terrible, nuclear nature of the war. To put it paradoxically, what some Europeans feared at that time was not only reckless American policies that might plunge Europe into war, but also the *credibility* of the American commitment to come to Europe's help in the event of attack, because this help was bound to be nuclear. Today, there still is fear that the United States may drag Europe into an unwanted war because of American policies outside Europe. Thus in his election speech of November 30, 1965, President DeGaulle raised the specter of France's becoming involved in a war against her will.[8]

Militarily NATO has grown stronger from year to year. During the past few years, while the political difficulties in NATO have been mounting, the increase in its military strength has been formidable. By the end of 1966 the stockpile of nuclear warheads in Western Europe will be twice as high as it was in 1961. There is less fear of Soviet aggression than there was in the early 1950's. Western Europe has attained considerable economic strength, with the Federal Republic playing the leading role. France has become a minor nuclear power, the third in NATO. And yet the burden of the main European argument about the need for a reform of the alliance has not been that the need for American protection has weakened because of Europe's increased ability and willingness to contribute to her own security more than in the past. Instead, it has been argued that (1) Asia, rather than Europe, has become the primary theater of American political and military engagement; (2) the American commitment to Europe, and thus the deterrent, has become *incredible*, since the United States cannot be expected to expose New York, Chicago, or Washington to Soviet nuclear attack for the sake of Hamburg, Paris, or Lon-

---

[7] It may be recalled that in the early 1950's, both President Eisenhower and John Foster Dulles spoke of tactical atomic weapons as "conventional" arms.

[8] *The New York Times,* December 1, 1965.

don; (3) given these two momentous changes on the international scene the United States and the Soviet Union are moving toward a new Yalta in which the former might bow to the latter's interests in Europe at Germany's expense; and finally, (4) that urging the Europeans to help provide conventional options of defense does not add to, but detracts from, the deterrent, again signalling an American intention to dilute its commitment to Europe (despite the increase in tactical nuclear weapons).

While these views are not shared by the Federal Government, they have been expressed in West Germany by responsible critics, and since no one is able to eliminate the uncertainties attending any assessment of international affairs, no one can afford to judge the merit of views deviating from his own by the lack of power their proponents wield in domestic politics. In my judgment, the critical views that I have mentioned are mistaken ones, and the real problems involving Germany and U.S. foreign policy must be differently stated.

It is true that in recent years U.S. policy has been increasingly preoccupied with the war in Vietnam and that for various reasons European problems awaiting a solution have not been acted upon with the same sense of urgency. A decision on the divisive issue of the MLF was postponed by President Johnson at the end of 1964. There has been no Western initiative on German reunification. Elections in the United States, the Federal Republic, and France have contributed to arresting the momentum of U.S. policy toward Europe. Domestic political issues have absorbed much of Washington's energy. But there has been no shift in the focus of American foreign policy from Europe to Asia. Whatever the meaning of "polycentrism," no communists have become reliable friends of the West. Nor has the Sino-Soviet rift or the explosion of two Chinese nuclear devices turned Red China into an adversary of the United States more dangerous than the Soviet Union. Red China's GNP is about one-fourth that of the Soviet Union; military outlays are closer to the ratio of one to eight; and the Soviet Union, not China, has a large nuclear arsenal. For good reasons China has been even more cautious than the Soviet Union in the use of military power. At his meeting with Kennedy in Vienna Khrushchev said that "if he were Mao he would probably have attacked Taiwan long ago."[9] At present, the Sino-Soviet rift obliges *all* noncommunist governments to consider the pros and cons of a differentiated diplomacy toward the communist states, but it is not absolutely certain that the rift will outlast Mao's life. And assuming the persistence or deepening of this rift, it is quite possible that for a long time to come the Soviet Union rather than China will remain the principal adversary of the West in Asia as well as Europe.

Mr. Sorensen, a man who was especially close to President Kennedy, once observed that Kennedy "did not expect the (Western) Alliance to hold tight in Vietnam, the Congo, Cyprus, *or similar side issues.* (Emphasis added.) But he was determined to hold it together on any major confrontation with the Soviet Union."[10] There is no indication that President Johnson differs in this regard from President Kennedy.

Some observers seem to believe that Europe can afford to relax because the two "nuclear giants" have attained a balance of power or terror and reached a stand-off in Europe, so that the time has come for the allies to turn to differences in their own ranks without fear of inviting calamity. On both sides of the Atlantic the optimistic appraisers of the prospects of peace take lightly the fact that it was in allegedly stabilized conditions of the balance of power that Khrushchev embarked upon his provocative missile venture in Cuba. Moreover, the appraisers seem to regard Kennedy's and Khrushchev's behavior during the Cuban missile crisis as a natural way of resolving conflict without war, that is, as a method which can be followed at will in any future contingency by any leader.

It seems likely to me that serious future conflicts — whether in Asia, Latin America, Europe, or elsewhere — will recur. They cannot be wished away. They must be guarded against

9 Arthur M. Schlesinger, Jr., *A Thousand Days* (Boston: Houghton Mifflin Co., Cambridge: The Riverside Press, 1965), p. 364.
10 Theodore C. Sorensen, *op. cit.*, p. 564.

with vigilance and in unity. Dissension within the Western
Alliance is, among other things, a sign that, for the time being,
all is quiet on the European front, but let us beware that dis-
array in the rear be not a luxury that sometime in the future
must be paid for at the front.

For two reasons all seems quiet in the frontiers of Western
Europe at present. First, since the resolution of the Cuban
missile crisis the communists have not exerted strong pressure
on West Berlin. Nor have they confronted the West with ultimata aimed at Western recognition of the German Democratic
Republic. Instead, they concentrate their political attack on
NATO, exploiting especially the sharp Western disagreement
on nuclear issues within the alliance. At the moment it is by
means of this concerted political attack that the governments
of the communist camp (regardless of "polycentrism") present
the Federal Republic as a menace to peace in Europe and as
the obstacle to international agreement on halting the spread
of nuclear weapons.

Second, the Western powers fail to insist that the Soviet
government concern itself anew with the reunification of Germany. At present, there does not seem to be a new Western
plan for negotiating with the Soviet leaders a political termination of World War II in Europe. United States policy on German reunification and on the illegitimacy of the Ulbricht regime
has not changed; it has been periodically and ritualistically
reaffirmed. Furthermore, despite its lack of initiative on reunification since 1959, the U.S. government has made it clear
that any attempt to Europeanize or de-Americanize the four-
power responsibility for reunification must reckon with American resistance. Not that a broader European framework for
settling the issue has been rejected. On the contrary, many,
though not all, views on this subject advanced by DeGaulle at
his press conference on September 9, 1965, were expressed also
by President Kennedy, for example, in his speech at the Free
University of Berlin in June 1963. He said at that time that a
united Europe on both sides of the Wall would provide the
best chance for attaining German reunification. President John-

son has spoken along similar lines, and unless I am mistaken, many German politicians are of the same opinion. But the United States will not renounce its coresponsibility for German reunification. Nor would I think it prudent if concern with the broader issue of the relation between East and West Europe were used as an excuse for halting political thinking about the narrower issue of German reunification. Certainly, from the German point of view this narrower issue is the more pressing one of the two; it has to be faced squarely lest the impression of a growing indifference toward it lead to predictable gains of the communists, if not to unpredictable consequences in Germany.

Ever since Mr. Rusk's background briefing of December 1964, if not earlier, it has become clear that the United States preferred German suggestions regarding a Western negotiating position on reunification and on related questions, such as European security and the frontier issues, to American initiative accompanied by German reluctance, not to mention German distrust and public criticism of U.S. efforts to explore with Soviet leaders the possibilities of a settlement.

Much more needs to be said on this subject than I can attempt to do in this context, but I shall confine myself to one observation. If reunification really is the fourth most vital concern of West German foreign policy — security, freedom, and peace being the first three — then it seems to me that reunification and the issues associated with it should indeed be a principal area of German initiative in international affairs. Only by a contribution to the settlement of these issues can the Federal Republic hope to attain more freedom of action in foreign policy than it now enjoys. Remembering that reunification involves a change in the territorial *status quo* in Europe, it is to be hoped that there will be careful and realistic German appraisals of (1) the conditions in which the Soviet Union might accept specified western terms, and (2) the political price which the Federal Republic itself (and the other powers involved) would be willing and able to pay should these conditions fail to materialize.

In their appraisals German political planners will also have to take account of the subtle but important difference in the American stake in Berlin, on the one hand, and in reunification, on the other. The primary U.S. objective in Berlin in maintaining the *status quo* with its well-known three essentials — allied presence, free access to the city, and political freedom of the West Berliners. The first two essentials are associated with certain prerogatives in relation to the Federal Government and with obligations that bind the Soviet Union as well as the three Western powers. Russian and East German communist leaders want to change the territorial *status quo* of Berlin in defiance of the three essentials and of Soviet obligations. Regarding Germany as a whole, however, they want to maintain and fortify the *status quo* by persuading noncommunist states to recognize the Ulbricht regime and the existing frontiers of Poland and the Soviet Union. In this regard, it is the Federal Republic that has a primary interest in changing the *status quo*: it wants reunification and not the sanctioning by international agreements of the communist three-state doctrine. The United States, being more powerful than West Germany's other allies and being a non-European state appreciates this German interest perhaps somewhat more fully or more easily than do the other NATO allies, but, even so, it is undeniably less of a tragedy for Americans to live with the present division of Germany than it is for the Germans to do so. From the German point of view, it is therefore fortunate that the future of Berlin is so intimately associated with the future of Germany as a whole.

Finally, I am sure, political observers in the Federal Republic appreciate the fact that the United States cannot pursue any policy on German reunification that would jeopardize the remaining cohesion of NATO. The Alliance may not last in its present form beyond 1970, but it would be calamitous indeed if its decline were precipitated by a policy on reunification that the Federal Republic or the United States or both powers jointly would wish to pursue against the strong objections of other allies, for example, Great Britain or France.

The Nuclear Issue

Probably the deepest cause of discord in NATO is the nuclear issue. It has two main roots, nuclear inequality among the members of the alliance and the conflict between the objectives of deterrence and *détente* in Western policy.

The political repercussions of nuclear inequality in NATO were formidable enough, as long as the United States was the uncontested protector of West European security, but in consequence of the spread of national nuclear capacities in the alliance this inequality has become more rather than less of a political problem. The nuclear dwarfs in NATO, being militarily more powerful than the nuclear have-nots in the alliance, either wish to maintain an especially close relationship with the United States or, proud of being nuclear rather than conventional dwarfs, occasionally try to defy the United States. At the same time they endeavor to maintain whatever superiority of power or prestige their nuclear arsenals give them over the nuclear have-nots. And the United States has not been eager either to help its allies to develop their own nuclear capacities. The proliferation of nuclear weapons in NATO has accentuated inequalities in the alliance, and if, in the absence of a united Europe, national nuclear capability is made the touchstone of influence in the alliance there inevitably arises the political dilemma of discrimination against the potential $n + 1$ country in NATO. The Federal Republic is affected by this dilemma.

In 1954 it made a pledge to remain a nonnuclear power. The German commitment of 1954 not to produce any nuclear weapons is limited in several ways: it covers only production and not acquisition by other means, such as purchase; it pertains only to production on German soil; it does not preclude participation of the Federal Republic in bilateral or multilateral nuclear arrangements that stop short of giving Germany a nuclear capability of her own; and, finally, the commitment was made only to West Germany's allies and not to governments of other countries, such as India, Egypt, or the Soviet Union. In September 1965, Mr. William C. Foster reminded the Soviet delegation at the end of the 18-nations conference on disarmament in Geneva that at present the Soviet Union has no *legal* basis from which to protest West German access to nuclear weapons, not to mention West German participation in a multilateral force; Soviet claims to the contrary notwithstanding, participation in a multilateral force would not necessarily give the Federal Republic such access.

Meanwhile the idea of a multilateral force has been withering on the vines of communist opposition, allied disunity, and — since December 1964 — greater American caution regarding the project. The intensity of the German interest in the arrangement — overestimated for a long time by many Americans — has weakened as well, as was evident in the debates of Dr. Erhard's government declaration in the Bundestag in November 1965. This does not mean, however, that the Federal Government can be expected to welcome seeing its pledge of 1954 turned into an instrument of allied discrimination against Germany. Nor would it be in the American interest to be indifferent toward such a turn of events, since it would give rise to justifiable German dissatisfaction.

The United States appreciates the German desire that any remaining discrimination against the Federal Republic within NATO be lessened. Indeed, it is desirable to establish among the members of the alliance as equitable a balance as possible of responsibilities and obligations, protection and risk, political influence and military contribution.

More serious than nuclear proliferation within the alliance has been the emergence and growth of nuclear capabilities in the communist camp. Directly and indirectly, nuclear proliferation outside NATO has had a considerable impact on the position of the Federal Republic. The growing Soviet nuclear capability has increased the possibilities that the Soviet Union may threaten the European NATO allies with nuclear blackmail as well as nuclear devastation. While the Federal Republic is as immune to blackmail as any other NATO ally as long as it can count on American protection, its vulnerability to physical attack is very great.

Furthermore, in conjunction with the Soviet long-range delivery capability, the nuclear might of the Soviet Union has led to mutual fear by the nuclear giants: the Soviet Union and the United States have a common interest in avoiding nuclear war. In European eyes this common interest has sometimes been misrepresented to mean that *détente* has replaced deterrence or that in the era of coexistence America's militant stand against communism has given way to a more conciliatory posture. There have even been irresponsible claims that the United States and the Soviet Union have developed a common interest in establishing a condominium in Europe. Fanciful as these conceits are in view of continued U.S. resistance of communism in Europe and elsewhere, given West Germany's nonnuclear status and the unsettled problem of reunification, the Federal Republic is understandably concerned about lasting American support of German military and political interests.

For several years, German concern over the U.S. policy of halting the spread of nuclear weapons has been particularly intense, since it is feared that an absorbing commitment to the goal of this policy may lead the United States to disregard German desires in order to attain formal agreement of the Soviet government on nonproliferation.

From the point of view of the United States the crucial question is how to reconcile the American interest in halting the spread of nuclear weapons with that of solving the nuclear problem in NATO. In the last six to eight months, three main U.S. positions on this moot question have emerged. They are not of equal importance in the U.S. government, but all of them have had adherents in the Executive and Legislative branches of the government. From the first position it is argued that reaching international agreement on halting the spread of nuclear weapons is a matter of such overriding importance that the United States should be willing to sacrifice nuclear sharing with other NATO powers in order to obtain Soviet consent to a nonproliferation treaty. From the second position it has been stressed that preserving or restoring the solidarity of the alliance is an aim of U.S. policy that ought to be accorded a higher priority than agreement on a nonproliferation treaty; at least a way ought to be found to reconcile the two interests. An attempt of this sort was indeed made in the form of the American proposal tabled at Geneva in the summer of 1965 for a nonproliferation treaty that would not preclude the formation of a joint nuclear force in NATO. The third position, which has attracted attention more recently than the other two, may be described as a compromise, which it is hoped might satisfy both the Soviet Union and the Western allies, particularly the Federal Republic; in any event it buys time. From this position special importance is attached to Secretary McNamara's proposal for a "select" planning committee within the alliance on nuclear matters. The idea was first advanced at a NATO meeting in May 1965, as a supplement to, rather than a substitute for, an MLF. It would enable the Germans to participate in nuclear deliberations and would at the same time de-emphasize the controversial aspects of physical access to the weapons.

Some Americans have argued with such desperate seriousness on the overriding importance of concluding a treaty on nonproliferation that they have come close to creating the false impression that the possible spread of nuclear weapons to new countries is a peril greater than the present possession of nuclear arsenals by communist powers. Few men have spoken more eloquently on the dangers of proliferation than Senator Robert Kennedy. On June 23, 1965, he declared on the floor of the Senate:

> . . . we cannot allow the demands of day-to-day policy to obstruct our efforts to solve the problem of nuclear spread. We cannot wait for peace in Southeast Asia, which will not come until nuclear weapons have spread beyond recall. We cannot wait for a general European settlement, which has not existed since 1914.[11]

Four months later, he voiced the same opinion even more desperately:

[11] *Congressional Record*, 89th Congress, June 23, 1965, p. 14051.

I do not care what progress we make, whether it be in education or poverty or housing, or even in Southeast Asia, in our relationships with Laos and Vietnam, or in the Middle East; if we do not find an answer to this problem, *nothing else means anything.* (Emphasis supplied.)[12]

Given the destructiveness of nuclear weapons no one will want to dismiss such statements as political rhetoric. Those who advocate subordinating all other tasks of U.S. foreign policy to the supreme task of preventing the spread of nuclear weapons mean exactly what they say and often do so for the most humane reasons. Their sense of responsibility for the future of mankind is born of the awe that U.S. control over the most fearful destructive power in the history of the race has created. It has created guilt feelings, too, prompting many nuclear physicists in the postwar years to take passionate flights into political roles. It made President Kennedy feel greater satisfaction about the nuclear Test Ban Treaty than about any other accomplishment in the White House.[13] And it made his brother Robert declare in the Senate "our responsibility and duty to act is plain. For we were the first to discover and use the atom's secrets."[14]

Nuclear terror or guilt, along with a disinclination to look back into the more distant past — the more distant past being un-American, as it were — may also be causes of the failure to learn discouraging lessons on nuclear dissemination from history. In the American literature one looks in vain for careful comparisons of the proliferation of nuclear capabilities — that has occurred and may unfortunately continue — with earlier phases of modern industrialization. Today, we are in a period of nuclear policy that resembles in some regards that of mercantilism when advanced states tried to keep secret those skills and techniques which augmented economic and military power. But on all levels of technology in the past the means of production have in the longer run influenced the means of de-

---

[12] *Ibid.,* October 13, 1965, p. 25900.
[13] Theodore C. Sorensen, *op. cit.,* p. 564.
[14] *Congressional Record,* October 13, 1965, p. 25890.

struction in an ever larger geographical area. This lesson of history seems to be lost on many deliberations about the spread of nuclear weapons. Perhaps this is so in part because the terrifyingly destructive use of nuclear technology preceded its peaceful application for constructive ends.

It is also noteworthy that American policy on halting nuclear proliferation by a general — preferably worldwide — treaty, rather than by specific — preferably bilateral and multilateral — arrangements has had predictable repercussions on the global balance of power. Today, it is no longer politically useful to divide the world into nuclear and nonnuclear countries. It is more realistic to distinguish among (1) the five powers that have nuclear arsenals (although the present inferiority of China and France — and to a lesser extent Great Britain — to the two nuclear giants must not be disregarded); (2) the aspirant powers, that is, the eight to ten powers that are most likely candidate members of the nuclear group of nations; and (3) those preindustrial countries which are likely to remain have-not powers for a very long time, if not forever.

Now the international debates on nonproliferation have shown that in addition to the cold-war division of the world, the East-West split, and the juxtaposition of the advanced and the underdeveloped countries, often referred to as the North-South division, a third alignment cutting across the former two divisions may be emerging. For a basis of possible common interest exists among the nuclear aspirant powers leading the other nuclear have-nots against the haves. This was expressed most pointedly by Mr. Trivedi of India at the Ninety-ninth meeting of the U.N. Disarmament Commission on June 14, 1965, when he said — in my view with a touch of political naiveté:

> Just as in the economic field we want the have-nots to be gradually assisted by economic advancement to assume the status of haves, in the matter of disarmament we want the haves gradually to become, in a contrary direction, have-nots.

Similarly, at the Geneva Conference the American delegation

encountered difficulties not only with the Russians, but also with the Indians, the Swedes, the Italians, and in a different context, with the Canadians and British.

The arguments against the U.S. position on nonproliferation were advanced without regard to the continued anticommunist role of the United States in the East-West conflict, but they were not entirely without foundation. For example, Mr. William C. Foster, the chief U.S. delegate in Geneva, had not confined himself to setting forth the humane arguments favoring a worldwide agreement on nonproliferation, but in his celebrated article had frankly admitted that Americans "should not lose sight of the fact that widespread nuclear proliferation could mean a substantial erosion in the margin of power which our great wealth and industrial base have long given us relative to much of the rest of the world."[15]

In Germany, the attack against the U.S. policy was waged most intemperately by Dr. Adenauer, on August 19, 1965; in the election campaign his views were echoed widely by his friends and even his critics. It was a generally pro-American weekly that commented:

> An atomic treaty, that would not be signed anyway by China, France, probably Indonesia and several other states, that would be imposed upon third nations with moral pressure and that would finally solidify the privileges of the atomically armed powers — such a "limited non-proliferation" could accelerate the decline of the Western Alliance without leading at the same time to an erosion of the Eastern coalition.[16]

Another German newspaper spoke of "the solidarity of accomplices (*Komplizenschaft*) of the atomic have-not powers" as "an answer to the solidarity of accomplices among the powers possessing nuclear weapons."[17]

Distinguished West German politicians have repeatedly

---

[15] William C. Foster, "New Directions in Arms Control and Disarmament," *Foreign Affairs*, Vol. 65 (July 1965), p. 591.

[16] *Die Zeit*, August 13, 1965.

[17] *Die Welt*, August 25, 1965; see also the article by Kurt Becker in *Die Welt*, August 23, 1965.

claimed that the commitment made in 1954 was the first promise given by the government of any nonnuclear state not to participate in the proliferation of nuclear weapons. This is literally true, though somewhat disingenuous, because in 1954 the Federal Government was concerned with Germany's political comeback, her military security, and her acceptability as a member of the Western family of nations; at the time it was not concerned with halting the spread of nuclear weapons. Thus, Foreign Minister Schröder, of course, stayed within the bounds of Germany's international obligations when he observed in July 1965 that the Federal Republic would not sign a general nonproliferation agreement, unless it was accompanied by progress on the issue of German reunification, and that West Germany could renounce to her allies acquisition of nuclear weapons only if she were protected against the more than 700 Soviet medium range ballistic missiles by the creation of a multilateral Atlantic deterrent force or by an equivalent arrangement.

It is another question whether or not it still is politically prudent of any German politician, no matter how distinguished he may be by virtue of advanced age or accomplishment, to assert German national interests in conjunction with an issue of arms control on which the communists and Germany's western allies may come to stand on common ground. It may be recalled that President Kennedy intimated to Mr. Adzhubei in December 1961 that the United States and the Soviet Union shared an interest in Germany's nonnuclear status; and in 1963, during the test ban negotiations in Moscow, the President instructed Ambassador Harriman not only to insist that the MLF was designed to prevent nuclear proliferation, but also "to explore without assurances whether our [U.S.] standing still on that project would help the Russians with the Chinese."[18]

At the present time (January 1966) the idea of a multilateral force no longer commands much attention. Conceivably, this may change again, since the future cannot be safely predicted.

[18] Theodore C. Sorensen, *op. cit.*, p. 736.

But at this time a different way has been chosen to demonstrate American interest in avoiding discrimination against the Federal Republic. Germany has become one of the five members in the important strategic subcommittee of Mr. McNamara's no longer so "select" committee, no less than 10 NATO nations now being represented on it. In addition, American-German cooperation in space ventures was agreed upon by Chancellor Erhard and President Johnson in December 1965.

The future will tell whether these two arrangements will satisfy German desires for political nondiscrimination and help to remove the obstacles to a viable policy on halting the spread of nuclear weapons. It remains to be seen whether the nuclear inequality in NATO can be politically de-emphasized. Much will depend on the nature of the issues to be discussed in the strategic subcommittee. If disunity and rivalry arising from nuclear inequality are to be mastered, interallied discussions in committees may not suffice to solve problems that are so intimately associated with physical arrangements. But such discussions may clarify the issues and, to repeat, they may buy time for the decisions that matter.

CHAPTER EIGHT

The Hallstein Doctrine

In 1955, when Chancellor Adenauer agreed to an exchange of ambassadors between Moscow and Bonn, the so-called "Hallstein Doctrine" became one of the touchstones of West German foreign policy. It was meant to deter by diplomatic means powers that were not aligned in the East-West conflict from recognizing the German Democratic Republic (GDR), i.e., Communist East Germany, as a second German state. In accordance with the doctrine, the Federal Republic of Germany (FRG) broke off diplomatic relations twice, with Yugoslavia and Cuba.

Although Gerhard Schröder, as a member of Chancellor Erhard's cabinet, prepared the ground for the erosion of the Hallstein Doctrine, its virtual abandonment occurred only under his successor, Willy Brandt, Minister of Foreign Affairs in Chancellor Kiesinger's coalition government. Schroeder established trade missions in various East European countries. Brandt proceeded early in 1967 to exchange ambassadors with Rumania, a state that had had diplomatic relations with the GDR all along. And in January 1968, Bonn resumed the diplomatic relations with Yugoslavia which had been severed in 1957 precisely because Tito had recognized the GDR in defiance of the Hallstein Doctrine.

Leaving aside the motives of the new "flexible" West German policy, it should be noted that Bonn had to find various pragmatic justifications for the doctrinal inconsistencies of its new policy. Despite its continued rejection of the communist claim that two German states exist side by side, both of which ought to be recognized, Bonn itself now entertains diplomatic

From *Survey*, London, No. 61 (October 1966).

relations with three communist states, which recognize the GDR as well as the Federal Republic. In each case Bonn has given a different reason for its own implicit acceptance of the Communist "two-state doctrine" and its own pragmatic disregard of the "one-state" Hallstein Doctrine.

(1) Ever since 1955 Bonn has justified the establishment of diplomatic relations with the Soviet Union, among other things, on the grounds that the Soviet Union is one of the four major powers legally obligated to bring about the reunification of Germany.

(2) The establishment of relations between Bonn and Bucharest has been justified on the grounds that the Hallstein Doctrine is not applicable to Rumania inasmuch as that country was a satellite of the Soviet Union when Bucharest recognized the GDR and could not possibly do otherwise. This second justification overlooks the fact that in recent years Rumania has found many ways of showing some independence from the Soviet Union but has chosen to remain a Russian satellite regarding adherence to the vital issue of the "two-state doctrine." The second justification, of course, removes an obstacle to the establishment of diplomatic relations between West Germany and four other East European states — Hungary, Bulgaria, Czechoslovakia, and Poland — despite the fact that all of them recognized the GDR.

(3) The second justification does not apply to Yugoslavia, for, when Tito in 1957 recognized the Communist regime in East Germany, his country was no satellite of the Soviet Union. Tito's independence from Moscow made his recognition of the GDR a challenge to the FRG and prompted Bonn's first demonstrative application of the Hallstein Doctrine to Belgrade: relations between Belgrade and Bonn were broken off. How then could the resumption of diplomatic relations in 1968 be justified? Bonn argued, among other things, that it wished to do what it could to relax tensions in Europe and make its contribution to the East-West détente, desired by all, that is, by Germany no less than by the United States, Great Britain, and France.

Bonn's new policy in Eastern Europe and its different justifications may have undesirable consequences both at home and abroad in the future. Certain West German circles and organizations no longer consider Bonn's new flexibility enough; they demand that Bonn recognize the GDR, which both Christian Democrats and Social Democrats still refuse to do. In 1968, Kiesinger himself, while acting in disregard of the Hallstein

Doctrine, found it necessary to criticize the "recognition party"
— an extra-parliamentarian opposition to the government —
that had formed among his countrymen.

Apart from domestic German political troubles that may lie
ahead in consequence of the new flexible policy, those Middle
Eastern, Asian, and African countries which do not — or not
yet — recognize the GDR no longer refrain from doing so be-
cause they respect the legal and moral position of the West
German government. How could they do so if Bonn itself no
longer acts in accordance with its legal position? They simply
find West Germany's economic might more impressive and
exploitable than East Germany's resources. In time, however,
Ulbricht's regime may well derive diplomatic benefits from
Brandt's and Kiesinger's pragmatism. Indeed, the time may
come when the one or the other of West Germany's powerful
Western allies will consider Bonn's claim to the right — or the
obligation — to speak for Germany as a whole to be anachro-
nistic, since it has been invalidated by Bonn's own pragmatism.

The following essay, written in preparation for a larger work
on German foreign policy in the post-Adenauer period, does
not deal with the political implications of the new flexible
policy. By confining the discussion of the Hallstein Doctrine to
the period from 1955 to 1966, the essay places Bonn's current
policies toward Eastern Europe in historical perspective.

Adenauer in Moscow 1955

THE SO-CALLED Hallstein doctrine, as formulated in December
1955, was primarily intended to warn neutral and nonaligned
states not to recognize the German Democratic Republic
(GDR) since the Federal Government, claiming to speak for
Germany as a whole, would regard such recognition as an unfriendly act. Heinrich von Brentano explained in the Bundestag on June 28, 1956:

The recognition of the "GDR" means recognition . . . of the
division of Germany into two states. Reunification would then no
longer be the elimination of a transitional disturbance in the
organism of our all-German state; rather it would be transformed
into the infinitely more difficult task of unifying two different
German states. . . . The recognition of the "GDR" by third states
would have to be regarded by the Federal Government as agreement to the unlawful splitting off of a part of the territory under

German sovereignty and as interference with domestic German affairs. Legally the unity of Germany as a state has not perished. . . .[1]

According to international practice, a government saying that another government has committed an unfriendly act is likely to break off relations with that government or take even more drastic counteraction. Thus the Hallstein doctrine is meant to put other governments on notice that their recognition of the GDR will adversely affect their relations with the Federal Republic.

The Hallstein doctrine was formulated in December 1955 in order to protect a principle of German foreign policy that three months earlier the Adenauer government itself had felt obliged to violate. In September Adenauer visited the Soviet Union and agreed to an exchange of ambassadors between Moscow and Bonn. Since that time the Soviet Union has been the only major power maintaining diplomatic relations with both German states. Should Bonn ever enter with East Berlin into negotiations more momentous than those conducted in the past via the West Berlin Senate, the *Treuhandstelle* in Berlin, and occasionally through Bundestag deputies or businessmen, it may yet become important that the Soviet government has ready access to both Bonn and East Berlin; the possibility of acting as arbiter between them may give to the Soviet government an advantage which the Western governments lack.

In 1955, Bulganin and Khrushchev were interested in stabilizing the political *status quo* in divided Germany by establishing diplomatic relations with the Federal Government as well as the GDR. Adenauer acted against the counsel of his senior advisers on foreign affairs — von Brentano, Hallstein, and Blankenhorn — and handed a diplomatic success to the Russians. He did not get much more in return than the review of a military honor guard, lavish banquets, and a per-

[1] Cited by Rudolf Schuster, "Die 'Hallstein Doctrine'," *Europa Archiv*, Vol. 18 (September 25, 1963).

formance of Prokofiev's ballet *Romeo and Juliet*. It is true the Soviet leaders undertook to release 10,000 German prisoners of war who were still being retained in the Soviet Union. The Russians denied knowing anything about an additional 80,000 German civilian internees mentioned by the German delegation, but promised to release them too, should they be found. It took nine months of negotiations and West German agreement to an expansion of Soviet-German trade to obtain the release of most of these civilians. Forty-eight hours after the departure of the West German delegation from Moscow, however, an East German delegation headed by Premier Grotewohl arrived in the Kremlin. After three days, it brought home a joint communiqué in which the Soviet government pledged the release of German prisoners of war in response to a written request by the GDR, dated 27 July, and of the more recently expressed wish of the Federal Republic. In addition, the Soviet government granted to the sovereign GDR the right to control civilian traffic between West Germany and West Berlin. On October 3, 1955, the Western powers formally protested against this relegation of control to the GDR. On October 18 the Soviet government rejected the protest, insisting on the right of the GDR to exercise sovereignty on its territory.

Adenauer negotiated in Moscow from a position of weakness in consequence of international events and for domestic political reasons. In order to maintain close rapport with the Western allies, the German Chancellor had to take account of the fact that at the time he went to Moscow his allies were under the spell of the spirit generated in July at the Geneva summit conference. As Anthony Eden has observed, "Each country present [at that meeting] learnt that no country attending wanted war and each understood why. . . . In the minds of the men who commanded power in the world, the lessons of the Conference might result in a reduced risk of total destruction to the human race."[2] Similarly, Wilhelm

[2] Anthony Eden, *Full Circle* (Boston: Houghton Mifflin Co., 1960), p. 340.

Grewe remarked, "Critics who were skeptical regarding the German question, as for example Walter Lippmann, considered the result of Geneva primarily to be a tacit renunciation of war by the atomic world powers on the basis of the *status quo*."[3] After the Geneva conference Adenauer could not afford to let himself be called, either abroad or at home, "the last Mohican of the cold war."

In West Germany, the Social-Democratic Party was at that time prepared to oppose the government's foreign policy, and could have made life difficult for Adenauer had he rejected the Soviet invitation to come to Moscow. In an opinion survey conducted in August 1955, before the Chancellor left for Russia, the majority of the respondents proposed that the Chancellor should discuss with Bulganin and Khrushchev the issue of reunification, while those recommending negotiations on the return of prisoners and the maintenance of peace were in the minority. Regarding the prospects of the Moscow conference, as many as 31 per cent believed that the visit would be crowned by success. Only 24 per cent expected the Soviet leaders not to make some concessions (45 per cent were uncertain regarding the outcome of the visit or expressed no opinion).[4] This public optimism had been stirred up by a large number of German journalists who in the summer of 1955 had returned from the Soviet Union with euphoric notions about the prospects of coexistence, lamenting Western cold war propaganda and its "fairy tale of 'the unhappy slaves' " in the East. They predicted that Soviet society would assume an "absolutely middle-class" character in the future.

In Moscow the going was rough for Adenauer and his delegation. Carlo Schmid, then SPD vice-chairman of the Bundestag Foreign Affairs Committee, appealed to Soviet magnanimity (for which Adenauer later thanked him) in order to make

---

[3] Wilhelm Grewe, *Deutsche Aussenpolitik der Nachkriegszeit* (Stuttgart: Deutsche Verlagsanstalt, 1960), p. 217.

[4] *EMNID-Informationen,* August 20, 1955, quoted by Gerard Braunthal, "An Agreement with the Russians," in *Cases in Comparative Politics,* J. B. Christoph, editor (Boston: Little, Brown & Co., 1965), p. 265.

some progress at least on the prisoners-of-war issue, but Adenauer did not succeed in getting a Soviet commitment in writing; this the Russians had reserved for Grotewohl. The issue of reunification was not discussed at all.

The only Soviet concession consisted in officially receiving a juridical reservation on which the Germans insisted in connection with their agreement to normalize diplomatic relations. The Soviet government restated in turn its position. This procedure was sufficient to make it clear that the Germans did not intend to recognize by implication the existing territorial status in Europe and that Soviet policy was in no way affected by the German reservation. Following Bulganin's suggestion, Adenauer read the German statement at a press conference on September 14, shortly before it was transmitted to the Soviet Government:

> The establishment of diplomatic relations between the Government of the Federal Republic of Germany and the government of the USSR represents no recognition of the present status of their respective territories. The final determination of the borders of Germany is reserved for the peace treaty.

The Soviet declaration was published by the Soviet Foreign Ministry the next day:

> With reference to the establishment of diplomatic relations between the Soviet Union and the German Federal Government the government of the USSR deems it necessary to declare that the question of the German borders has been solved by the Potsdam Agreement and that the German Federal Republic exercises jurisdiction on the territory on which it has sovereignty.[5]

Note that the Soviet declaration did not speak of the Federal Republic of Germany, but of the "German Federal Republic," thus putting West Germany even in name on a par with East Germany.

Purpose

The Hallstein doctrine was formulated in December 1955 at a conference of German ambassadors who were called to Bonn

[5] Cited by Wilhelm Grewe, *op. cit.*, p. 221.

in order to consider how to prevent other states from recognizing both German states. The fact that Adenauer himself had enabled Moscow to set this example was seen as inevitable, since cooperation of the Soviet Government would be needed for the restoration of German unity. This argument has been repeated many times; to this day it is not quite conclusive. It was not the Federal Republic but the Soviet Union which sought the exchange of ambassadors, and it did so in furtherance of its contention that two German states existed. Brentano considered tendering his resignation in disapproval of the poor bargain that Adenauer had made. The arrangement that was reached may have been a politically inevitable consequence of the spirit of Geneva, given West Germany's dependence on her allies, or of West German domestic politics, but it was not sought by the Germans in order to create one of the preconditions of reunification. If anything, this agreement reduced the chances of reunification by helping to confirm the *status quo*.

The main question before the conference of ambassadors in Bonn was how to prevent other governments from establishing diplomatic relations with the rival regime of the GDR. The Western allies were pledged to consider the Federal Government as the only legitimate German government, and they presented no problem. With regard to Russia's allies, which had already recognized the GDR, the principal question was whether the Federal Government should refuse to exchange ambassadors with any of these states (even with the reservation filed in Moscow) in order to prevent dual representation in the capitals of eastern Europe, or whether it should rather seek to establish such embassies, if an opportunity arose, in order not to leave the field to the GDR. The second alternative gained some favor only in the 1960's, especially after the Middle Eastern crisis in 1965. To many Germans, this alternative appeared preposterous ten years earlier. Wilhelm Grewe, the architect of the misnamed Hallstein doctrine, strongly argued as late as 1960 against establishing diplomatic relations with communist states that had such relations with the GDR.

If the Federal Government were to do so, he wrote, the allies of West Germany and a few other states would probably continue not to recognize the GDR, but "about thirty to fifty states of the neutral and non-aligned world" would undoubtedly follow a different course by recognizing the GDR. The Federal Republic would simply have no pertinent argument to deter Cairo, New Delhi, or Jakarta from entertaining diplomatic relations with both German states, if it enabled Warsaw, Budapest, and Prague to have such dual representation. Grewe characterized the successful application of a double standard based on the distinction between communist states that have recognized the GDR for years and other, neutral or nonaligned, states that have not, as "pure utopia."[6]

As far as the nonaligned states are concerned, the Federal Republic has been remarkably successful in asserting its claim to represent Germany; this is true at least if diplomatic recognition is used as a criterion of success. By 1956, the year in which the first West German ambassador arrived in Moscow, the Federal Republic had established 47 embassies and 21 legations. Nine years later, West Germany had diplomatic relations with 97 sovereign states which on their part did not entertain such relations with "the Soviet Zone of occupation."[7]

This growth in diplomatic representation of the Federal Republic abroad has been a consequence of the process of decolonization, of Western economic power, and of the Hallstein doctrine. Given their neutralist leanings, many of the new states might have established diplomatic relations with both Germanys had it not been for the doctrine. Such a development would have been a marked setback for the Western policy on Germany; by lowering the international standing of the Federal Republic it would have added considerable political weight to the two-state theory in the noncommunist

---

[6] Wilhelm Grewe, *op. cit.*, p. 151.

[7] Auswärtiges Amt, *Vertretungen der Bundesrepublik Deutschland im Ausland*, September 1, 1956; Communiqué of the Federal Government of March 7, 1965, *News from the German Embassy*, Washington, D.C., March 11, 1965.

world. It would also have made inevitable the entry of the GDR into international organizations, in which it now has but a few seats; as matters stand, the GDR has been most successful in gaining recognition in international sports organizations.

By recognizing the Federal Republic and not the GDR, the new nonaligned states in fact aligned themselves on the side of the West. The facts do not appear to be fairly assessed in Rüdiger Altmann's observation that "the neutralist states of Asia and Africa, when denying international recognition to the zonal State, were able to refer to their neutralism — their refusal to participate in the East-West conflict".[8] They did recognize only the Federal Republic, which lies on this side of the dividing line.

It is true that several new states, such as Guinea and Mali, went through intense conflicts with the colonial powers from which they gained their independence and were therefore tempted to move closer to the GDR rather than the Federal Republic. In some other neutral states, security considerations arising from geography led to prudent respect for communist interests so that the stock of West Germany fell; this was true, for example, of Burma, Cambodia, and Afghanistan. Sukarno came close to recognizing the GDR in exchange for Soviet support of his territorial ambitions. India seemed to believe that utterances favouring the Soviet two-state theory on Germany furthered the cause of world peace. And yet, by 1966, the GDR had embassies only in communist countries, including China, Mongolia, North Korea, North Vietnam, and Cuba.

Tito permitted a legation of the GDR to be established in his country in 1957. This led to the diplomatic break between the Federal Republic and Yugoslavia. Albrecht von Kessel, then a high official of the West German foreign service in Washington, had the impression that Georg Pfleiderer, a vocal opponent of the Hallstein doctrine and at the time West German ambassador in Belgrade, was not forceful enough in trying to

[8] Rüdiger Altmann, "Überlegungen zur deutschen Aussenpolitik," *Der Monat,* Vol. 17, April 1965, p. 11.

dissuade Tito from recognizing the GDR. "Until the end, the Yugoslav government did not believe that Bonn's warnings and threats were meant seriously."[9] But neither Tito nor the heads of other communist governments have succeeded at any meeting of the nonaligned governments or at any Afro-Asian conference in persuading other states to follow Tito in recognizing the GDR.

In January 1963 the Federal Government broke off relations with Castro. Occasionally, Bonn took less drastic retaliatory measures against lesser "unfriendly acts"; for example, economic aid to Ceylon was terminated in the spring of 1964, in response to the establishment of a GDR consulate-general in Colombo, and military aid to Tanzania was cancelled in February 1965 in answer to the opening of an East German consulate-general in Dar-es-Salaam.

Nine years earlier, when the doctrine was formulated, economic means — technical, economic, and military assistance, or its punitive withdrawal — for gaining in the new nations respect for Bonn's all-German interests, played virtually no role. The Ministry for Economic Development was created only in 1961. Since then, German economic aid has become a politically usable, if often economically wasteful, instrument supplementing the diplomatic instrument of the Hallstein doctrine.

It is often pointed out that the Hallstein doctrine makes the Federal Republic vulnerable to blackmail. Certain nonaligned countries, it is said, can extort economic aid from West Germany merely by threatening recognition of the GDR or nonrecognition of West Berlin as part of the Federal Republic, or they can threaten to accept East German offers of aid in the hope that West Germany will then outbid the GDR. To be sure, facts can be cited in support of these arguments, for example in respect to relations with Ben Bella and Sukarno; but it is not quite clear what the argument is supposed to prove. Is its meaning that for moral and legalistic reasons the

[9] Albrecht von Kessel in *Die Welt*, February 26, 1964.

GDR ought not to be recognized, but that the decision to abstain from such recognition becomes worthless if taken by the new states on grounds of economic expediency? Correlatively, should West Germany refuse to pay a price for asserting its claim to exclusive legitimacy among neutral and nonaligned countries? Clearly this would be an absurdly purist view to hold.

The new nations are faced with political and economic problems of their own, which to them have a great deal more meaning and weight than has the division of Germany. There is nothing surprising or shocking in the fact that German economic or military aid to a new state can be used to impress upon that state the importance of political interests which the Federal Republic considers vital. The only sensible criteria for judging whether or not such a "bribe" for political ends is worth the price seem to be its political success and the value put on that success. The critics who attack the Hallstein doctrine because it renders the Federal Republic vulnerable to economic blackmail fail to recognize that such vulnerability would exist even in the absence of the doctrine, so long as both West and East Germany in pursuit of their respective political interests are willing to offer "bribes" in the form of aid. The GDR cannot hope to match West Germany's economic resources, but in giving aid to Africa it occupies the third place among the communist countries, preceded only by the Soviet Union and Czechoslovakia.

In vying with the Federal Republic for diplomatic recognition abroad, the GDR has failed, but it has made determined efforts to assert its presence in Asia, Africa, and elsewhere, if only below the ambassadorial level. To the extent that these efforts have been successful they testify to the gradual, partial erosion of the Hallstein doctrine; paradoxically they testify also to its efficacy. Wherever the GDR established a legation, a consulate-general, a consulate, a trade mission, or a lesser foothold, Ulbricht would have preferred to have an ambassador accredited. Conversely, whenever the GDR did succeed in making its presence felt, if only in the form of a trade mission or a consulate, the Federal Republic would have preferred total failure of the GDR.

In addition to the twelve communist states in which the GDR has embassies, and to Yugoslavia where it maintains a legation, the GDR has established its presence in the form of consulates-general in Burma, Ceylon, Indonesia, Iraq, Yemen, Cambodia, and the United Arab Republic; a consulate in Syria; trade missions with consular rights in Algeria, Finland, Ghana, Guinea, India, and Mali; trade missions without consular rights in Lebanon, Morocco, and Sudan; a representative of the Ministry for Foreign Trade in Tunisia; representatives on the basis of agreements between the state banks in Brazil, Colombia, and Uruguay. In addition, the "Chamber for Foreign Trade with the GDR" is represented in the following countries: Belgium, Denmark, Great Britain, Iceland, Italy, Netherlands, Norway, Austria, Sweden, and Turkey.[10]

Nor does the list of countries in which the GDR is represented in some form reveal the full extent of East German influence abroad. For example, in Algeria, Tanzania, Ghana, and the UAR, more persons are assigned to the GDR missions than to the respective embassies of the Federal Republic.[11] In Africa the GDR exerts influence also through foreign correspondents, all of them members of the East German communist party; they are permanently assigned to Accra, Algiers, Bomaco, Dar-es-Salaam, Zanzibar, Cairo, and Alexandria. Furthermore, the GDR operates abroad through its labor unions and youth organizations; through invitations and stipends, at scientific and cultural conferences, and through printed materials sent to Africa in Spanish, French, English, and Arabic.

---

[10] The GDR Embassy on Zanzibar was closed by President Nyerere of Tanzania after the union of Zanzibar and Tanganyika, and a Consulate-General was established in Dar-es-Salaam. In Cairo the GDR has also a "delegate" to the Arab states. Cf. Jens Hacker, "Zonen-Diplomatie," *Die politische Meinung,* Vol. 10 (February 1965).

[11] Harald Ludwig, "Die 'DDR' in Afrika," *SBZ Archiv,* Vol. 16 (March 1965), p. 84.

Erosion

By 1965 various inconsistencies had developed in the West German policy of defending its rights by means of the Hallstein doctrine and by using the carrot of giving aid or the stick of withholding it. For example, it was noted that West German economic aid to Ceylon amounting to DM 13 million was suspended because the GDR had been permitted to establish a consulate-general in Colombo, whereas economic aid to Syria amounting to DM 350 million continued despite the establishment of an East German consulate-general in that country. Some Germans considered the diplomatic reprisals against Tito in 1957 to be weak, since consulates-general in Hamburg, Munich, and Zagreb survived the diplomatic break; in addition, substantial German economic aid continued to flow to Yugoslavia. More recently, the case of Tanzania was especially puzzling.

Tanzania, newly formed by the union of Zanzibar and Tanganyika, announced on February 19, 1965, that the GDR embassy on the island of Zanzibar, where the Chinese have a strong foothold, had been closed and in its stead a GDR consulate-general had been opened in Dar-es-Salaam on the mainland. Although this measure did not involve diplomatic recognition of the GDR, as President Nyerere pointed out, and actually downgraded the GDR representation, the Federal Government took a jaundiced view of the change, since before joining the union, Tanganyika had had diplomatic relations only with West Germany. In an effort to thwart the first attempt of the GDR to establish itself in Black Africa, Chancellor Erhard had written to President Nyerere on February 11, 1965, that the establishment of a consulate-general would jeopardize the friendly relations between West Germany and Tanzania. The Federal Government had not taken retaliatory action against any of the states in Asia and the Middle East which had admitted consulates-general of the GDR, but when Nyerere disregarded Erhard's warning Bonn discontinued its *military* aid. Thereupon Dr. Nyerere, concerned about his reputation of nonalignment, angrily announced that he would accept no further *economic* assistance from West Germany. And yet the Federal Republic did not break off *diplomatic* relations with Tanzania. *The Economist* (April 24, 1965), reviewing Dr. Nyerere's Easter visit to Great Britain and his statements on the West's relations with Africa, came to the conclusion that "Bonn seems to Tanzanians to look silly." In West Germany at least one leading newspaper considered Bonn's action against Dar-es-Salaam to be the result of frustrations which Colonel Nasser had inflicted upon the Federal Government. "In their quarrel with Egypt they had manoeuvred themselves into a corner, and so Tanzania suddenly became a welcome lightning conductor for Bonn's wrath."[12]

The crisis of 1965 in West Germany's relations with the Arab states revealed that the original Hallstein doctrine had become a blunt instrument. In order to induce President Nasser to cancel Walter Ulbricht's visit to Cairo, the Federal Government discontinued West German military aid to Israel, but Nasser, not content with having embarrassed the Federal Government, proceeded to humiliate it by upholding his invitation. When Ulbricht arrived in Egypt at the end of February he was treated like a head of state, although Nasser maintained that he had not recognized Ulbricht's regime. He had recognized it *de facto*.

After Ulbricht's visit to Cairo, ominous warnings were uttered in Germany about the future of German foreign policy. Franz-Josef Strauss declared that Ulbricht could be expected to visit Jakarta before the end of the year, and Rainer Barzel considered it possible that Ulbricht would soon visit Latin American countries as well. Until March 7, the sixteen members of the German Cabinet were almost evenly split on what to do. Those who counselled caution argued that if Bonn were to apply the Hallstein doctrine and break diplomatic relations with Cairo, West Germany would lose the right to sole representation of the German people in the Middle East, since

[12] Werner Holzer in *Süddeutsche Zeitung,* March 30, 1965.

Nasser would establish diplomatic ties with East Berlin and at least five other Arab states would follow suit. The cautious policy was championed by Gerhard Schröder, four CDU ministers, including the defense minister, and four of the five cabinet members belonging to the Free Democratic Party. This party, which had always been critical of the Hallstein doctrine, now contended that the doctrine immobilized German foreign policy and would lead to the gradual retreat of the Federal Republic from Asia and Africa. Caution was also strongly urged upon Erhard by Allied ambassadors, especially U.S. Ambassador McGhee, for fear that a break with Egypt would disturb the balance of power in the Middle East.[13] Between March 4 and 6 Erhard was inclined to take drastic action against Egypt. He was supported by four Bavarian ministers, who followed Strauss, and by at least two CDU ministers — Paul Lücke and Ernst Lemmer. Adenauer, Hallstein, and Westrick were said to have urged the application of the Hallstein doctrine to Egypt, and many members of this faction pointed to the need to repair the damage done by the earlier German action against Israel.

After protracted cabinet deliberations, Erhard reversed himself on March 7. His decision, which surprised many, including the Israeli mission in Cologne, was a compromise that could be supported by all the feuding factions in his government. Some were pleased because an open diplomatic break with Cairo had been avoided; others were pleased with the renewed refusal to give aid and credit guarantees to Egypt in the future; still others with the announcement that the Federal Republic would seek to establish diplomatic relations with Israel.

Ten states of the Arab League broke off diplomatic relations with the Federal Republic; only Morocco, Tunisia, and Libya did not follow suit. Economic and cultural relations, however, were maintained, and the staff of the German embassies continued to work in the embassies of the western countries which assumed the functions of protective powers.

On May 15 the official Cairo newspaper, *Al Ahram*, declared

[13] *The New York Times,* March 7, 1965.

that Egypt did not plan to recognize the GDR, since at best only Algeria, Iraq, and Yemen would follow suit and thus Arab disunity would be manifest. On the next day, in response to a letter that Erhard had sent to the Arab heads of state and government on May 9, Nasser informed the Chancellor that Egypt would continue to support the striving of the German people for reunification and to be interested in preserving German friendship.

After many months of uncertainty and disquiet, during which individual officials and the government as a whole had been publicly criticized, it was almost an anticlimax when on May 25, 1965, Professor Carstens, Undersecretary of State, informed the Bundestag that the Federal Government expected diplomatic relations with the Arab states to be resumed in the not too distant future.

What had happened in the crisis to the Hallstein doctrine? Although many German politicians and observers maintained that the doctrine had always permitted a flexible application, it can hardly be disputed that according to its original meaning diplomatic relations with Egypt should have been severed in February 1965. Erhard left the initiative of making the break to the Arabs. Since he responded to Nasser's provocative acts only with economic sanctions and with the recognition of Israel, the original doctrine had been quietly put aside. But on March 7, referring to "the self-evident right of every people to self-determination," the Federal Government reasserted the Hallstein doctrine in these terms: "An upgrading of this despotic regime [i.e., the GDR] is regarded by the Federal Republic of Germany as an unfriendly act to be answered by appropriate measures in each individual case."[14]

Prospects

The demise of the Hallstein doctrine, so ardently desired by the communists, will not result from alleged inconsistencies in its application to one or the other new state. A mortal wound

[14] *Bulletin des Presse- und Informationsamtes des Bundesregierung,* March 9, 1965.

can be inflicted on it only by a Western power, or by a future Federal Government finding it politically prudent to do so. In the latter case the German "right" to reunification, which the doctrine helps to assert, would expire. To be sure, rights are not subject to the judgment of history, but world events affect the political worth attached by friend and foe to the moral and legal rights of others. In the 1960's, the insistence of the Federal Government that the Allies take an active interest in reunification — an "initiative" — no longer occurs in the political climate of the early 1950's, but in the face of hardened Soviet determination not to change the *status quo* in Europe, of American interest in avoiding acute political conflict with the Soviet Union, and of French defection from NATO. The claim that Ulbricht's regime lacks legitimacy did not then, but now does, refer to the government of a country that has had remarkable economic success and boasts many political and economic contacts with the Federal Republic and its allies.

The Hallstein doctrine could fall into abeyance if the Western powers, without necessarily changing their declaratory policy on German reunification, were to abstain from the active pursuit of this policy over a long period of time. It may, in fact, be argued that such inactivity has prevailed ever since the end of the Geneva conference of 1959. At the end of 1964, Secretary Rusk, in a background briefing, urged the West Germans to re-examine their own ideas on reunification. Without withdrawing American support of the German interest in reunification, he passed to the Federal Government the responsibility for taking the initiative which Bonn had so often demanded of her powerful allies. Only a few months later, General de Gaulle attempted to remove the cornerstone of Western policy in Central Europe by viewing the reunification of Germany as a purely European concern. Had he been successful, the principle of four-power responsibility for German unity would have been abandoned. Erhard declared at the time, "A Europeanization [of that responsibility], with the practical consequence that the United States would have diminished rights and a lesser rank in respect of guaranteeing the restoration of German unity, is firmly rejected (*indiskut-abel*) by the Federal Government."[15]

In 1965, when relations between the Federal Republic and Egypt deteriorated sharply, puns about the "Hallstein epoch" gained currency in West Germany, suggesting that the doctrine had become as remote as the prehistoric Hallstatt epoch. Several prominent members of Erhard's cabinet were known to favor the establishment of diplomatic relations with communist states of eastern Europe. In particular, Vice-Chancellor Erich Mende urged that the Federal Government abandon the Hallstein doctrine in its relations with the communist regimes in Europe,[16] and many other Germans in positions of authority regarded such a development as the desirable extension of Schröder's trade policy. On this issue as well the orthodox principles of West German diplomacy prevailed. Moscow remained the only communist capital with diplomatic representations of both German states.

While the modified Hallstein doctrine still is officially held to provide some guidance for the future foreign policy of the Federal Republic, it has become increasingly evident in the past years that Bonn is pondering the obstacles to Western action on the issue of reunification. Early in 1965, Gerhard Schröder hinted in somewhat obscure language at these obstacles when he said:

> Today the predominant and general interest in preserving peace has gained pre-eminence over the specific interest in reunification. True, agreement on the goal still exists; but it has become more difficult for German foreign policy to conserve the close interdependence of the two problems down to their practical consequences.[17]

[15] *Berliner Morgenpost,* May 1, 1965, republished in *Bulletin des Presse- und Informationsamtes der Bundesregierung* (May 4, 1965), p. 610.

[16] Interview in *Der Spiegel,* April 14, 1965.

[17] Speech at the CDU Conference in Düsseldorf, March 30, 1965; cf. *Süddeutsche Zeitung,* March 31, 1965.

CHAPTER NINE

On War Games

The following two chapters deal with the simulation of international conflict. Chapter 9 contains some observations on the history of war games. Chapter 10 reports on an exercise developed by the Social Science Division of the RAND Corporation in the 1950's, in which the course of an international political crisis was simulated. In the meantime, this procedure has been widely used and further developed both in academic institutions and by U.S. Government agencies. The report in Chapter 10 also contains an appraisal of the value this gaming procedure has in furthering cooperation among experts in different fields, in teaching and training, in research and in predicting the future. It should be said at the outset that the predictive value of such games is, if anything, very low, but the game challenges players to concern themselves with contingencies they might overlook or neglect in a solitary analysis of foreign affairs.

War games have a longer history than political games. It is easy to understand why this is so. Those who make political decisions perform their functions in peacetime as well as in war. Many wars in the past and all wars after World War II have been limited in character. On any given level of technology, limited wars are inefficient wars in the sense that the available means of violence are not fully utilized. Those who make political decisions against an escalation toward unlimited war insure such inefficiency in the interest of overriding political, long-range considerations.

The military perform their function in earnest only when

From a paper presented at the annual meeting of the American Association for Public Opinion Research, Berkeley, California, May 1961.

their country is at war. In peacetime, they merely prepare for the execution of the tasks, the performance of which is the reason for their existence. This is one of the decisive differences between the armed forces and all other professions in society, the other being that the military when performing their duties in earnest are expected to accept a high risk of violent death. The highest virtue of the soldier is therefore courage, while we hope that statesmen will excel in wisdom and prudence.

Military maneuvers, war games, map exercises, and the like, pretest and in a sense rehearse the efficient performance of wartime functions that to a society devoted to its peacetime pursuits are extraordinary in the true sense of the word, and these functions lie in the future. Such tests and rehearsals necessarily are simulations.

As the historical record shows, there are two basic types of war games, the "rigid" and the "flexible." In the rigid war game the effect of each move is assessed according to a scale of pre-determined, quantitative values, and sometimes the universe of possible moves itself is fixed. In the open or flexible game, measurement of success or failure is replaced by the judgment of knowledgeable umpires. The initiative and imagination of the players is taxed by providing them with a greater latitude of moves.

The political exercise described in Chapter 10 is an "open game." It was invented because of disappointing experiences with attempts made by some mathematicians at RAND to construct and play a rigid political game, which suffered from lack of realism.

WAR GAMES have been put to three major uses: (1) training and rehearsal, (2) testing of the ability of officers, and (3) testing of doctrines, combat principles, and operational plans.

(1) *Training and rehearsal games* are military exercises (without the use of troops as in maneuvers) which give advanced training to officers of all ranks in making decisions. The simulated tasks which the officers have to fulfill are either especially designed for the game or taken from an operational plan in order to acquaint the participants with the missions they may be called upon to carry out in real war. In the latter case, the game is a rehearsal. In either case, the objective is to improve the ability of officers to perform wartime functions more intelligently, imaginatively, resolutely, and at a lower

risk of failure. The officers learn to appreciate the conditions
under which they may have to act, get practice in facing the
responsibility of making decisions, and witness the simulated
effects of their actions in consequence of simulated counteraction by the opponent.

Rehearsal through war games need not extend to actual encounters with the enemy, but can be confined to special components of action on one side. In this case the participants
do not compete but cooperate. For example, communications
procedures or logistic support operations have been the focus
of war games, and so has the cooperation of different branches
of the armed services, e.g., air support of ground action,
armored units operating in conjunction with infantry, etc.

The modern war game played for purposes of training and
rehearsal is a German invention. Von Reisswitz, Jr., a First
Lieutenant in the Prussian Guard Artillery, who continued the
work of his father, is usually credited with having been the
originator of the modern war game in the 1820's. Von Reisswitz, Sr. had transferred war games from the large boards on
which they used to be played[1] to a sand table, and his son
improved and formalized the game; it dealt with tactics. He
introduced maps representing actual terrain; differentiated
the representation of the various branches of the armed forces
by pieces of lead and by symbols; prescribed written moves,
reports, and orders to be transmitted through an umpire; gave
careful attention to the relation between game time and real
time; and imposed calculations of the rates of movement and
losses. The impact of incomplete information or intelligence
was simulated in his game, and the outcome of engagements
was determined by throws of dice. When von Meffling, the
Chief of the Prussian General Staff, witnessed an exhibition

---

[1] The most notable invention made prior to von Reisswitz was that
of Georg Vinturinus in 1798, who employed a chart divided into 3,600
squares and pawns representing troops. On the chart war games were
being played according to rules that governed the simulation of movement and fighting, the book of rules taking up more than 60 pages of
instruction.

of the game in 1824, his initial skepticism disappeared quickly. He burst out saying, "It is not a game at all! It's training for war! I shall recommend it most emphatically for the whole army!"[2]

With further improvements, von Reisswitz's game became ever more complex, *rigid,* and formalized, and hence less useful in training. It continued to be a favorite pastime of German officers in clubs especially organized for that purpose well into the latter half of the nineteenth century.

Interest in war games for purposes of training and rehearsal was reawakened by a new departure in the 1870's. In the new, *free* game, the judgment and experience of the umpire replaced the tables, charts, and calculations of the former war games.[3]

The victories of Prussia in the wars of 1864, 1866, and 1870–1871 did much to popularize war games outside Germany. By 1882 Captain W. R. Livermore, in his book, *The American Kriegsspiel,* pointed out that the game was now played not only in Germany but also in Russia, Italy, France, Belgium, and elsewhere. In the United States, war games for training purposes have been used in the armed forces at least since 1880 when Secretary of War Alex Ramsay approved the issue of the Rules and Tables of *Strategos — The American Game of War,* a book written by Charles A. L. Totten. The rules set forth by Totten were based on statistics derived from the Wars of the Rebellion.

In the period between the two world wars, the War Plans Division of the U.S. Army war-gamed American mobilization plans each year, beginning in 1934. At Leavenworth in the 1920's and 1930's students played war games with forces varying in size from a brigade to Army groups. At the Army

---

[2] Cited from C. P. Young, "A Survey of Historical Developments in War Games," in M. Weiner, "An Introduction to War Games," RAND P-1773 (August 17, 1959), p. 8.

[3] The main landmarks in this new development were works by Meckel in 1873 and 1875 and especially General Verdy du Vernois' *A Contribution to the War Game,* 1876.

War College one group of students functioning as the Japanese General Staff prepared a simulated Japanese war plan while another group drew up an American war plan. Then the two groups reversed their roles and executed the plan prepared by the opposing team.

Today, war games and other techniques of simulating military conflict are still more widely used in this country, although most of them must be regarded as research games, on which I shall comment presently.

One of the most notable instances of rehearsing a supreme military command decision in World War II was the exercise through which General Eisenhower went many times prior to the landing of the Allied forces in Normandy. Repeatedly, he assembled all of his subordinate commanders, listened in their presence to "live" reports and forecasts of the specialists on weather, tides, enemy capabilities, etc. Given these "live" conditions, he then heard the views of his subordinate commanders concerning the risks and the expected losses of their forces and their assessments of the probability of a successful invasion. All this was done in order to enable General Eisenhower to rehearse the vital decision that he was soon obliged to make in earnest, namely that of ordering that the invasion be either launched or postponed.

(2) War games have also been used to *test the ability* of staff and line officers. In that case, the game directors, who are usually senior officers, can observe the fitness of the participants as commanders, their strength and weakness, and certain qualities of mind and character. But even the best designed war games fall short of simulating the reality of war in a completely satisfactory manner. The rehearsal of a stage play or the training of an athlete differs from the training which young staff officers receive through participation in war games. In the theater or in sport, preparatory and final activities — the rehearsal and the rehearsed performance — are very much alike, but this is not true of war games in relation to wars. War games can merely simulate certain especially selected conditions of armed conflict. Neither the hazards nor

the psychological effect of the imponderables of war can be fully simulated. For this reason no war game can test the ability of future commanders reliably. A German officer who prepared an interesting account of German war games after the end of Warld War II observed on this point:

> . . . (war games) can no more simulate real warfare than can maneuvers. For what is missing are the impressions of combat, the live ammunition, the genuine tensions and the far-reaching responsibility . . . there are officers who felt constrained and nervous when under the spotlight of a war game, but who later proved to be clear-thinking and decisive commanders in war. In the same way an intelligent participant in a war game who has perhaps known the director for a fairly long time can sometimes guess the latter's intention exactly; this same man, who is so brilliant in a game, may be unsure of himself and fail when actually under fire. The imponderables which make up one part of war and combat and the psychological factors can never be completely represented in a game. Thus, an officer's performance during a war game can only be used to judge a fraction of his actual military ability.[4]

(3) *Research games* are exercises that test or improve doctrine derived from past wars or are used in the development or plans of future operations. Like the value for training and rehearsal, the research value of war games is definitely established. Research games are in wide use. I shall confine myself to a few observations on the use of games for the improvement of plans.

The execution of plans can be rehearsed with the help of gaming procedures. If in such rehearsals certain flaws of the plan are discovered and the plan is subsequently changed, rehearsal and research are combined. An analogue would be changing the script of a play in consequence of a rehearsal prior to the actual performance. But pure research games are often played for planning purposes. For example, during the Nazi period the Germans played them in developing the plans for the invasions of France and the Soviet Union, and the

---

[4] U.S. Army War College, *War Games. An Anthology* (January 6, 1958), p. VIII–19.

Japanese did so prior to the battle at Midway. An account of the German exercises states explicitly that the games ". . . were not played for training but for research purposes."[5]

Rehearsal as well as research purposes were served in games subsequently played prior to the actual invasions. The account that I have just quoted points out that after plan "Barbarossa" for the German invasion of the Soviet Union had been developed,

> . . . the presumable operations were so thoroughly rehearsed in advance in war games and map exercises that actually every single commander down to company level was thoroughly familiar with his initial missions, with the difficulties which were presumably about to confront him, and with the enemy forces situated opposite him.

> The procedure adopted in these cases was approximately as follows: First, in a war game the army group commander briefed his army commanders and corps commanders and their tactical assistants as to their missions. On the basis of the same situation, but on a correspondingly smaller scale, the army commander acquainted his corps commanders and divisional commanders with their missions. Then the corps commander held a theoretical exercise and so forth. In the end it was the task of the battalion commander to instruct his company commanders and the majority of his platoon leaders by means of a map exercise. This procedure had the great advantage that new views for the disposition and employment of the troops were constantly brought up for discussion and that the orders for attack could be revised accordingly.[6]

In the postwar era the importance of research games has, if anything, been enhanced. This is a result of the new revolutionary weapons systems, which have rendered past war experiences almost totally irrelevant for the planning of future operations in unlimited war. It would have been absurd for the Germans or the Japanese in World War II to have based their research games on planning factors derived from naval engagements in ancient Greece or from siege warfare in medieval Europe. Correspondingly, the war games involving

[5] *Op. cit.*, p. VIII–17.
[6] *Ibid.*

the use of modern aircraft, missiles, and nuclear warheads cannot glean much strategic or tactical insight from the study of wars waged earlier in this century. This means that military planning must now rely more than ever on research, and research games — many of them now making use of high speed computers — play an important role in this effort.

The number of factors which decision makers can keep in mind is often smaller than the number of factors that should bear on the decision they are called upon to make under modern conditions. One of the invaluable contributions of high speed computers to war games is their capacity for the replication of any one game with different players within an immensely shortened time period; a third is the capacity of computers to test, again very rapidly, the outcome of games by varying assumptions, objectives, strategies, or tactics.[7]

"Research" in nuclear war games, however, has little to do with searching out from past experience empirical facts that may bear on a future situation. Since bilateral nuclear war has never been fought, research on this subject inevitably consists in the manipulation of assumptions and calculations of cost, performance, and effect derived from theories, tests, analogies, extrapolations, and projections. The experts in research games of nuclear war are experts on a kind of war that has never been fought. The only ingredient that pre-nuclear and nuclear conflicts have in common is the involvement of human beings making and executing decisions and surviving or dying. Usually experts on nuclear war have no need or vocation to study man, the only "independent variable" on which empirical knowledge abounds. Their colleagues in the social sciences are not of much help either, often because they proclaim to be experts on human "behavior" rather than on man. They profess ignorance on the "relevant behavior" because it has never been observed under the ap-

---

[7] For a brief account of a use to which strategic war games have been put, see C. J. V. Murphy, "The Revolution Gets Revolutionary," *Fortune,* Vol. 54 (May 1956).

propriate conditions (of nuclear war). Or else, overwhelmed by the precision with which the experts on nuclear war express themselves, those who have reflected on human affairs do not dare to speak in plain English about the intrinsic uncertainties hidden beneath the veneer of expert rigidity.

CHAPTER TEN

Some Observations on Political Gaming

FROM 1954 TO 1956, the Social Science Division of the RAND Corporation developed a procedure for the study of foreign affairs that we called "political gaming."[1] This paper gives a brief description of the technique and some of our observations about its utility.[2]

Descriptions of RAND Game

Political gaming has antecedents both outside and within RAND. Prior to World War II, political gaming was applied to questions of foreign policy in Germany and Japan, although

Co-author: Herbert Goldhamer. From *World Politics,* Vol. 12 (October 1959).

[1] This work was made possible in part by funds provided by the Ford Foundation.

[2] The Social Science Division of RAND prepared a series of internal papers on gaming. Several of these were made available to persons outside RAND who expressed an interest in experimenting with the technique. Some of these papers are: Goldhamer, "Toward a Cold War Game" (1954); P. Kecskemeti, "War Games and Political Games" (1955); H. Goldhamer, "The Political Exercise: A Summary of the Social Science Division's Work in Political Gaming, with Special Reference to the Third Exercise" (1955); J. M. Goldsen, "The Political Exercise: An Assessment of the Fourth Round" (1956); Social Science Division, "Experimental Research on Political Gaming" (1958). The present article has incorporated some material from the papers listed above, particularly from the last-mentioned item.

we were not aware of this at the time that we started our own experimentation.

Before Hitler assumed power in 1933, the leaders of the German Reichswehr were much concerned about Polish military strength and political designs. The German armed forces were then restricted to 100,000 men in strength. In 1929, a young staff officer, later to be General Erich von Manstein, charged with the responsibility for the organization of a war game involving German defense against a Polish attack on East Prussia or Upper Silesia, realized that the outbreak of war would be preceded by mounting political conflict. In that conflict, he thought, Germany would have to avoid giving France and Czechoslovakia cause for entering the war as Poland's allies and the League of Nations a pretext for not declaring Poland the aggressor. Manstein proposed that the strictly military exercise be introduced by a political game in order to let political and military leaders learn from each other. High-ranking members of the Foreign Office played the roles of the president of the League of Nations Council and of the Polish and German Foreign Ministers. In his memoirs, Manstein writes that the inventiveness of the player representing Poland in alleging German provocations left his German counterpart "completely speechless" and that the skillfully simulated procrastination of the League was grimly appreciated by all participants. "We had the impression also," Manstein reports, "that the gentlemen from the Foreign Office, to whom such a playing-through of possible conflicts seemed to be completely novel, were thoroughly convinced of the value of the game."[3]

According to exhibits offered in evidence at the Tokyo War Crimes Trials, the Japanese Total War Research Institute, established in 1940, engaged in games of aggression that involved having teams of high-ranking specialists in the Japanese government play the political and military roles of leading powers in the Pacific area. In these exercises Japan was rep-

[3] Erich von Manstein, *Aus einem Soldatenleben* (Bonn: Athenäum Verlag, 1958), pp. 131–133.

resented not by one team, but by several — Army, Navy, Cabinet — and the views of these teams had to be co-ordinated before Japan as a whole could act. Some of the moves in this game anticipated actual measures taken by the Japanese government after Pearl Harbor.

In a German report written for the Office of the Chief of Military History, U.S. Army, in 1951, we read that in Nazi Germany the Wehrmacht Academy "held a big military-political game every year followed by a training trip. Representatives of all branches of the Wehrmacht, as well as of politics, business, the armament industry and the Propaganda Ministry, participated in it."[4]

From an article in the Sunday *Times* (London), December 9, 1956, it appears that the Soviets may have made use of a similar procedure. Alexandre Metaxas, who is identified as a Russian-speaking French journalist, reports that Soviet political specialists try to anticipate the results of international political moves by putting themselves in the role of each interested party in turn. Metaxas claims that the course to be followed by the Soviet Foreign Office is determined in part by the results of this simulated interaction. It is not clear from his account whether actual gaming procedures are involved.

RAND's interest in political gaming grew out of work in political analysis and previous experimentation with the use of gaming techniques for other purposes. For several years RAND had worked extensively with various sorts of highly formalized war games. At one point an attempt was made to devise a "cold war game" in which a few political and economic factors were assigned numerical values so that the relative worth of alternative strategies could be assessed quantitatively. Players were allowed only a limited choice of specified moves. This experiment was abandoned when it became clear that the simplification imposed in order to permit quantification made the game of doubtful value for the assessment of political strategies and tactics in the real world.

[4] U.S. Army War College, *War Games. An Anthology* (January 6, 1958), p. VIII–6.

The first proposal for a political game of the type with which we have been working was made by Herbert Goldhamer in 1954.[5] He suggested a procedure that avoided schematic simplifications of the international political situation and attempted to simulate as faithfully as possible much of its complexity. The government of each country was to be represented by a separate player or group of players. (In practice, of course, all countries never were represented, but only those regarded as most significant for the geographical or problem area around which the game was centered.)

In addition, "Nature" was to be represented by an individual or a team, and there was to be a team of referees. The role of "Nature" was to provide for events of the type that happen in the real world but are not under the control of any government; certain technological developments, the death of important people, nongovernmental political action, famines, popular disturbances, etc.

Participants in the game were to be area specialists who could draw on their knowledge and accumulated area experience.[6] With the exception of the American Team, all government teams were to act as they judged "their" governments would in the circumstances prevailing at any given time of the game ("predicted strategy"). The American Team was less restricted; it was permitted to pursue any strategy which it judged to be optimal; in particular, the United States Team was not required to follow the foreign policy line of any administration or to have special regard for the constraints placed upon American foreign policy in reality by domestic considerations. The game was thus designed to permit tests of a wide range of United States strategies.

The referees had the task of ruling on the feasibility of each move; that is, they were to disallow any move that they did not regard as within the constitutional or physical power of the

---

[5] H. Goldhamer, "Toward a Cold War Game" (1954).

[6] All players had spent some time in the country whose government they represented and were familiar not only with its political system but also with many members of its ruling groups.

government proposing it. For three reasons the referees also played the role of "Nature." This arrangement saved manpower; it restricted the number of arbitrary moves which might have been made had full-time players represented "Nature"; and it permitted the referees to make certain nongovernmental moves which constituted indirect, partial evaluations of the state of affairs that had been reached at any chosen point of the game. For example, the referees could introduce such evaluations in the form of press roundups, trade union resolutions, intelligence reports, speeches made in the United Nations, etc. (The governmental players were permitted, however, to challenge the plausibility of such moves.)

In the course of 1955 and early 1956, four political games were played, starting with the rules suggested by Goldhamer and gradually developing additional refinements. The first two games extended over only a few days. The third game lasted four weeks in the summer of 1955, and a dozen RAND staff members devoted approximately half time to it. The fourth was conducted during the month of April 1956. Three senior Foreign Service Officers from the Department of State participated in the fourth political game, along with specialists from RAND's Social Science, Economics, and Physics Divisions. In the fourth game, unlike previous plays, all thirteen team members devoted practically full time to the exercise, one of them spending part of it on liaison functions. In addition, a number of consultants were called upon whenever the development of the game required competence in fields of which the full-time players did not have special knowledge. The players were assisted by a sizable secretarial staff. Prior to the start of gaming, considerable time was spent on the preparation of a "scenario" and "strategy papers."

Since the fourth game is by far the most exhaustive test we have given this technique thus far, the following observations refer primarily to it. One reference to the earlier games will, however, be useful in order to explain what is meant by the "scenario." In our first attempts at political gaming, we started with the historical present as a backdrop. From then on, game events moved into the future under their own momentum. It sometimes proved difficult to prevent the initial action in the game from being overtaken by or becoming entwined with developments reported in the daily newspaper. The fourth game, therefore, was projected further in the future, with the opening moves to be made as of January 1, 1957. The "scenario," written in March 1956, represented an effort to describe how the world of January 1, 1957, would look. It provided the players with a common state of affairs from which to begin. The scenario rid them of the intrusion of current news into the game and served to focus it on problems of special analytical interest.

In this game, as in the third, all moves by national teams were made in written form and submitted to the referees for clearance prior to distribution. The government teams were generally required to state (to the referees) the motives of their moves and the expectations on which they were based. The referees could challenge not only the feasibility of the moves but also their plausibility or the reasoning behind them; and if the government teams so desired, the referees could be asked to state their objections in writing.

Some moves were "open" and available to all teams; others were "game classified." The referees determined the distribution of each paper and, as controllers of information, could "leak" the contents of "game classified" papers, in whole or in part, sooner or later, accurately or in distorted form; thus the referees served as surrogates for the intelligence function in the political process or for actual "leaks" of classified information in the free press. They did not act for the Communist press, since it is government-controlled.

Prior to the April 1956 session, the government teams drew up strategy papers. These were "game classified" and were distributed only to the referees. Also certain parts of the scenario were "game classified" — e.g., sections containing descriptions of certain weapons developments.

During the three weeks of actual play, 150 papers were

written by the participants. Many of these consisted of moves by government teams; moves were dated in "game time" and numbered sequentially with reference both to the action of each team and to the game as a whole. "Game classified" background papers served to give the referees a basis for judging the motivation of any given move, and to provide a written record of the analytical thought relating the move to the strategy paper of the actual team.

The fourth game was focused on the activities of the United States and the Soviet Union with respect to each other and to Western Europe. In the first week some major activity did develop involving the Middle East and some minor activity involving North Africa and Asia. But on the whole these areas received secondary attention because of limitations in time and a determined effort to keep the game focused (and not because of an *a priori* judgment about the political importance of these areas).

Events of the game carried well into the summer of 1957 (game time). After three weeks of play, the complete set of records was thrown open to all participants, including the strategy papers and all other "game classified" documents. Time was allowed for the study of these papers, and then a few days were devoted to meetings of all participants to assess and evaluate the game.

In short, the game was so designed as to meet six main requirements:

(1) *Minimal formalization*: The government teams were not limited to any prescribed set of moves, as is the case in a game like chess and in some war games; nor did the game contain any pre-established prescriptions automatically entailing certain consequences from particular types of moves.[7] Such formalization would beg many questions that we regarded as the proper subject of discussion and inquiry within the exercise itself or as resolvable only by research outside

---

[7] In war games, these prescriptions are called "planning factors."

the game. Rather than work from highly simplified and schematic assumptions up to a richer and more complex game world, we followed the opposite approach.

(2) *Simulation of incomplete and incorrect information*: In foreign affairs, state secrets, which all governments keep with varying degrees of success, are important obstacles in the process of decision-making. In our game the introduction of "game classified" moves and their unpredictable handling by the referees tried to take account of this factor.

(3) *Simulation of contingent factors*: In political life many events are beyond the control of the most powerful actors, a fact designated in political theories by such terms as *fortuna*, "chance," "God's will," "changes in the natural environment," etc. We tried to simulate this fact by moves of "Nature."

(4) *Plausibility of game events*: We vested insurance against implausible game events not only in the political judgment of the referees but also in that of the participants responsible for governmental moves. We found no tendency for politically knowledgeable and responsible players to invent "wild" moves in order to relieve the tedium of the often slow and deliberate maneuvering of the governments involved in the game. Indeed, we found that some players in their desire to behave responsibly were at times unnecessarily cautious in their moves. We believe that continuing participation in political games resolves this difficulty.

(5) *Clarification of issues*: Our aim was not to move on rapidly from point to point of the game but to clarify by discussion the issues raised in the course of the play. Such discussions took place during the game within each team before a move was proposed or on occasion between a government team and the referees, and after the game among all participants. Furthermore, we directed effort toward the clarification of intellectual issues by providing a focus of the game in the scenario and the strategy papers, by restricting the number of teams participating full time, and by selecting highly qualified specialists as players.

(6) *Exploration of novel strategies*: We tried to stimulate

efforts to meet this requirement by prescribing "predicted" and "optimal" strategies respectively to various teams in advance of the play.

Assessment

The Social Science Division has carried on several discussions to assess whether the game procedure is worth the substantial investment of time and energy that it requires. The immediate stimulus to the Social Science Division's venture in this field was the difficulty of deriving from the results of research and from general political and military knowledge a sense of the probable trend of future international affairs and the most likely consequences ensuing from policies and military postures that might be adopted by the United States or other countries.

Evidently the principal difficulties here are those inherent in scientific and applied scientific work, especially in the social sciences. Any basic improvement in our ability to forecast the consequences of an actual or hypothecated change in the political-military world will surely depend on advances in our theoretical and empirical knowledge. Granted this, there still remains the problem of making the most effective use of any given level of empirical knowledge and theory. In this connection the political game was primarily envisaged as a means for securing a more effective collaboration of the specialized skills involved in political-military analysis. The political game provided an easily and sharply defined division of labor for the participants, and it gave them a more systematic means of adjudicating the conflicting claims of different lines of argument. It also demanded of them extensive and explicit statements of the political and military assumptions from which they argued. In these ways it helped the participants to achieve a more effective co-ordination of the knowledge and intellectual talents at their disposal. In addition the game provided, through its sequence of moves and countermoves, a "calculation" of consequences (anticipated and unanticipated). In this respect the political game is somewhat similar to the use of Monte Carlo methods, whereby machine stimulation takes over the job of a purely mathematical derivation of results.

It should not be supposed, however, that the political game displaces customary forms of intellectual collaboration such as the writing of political analyses, by individuals or jointly, and seminar-style discussions. On the contrary, we found that one of the most useful aspects of the political game was its provision of an orderly framework within which a great deal of written analysis and discussion took place. In describing our experience to others, we have continually emphasized that oral or written discussion of political problems that arise during the game is one of its most valuable features.

Making effective use of a given level of knowledge and theory does not, of course, preclude advancing knowledge and theory through gaming. While obviously such benefits will vary from player to player and from problem to problem, participants in our games did find opportunities to check their suppositions, both of a factual and of a more theoretical character, against the game events. It is not easy, however, to derive these benefits, and we suspect that they often get lost in the process of playing the game. A critical and self-conscious effort is needed to retain these benefits in a more lasting and transmissible form.

We did not expect and we have not so far found that the political game enables us to test strategies or to forecast political developments with any real degree of confidence. Unlike a written analysis, however, the game does provide some testing of a strategy prior to the test made by history itself (if that strategy is indeed followed in the real world). However, the political analyst working in his study "controls" not only the political maneuver he is analyzing but also the responses of hostile, neutral, and allied countries. In the political game, the analyst must contend with responses made by other players and not those which he assumes will follow from the line of action he is proposing. In a fairly comprehensive political game, there are numerous plausible alternative moves that governments may make, and the one line of many branching lines of development pursued in a single game cannot usually be accepted as an adequate test. To test strategies and to forecast political developments would require several replications of the gaming problem. This we have not yet attempted. On the other hand, our experience does show that even though an over-all strategy may not be tested (in terms of a clear payoff) by a single game, players do become aware during the game of pitfalls and problems that surround a strategy or some aspect of it.

The requirement of the political game that the participants make definite acts on behalf of their governments provided a very real stimulus to political inventiveness and a keen realization of possible contingencies that in analytical work might have seemed less important or less likely. On several occasions in our fourth game, certain developments in the game suggested the need for particular types of contingency planning in the real world or anticipated events that did occur later.

We hoped that the political-military questions arising in the game would indicate problems for further research and that gaming would thus help to shape our research program. This proved to be the case, but probably the major benefit lay in the fact that the game served to suggest research priorities for problems of which we were already aware and to define these problems in a manner that would make the research more applicable to policy and action requirements.

We believed when we began our work in gaming that the political game would prove to be a useful educational device. Our experience (and that of academic institutions with which we have collaborated) has increased our conviction in this regard.

First, the political game provides a lively setting in which students of politics, acting as observers or apprentice participants, can learn a good deal about the structure of the contemporary world and about some of the reasons behind political decisions. Factual information takes on a new interest and importance when it is required for intelligent participation in the game, and political principles assume special significance when they are illustrated by political actions and situations with which the student is associated as a participant. Needless to say, these benefits are realized only if the students receive continuous criticism from politically knowledgeable persons or participate in a game with such persons.

Second, the political game performs an educational function also for individuals with considerable political training and knowledge. We found that the game provided excellent opportunities and incentives for such participants to acquire an overview of a political situation and to amass relevant information that the ordinary intellectual division of labor and specialization by area or discipline do not make available. Some players found that they were exploring new fields of knowledge, some of which they had not previously associated with the conduct of foreign policy, such as developments in weapons technology. Area specialists were not infrequently made more keenly aware of the specific ways in which the world outside their area of specialization affected the politics of countries within their area.

A third educational benefit of the political games we played was to give players a new insight into the pressures, the uncertainties, and the moral and intellectual difficulties under which foreign policy decisions are made. This, of course, is in part a tribute to the earnestness and sense of responsibility with which the participants played their roles, since otherwise these pressures and perplexities would not have made themselves felt.

Experiences Elsewhere

Even before the first four games had been completed, RAND began to receive requests for information about its political gaming procedures, and staff members have by now taken part in a substantial number of discussions about it. In the summer of 1956, Hans Speier presented a summary of our experience as of that date to a Social Science Research Council summer institute in Denver, and in 1957 to the Fellows at the Center for Advanced Study in the Behavioral Sciences at Stanford. On several occasions during 1956–1958, Herbert Goldhamer lectured on the political game at the Army War College, and Joseph Goldsen discussed it at faculty and student gatherings at Yale and at a conference sponsored by the Carnegie Endowment for International Peace at Princeton. Informal discussions about political gaming have been held with personnel of the Department of State, the Center for International Affairs at Harvard, the Brookings Institution, Northwestern University, and the Massachusetts Institute of Technology. In June 1959, the Social Science Research Council held a conference at West Point, N.Y., on teaching and research in the field of national security. At one of the sessions Hans Speier described the RAND experiments in political gaming, and several social scientists from various academic institutions, including all those mentioned immediately below, reported on their own experiences with such games. Finally, in September 1959, Herbert Goldhamer presented a paper on political gaming at the annual meeting of the Political Science Association in Washington, D.C.

We have not attempted to collate the experiences other institutions have had in using political gaming techniques derived from the RAND experiments or worked out independently.[8] Such a collation might be useful at some future time.

Because of RAND participation we do, however, have rather detailed information about various experiments with political gaming at MIT. During the academic year 1957–1958, W. Phillips Davison of the RAND staff served as visiting professor at MIT, and while there tried out political gaming in his graduate seminar on international communications. This game was conducted according to greatly simplified rules. Players sat

---

[8] Work in this area at Northwestern University is partially summarized in a paper by Harold Guetzkow, "A Use of Simulation in the Study of Inter-nation Relations" (mimeographed).

around a large table and could make their moves orally, although a fairly detailed written record was kept. The instructor acted as referee and "Nature."

In spite of the limitations imposed by the simplified procedures and the brief time available, Davison concluded that the experiment achieved worthwhile results from an educational point of view. While it did not approach the realism of the RAND games, it showed that even with less expert players the game could provide real benefits. Perhaps the most outstanding of these was the intense interest generated among the students. When formal gaming came to an end, students continued the game at lunch and at other informal gatherings. A related benefit was the increased sophistication with which students approached their research problems.

Later in the same year Professor Lucian Pye — also at MIT — assisted by Professor Warner Schilling (now at Columbia), adapted the RAND technique to the requirements of his course in American diplomacy. During the term each student was asked to write a paper setting forth the major foreign policy goals of some country and to outline a foreign policy for achieving these goals. Then, during the last four meetings of the course, political gaming was conducted, with students taking the parts of the countries whose foreign policies they had discussed in their term papers.

This experiment appeared to be a highly successful pedagogical enterprise. In many cases students found that the foreign policy they had constructed in their term papers proved unrealistic when they attempted to follow it in the game. The game thus provided a means of obtaining critical insight into their own previous thinking. Both Pye and Davison have noted that political gaming, when conducted with students, places a very heavy burden on the instructor (who acts as referee and "Nature").

A further use of the gaming technique at MIT was made by the Center for International Studies, in connection with a research project on the United Nations headed by Professor Lincoln P. Bloomfield. One session took place in September

1958. Several RAND staff members discussed the plans with Professor Bloomfield, and the informal records on RAND's gaming experience were made available to him. Paul Kecskemeti of the RAND staff participated in this game. Professor Norman J. Padelford, also at MIT, has since organized various other games for undergraduate students, in some of which political scientists from other institutions have participated.[9]

We believe that there are a great many political questions and questions of technique that could be clarified by more work in political gaming, but that this should not lead to a neglect of customary research and study. Gaming is most productive if one is able to bring to it the results of continuous research in the field of foreign affairs and weapons development.

Variants of the Game

In conclusion we are setting forth a few variants in the form and content of the game that any thorough exploration of this procedure ought to test.

(1) *Time*: In our experiment the initial scenarios with which the games began still resembled reality rather closely. The effect of more extreme deviations from current political and military reality in the game remains to be tested. For example, the character of the game might be strongly modified by a scenario in which NATO had been dissolved, various national states in addition to the present three nuclear powers were in possession of nuclear weapons, and the political leaders of the major powers of the world were replaced by unknown persons. Such a game, removed from immediate political reality, could conceivably lead to the discovery of entirely new problems and to new insights and provide a greater emphasis on analytical results or generalizations. It might also be of interest to play games covering *past* history.

(2) *Tempo*: While the groups involved in the exercise at

[9] For one of these, cf. Norman J. Padelford and Seth P. Tillman, "Report on Political Exercise on Berlin Crisis," January 1959 (mimeographed).

MIT played the game in rapid-transit fashion, this procedure has not been tried out by senior players. The best "tempo" of the game remains to be determined.

(3) *Replication and variant strategies*: Fast games would lend themselves especially well to replication, and without replication certain results of the game cannot be validated. Alternatively, it would be desirable to have two or more sets of teams play simultaneously a game with the same scenario,[10] or else to begin a single game with sufficiently large teams so that they could be split to explore branching strategies when important alternative continuations develop at any stage of the game.

(4) *Predicted vs. optimal strategies*: Our own experience has been largely, though not exclusively, based on allowing the United States Team to pursue any strategy it deems optimal, but requiring other government teams to pursue the strategies to be expected of them ("predicted strategy") in the given circumstances of the game. More experimentation would permit games in which the United States plays expected strategies and other governments optimal strategies, or in which all governments play expected strategies or all governments play optimal strategies.

(5) *Scope*: There are a number of variants to be explored in which the scope of the game is changed so as to encompass smaller or larger political-geographical areas or more or less specialized policy problems. It is possible that the value of the game to students increases when its scope is enlarged, while the inverse relation may exist regarding the value of the game to decision-makers. The latter, however, will want some assurance that specialization of the game problem does not obscure important side effects of the policies involved in the game.

(6) *Political behavior*: The game offers opportunities for studying problems other than policy choices and their conse-

---

[10] In 1959, such an attempt has been made on the undergraduate level in three institutions — Columbia University (Warner Schilling), MIT (Lucian Pye), and West Point (Major Abbott Greenleaf).

quences. For example, by simulating international conferences within a given game (which we have tried on occasion), additional data can be developed for the study of negotiatory behavior. To be sure, special arrangements toward this end for observation and recording have to be made in advance. Similar opportunities exist with regard to the study of, and training in, specialized political and economic warfare problems, the drafting of diplomatic notes, the study of the effect of uncertainty and stress upon decision-making, and a host of other problems that arise in the conduct of foreign affairs.

(7) *International participation*: It would be desirable to have a few foreign political analysts play the roles of their own governments so that close consideration of each nation's interest would be increased. (Teams representing Communist governments could be composed of both American and foreign specialists.) It is to be expected that such a game, if carefully prepared, would substantially enhance among all participants the understanding of national "bias," collective security, the nature and problems of coalitions, and the viewpoints of neutrals.

CHAPTER ELEVEN

The Pitfalls of Political Humor

Since the end of World War II there has been intense interest in the more elusive forms of resistance to modern totalitarian regimes. Such resistance includes clandestine publications, the use of Aesopian language — writing allusively between the lines — whispered jokes and even dreams. These responses to oppression do not serve exclusively the aggressive ends of protest and resistance. They may also protect the self-respect of the oppressed, who escape from reality by flight into imaginative protest. By the same token, the new German preoccupation with the political jokes circulating during the Hitler era, is in part an attempt to prove that German resistance to Hitler was more widespread than its overt manifestations indicated.

In Germany there have been redundant publications of data on writing between lines, jokes, and even of dreams as forms of political resistance to the Nazi regime. The analysis of the data has been more halting. By no means every German editor introducing his collection of jokes to a post-Hitlerian public has appreciated the fact that certain anti-Nazi jokes were launched by the regime itself in support of its policies, and others were tolerated on the assumption that after letting off some steam the engine might run more smoothly. Furthermore, telling clandestine jokes may well be an act of accommodation to suppression rather than an act of aggression. Whispering a political joke against the authorities may be more courageous than remaining silent, but it may also assuage pangs of conscience caused by one's unwillingness to do something that taxes his courage. An author writing, say, animal fables that he thinks subtly condemn the regime may delude himself about

Written for Paul Kecskemeti, October 1966.

both the extent of his daring and the number of readers who understand him. A person hating the regime in his waking hours and perhaps revealing some of his hatred to close associates may be the victim of anxieties appearing in his dreams that show him abjectly cooperating with his persecutors. Much analytical work remains to be done on esoteric forms of resistance and accommodation to tyrannical rule.

The following essay merely points to some of the gaps that need to be filled. In addition, it is a call for paying close attention to the relationship between seriousness and humor in high politics, democratic as well as dictatorial. Paul Kecskemeti, a friend for whom these pages were originally written, replied among other things, "Ridicule is indeed a weapon, and, as you show, a double-edged one. It may ruin its wielder, showing the latter's inferiority instead of demolishing the superiority of the intended victim."

The reader is also referred to the last chapter in this volume, which contains some data reflecting on the use of subversive humor in predemocratic society.

A BRAVE MAN may be admired for his courage, but beloved he will be only if he admits that sometimes his heart is gripped by fear. By admitting that he has trembled like everyone else, he makes his excellence tolerable to men who admire but do not resemble him, because unlike him they are not brave enough to conquer their fears. By the same token, an exceptionally judicious man gives less discomfort to the guardians of egalitarianism if he is known to have confessed to errors committed in the past. It often happens that he who is pleased by the fallibility and imperfection of judgment readily overlooks that admitting error may betoken good judgment rather than respect for equality, just as those who like a brave man to be candid about his weakness often fail to realize that without fear there could be only recklessness, but never courage.

Virtue and power establish distinctions. In democracy the cult of equality demands of the virtuous and the powerful a tribute to egalitarianism in the form of a show of modesty, if not self-effacement. The powerful must not give the impression that they are free of weakness, or worse, that they shun the company of the weak. He who holds much power had better behave like a good fellow, or at least be known for his capacity to enjoy the diversions of the multitude. Nor must his taste remove him too far from his fellow men. Harry S. Truman's remark that modern art reminded him of ham and eggs did not harm him politically. Chancellor Erhard did not lose any votes by referring to intellectuals who had criticized his policy as "little terriers." For better or worse, the laughter of those who do not paint or reflect was the reward for showing poor taste in either case.

When the good political life is held to be egalitarian in nature, the powerful must be able to laugh at themselves, and are expected to prove this ability by permitting others to laugh at them. For although low tolerance for ridicule may protect the dignity of an office or person, it may also betray an autocratic disposition, whatever the role of the man who hates jesting: father, officer, bureaucrat, or ruler over large masses of men. Hitler's or Stalin's table talks provided no relief from the solemnity and ruthlessness of their public careers, for these men were humorless. Even Khrushchev, who liked to demonstrate with varying degrees of skill that he was fond of folk humor, never gave the impression that he would have laughed, had anybody dared to laugh about him.

Ridicule is indeed a weapon. Tyrants who do not permit jokes to be aimed at themselves use it against their enemies. When the National Socialists persecuted the Catholic Church, they circulated anticlerical jokes; they planned their distribution as though jokes were news: jokes became an instrument of propaganda.

Members of a totalitarian elite who have not yet been killed or ousted can be ridiculed only at a grave risk, including that of torture and death, because jokes about them are treated as expressions of hostility toward the regime. And yet, no totalitarian rule has ever succeeded in suppressing all political humor. Jokes help the victims of repression and persecution to bear their suffering, to vent aggression against their tormentors, and through whispered words and clandestine smiles to discover friends.

Regardless of time and circumstances, the same whispered jokes against the abuse of power by tyrants reappear again and again. It is futile to search for the way in which they were transmitted from period to period or from one country to another. Rather than being remembered these jokes seem to be rediscovered spontaneously. They meet identical, profound needs of the imagination. In such jokes the tyrant commits blunders and is blind or stupid or mortal; the powerful are impotent, and those adorned by the symbols of majesty stand naked. When Hermann Goering got married a story circulated in Germany to the effect that his wife had left the Church. Why? "Because she no longer believed in the resurrection of the flesh." Toward the end of the seventeenth century the same joke appeared in one of Grimmelshausen's anecdotes, and long before that in Rabelais' *Gargantua and Pantagruel.* Presumably very few Germans who grinned at the whispered suggestion of Goering's impotence had read the old books in which blasphemous use was made of the identical phrase.

In democracy the same people who like their leader to join in harmless laughter at his weaknesses resent any ridicule of sacred symbols, such as the flag or the national anthem. Similarly, time-honored views are not proper subjects of humor. There had better be no joking about the superiority of democratic institutions to nondemocratic ones, or about God. God is very seldom laughed about in any society, because most people are shocked by blasphemous humor. One wonders how many people today, more than 400 years after the event, appreciate Rabelais' wit on his deathbed, when he asked to be dressed in a domino cloak, as though he was about to attend a carnival, and then uttered his last words, *"In Domino morior."*

A democratically elected leader is expected, on appropriate occasions, to express in solemn and memorable language that rings true the cherished, traditional beliefs of his listeners. He must be careful never to permit this edifying performance to lower his tolerance for ridicule, which is also expected of him. He must reserve each of the two contradictory abilities for the proper occasion. Perhaps this is not asking too much.

None of us peels potatoes in church, gets dressed up for a swim, tells jokes in a house of mourning, or weeps while watching comedians. The democratic leader who is blessed with a sense of humor as well as skill in solemn eloquence is likely to enhance his political fortune if he is jocular and serious, each at the proper time. By lack of discernment, tactlessly confusing the solemn occasion with the time for jokes, he lowers the standards that he ought to set as a leader of men and may even ruin his career.

The pitfalls of humor in democracy may be illustrated by two incidents. John F. Kennedy, widely admired for his serious eloquence as well as his nimble, sharp wit, captured the imagination of all Americans by the patriotic exhortation in his inaugural address, "Don't ask what your country can do for you. Ask what you can do for your country." Not very long thereafter, he attended a dinner in New York. On this occasion he used the same precept humorously in order to persuade the affluent guests to make financial contributions to a partisan cause. It may be suggested that the young President suffered the fate of the reckless wit who could not suppress a joke, although he amused his listeners at the expense of somebody in their midst. Such humor is permissible and politically on the mark if the target is an adversary. Perhaps as apt an illustration as can be found is Churchill's calling his rival Attlee, "a sheep in sheep's clothing." While Churchill hurt Attlee, and undoubtedly meant to do so, John F. Kennedy in New York cast the shadow of irony on the patriotic feeling he had expressed and aroused in Washington; he was carried away — into the pit of humor.

Another illustration involves Lyndon B. Johnson, at the time of his Vice Presidency. When the Berlin Wall was erected in August 1961, the West Berliners were disappointed by the failure of the Westen powers to take counteraction. The anti-American mood in the city grew ugly; on August 16 Mayor Willy Brandt appealed to President Kennedy in Washington, using strong language in his letter. The situation, he said, called for action rather than words. The President was angry, but finally decided, among other things, to send to Berlin as distinguished an emissary as Vice President Johnson to assuage the resentment in the city. The grateful Berliners received their guest with jubilation. After the official business had been successfully transacted, the Vice President spent some time socially with Brandt and other dignitaries on a Saturday afternoon. He noticed admirably the shoes that the Mayor was wearing and asked where he could buy a similar pair. Brandt informed him that the stores were closed over the weekend, but the Vice President retorted that Brandt had insisted on "action, not words": now it was his turn to *act*. Willy Brandt did. Special efforts were made to contact the keeper of the shoe store, and Lyndon Johnson got his footwear.

The Vice President had humorously equated his desire to obtain a pair of shoes for his personal use with Brandt's desperately serious insistence on American action against the communists. The point could be made that by misplaced humor Johnson depreciated ever so subtly the importance and success of his mission. Willy Brandt reported the incident, perhaps with a smile, but certainly without a frown, in his book *Begegnungen mit Kennedy*. This fact is as instructive on the pitfalls of political humor in democracy as is the incident itself.

II

Folly

Introduction

Readers interested in foreign affairs may be baffled by finding essays assembled under the heading of "Folly" following Part I, which deals with force and international conflict in the nuclear age. A word of explanation may be in order.

Instead of discussing the tedious subject of specialization in institutions of higher learning and the related much-talked-about need for "interdisciplinary research," I shall set forth the specific reasons I had for concerning myself as a student of international conflict in the nuclear age also with seventeenth century literature and ideas even further removed from the current scene.

Nuclear war is "total war" on the highest level of technology man has ever attained. While a nuclear World War III cannot be examined empirically, it is possible to study on the basis of empirical data total wars of the past. To be sure, all these wars were waged on lower levels of technology, but an examination of historical facts permits an approximate understanding of what happens to man and society in consequence of total war. Specifically, we learn quite concretely that total war is not only a matter of death and destruction. It rather throws into relief issues of momentous moral and religious significance which we often evade under less distressing peacetime conditions of life. War forces man to plumb the depths of despair and enables him for a while to be ruthless as well as righteous. It makes him wrestle with God and leads him — if there is time — to reflect on the forces he has unleashed. Perhaps this is particularly true of the Thirty Years War in the seventeenth century — a total war — when religion and religious controversy still exerted a powerful influence on the minds of men; at that time even eschatological expectations seized the imagination of many people.

In connection with earlier studies of the history of war, I had been familiar with some of the books by Grimmelshausen, whose

189

writings had long been regarded as a major source of information on social conditions in Germany at the time of the Thirty Years War. Grimmelshausen, perhaps Germany's greatest writer between Hans Sachs and Goethe, was a humble soldier in that war, which retarded more than any other event in modern history the political and social development of Germany. Grimmelshausen wrote about war from personal experiences in his youth, publishing his novels and tales twenty years after the Peace of Westphalia had finally been concluded. Today it is generally accepted that Grimmelshausen, for all the light he throws on the cruelty of that war, practiced by soldiers and peasants alike, and for his marvelous depiction of popular superstitions, cannot be regarded as a dispassionate observer. He was a satirical writer of the highest ability, and despite his preoccupation with morality, a profound humorist. As an observer, he was far less concerned with the affairs of state than with the life of simple people. The main character he created in his novels was called Simplicissimus, who became something of an immortal figure in German imagination: Simplicissimus — "the most simple one," adventurously yielding to the temptations of life, participating in its follies, waxing in his powers of discernment as he grows older and always, in war as well as in peacetime, searching for the truth about man and man's struggles with man and God.

My own interest in this writer, dating back to student days, was revived in 1956 at the Center for the Advanced Study in the Behavioral Sciences at Stanford when Carl Bridenbaugh encouraged me to translate more of Grimmelshausen than the few pages I read to him. I translated two tales by that author, subsequently published by Princeton University Press under the title Courage, the Adventuress *and* The False Messiah *(1964). For the last ten years I have spent in this connection many leisure hours studying the social conditions and the literary scene of the late seventeenth century in general, as well as Grimmelshausen's writings in particular.*

Simplicissimus was one of the great Fools in Western literature. He belongs in the good and colorful society of other Fools of distinction: Stultitia, Til Eulenspiegel, Falstaff, Prince Myshkin. Less learned than Stultitia; as full of mischief as Eulenspiegel; healthier, more active, and less of a mystic than Myshkin, he holds his own in their company. Through Grimmelshausen's Simplicissimus I became interested in the literature of Folly.

To the extent that certain kinds of foolishness stem from lack of education, the spread of literacy has lowered the incidence of folly in society. Similarly, mentally ill persons, especially those suffering from epilepsy, who in the past were regarded as divinely inspired, have ceased to be fools and become patients in need of psychiatric care. In a civilized, progressive climate, the Fool no longer holds the fascination that he commanded in earlier times when he played a prominent social role at court, in towns, and in villages. A study of Folly in its classical form is nonetheless rewarding not only because of the intrinsic importance of the subject or for understanding certain social consequences of the Christian paradox that wisdom is folly, but also for the insight it affords into the nature of public order. For apart from entertaining people by outrageous pranks and daring words, the Fool throws light on the social order through his nonconformism. He not only defies the values embodied in a given order, but may be said to question more radically the value of order itself. He treats with natural disrespect the constraints and tabus that conformists violate only in secrecy, on special, socially sanctioned, occasions, or in their dreams. It takes the daring of a gay fool to make a virtue of stealing rather than working, of cowardice rather than courage, of the appetites rather than authority, whether human or divine.

The Fool is as unwarlike as he is antiheroic. Falstaff outrageously mocks honor and courage on the battlefield. An enemy of public order, the Fool scorns all efforts to protect the security of the community against external threats.

The nonconformism of the great fools of the past and of associations of fools is of additional interest today when the word conformism has assumed a pejorative meaning in some circles and when its social worth is sometimes attacked with impunity. In Chapter 12 the Fool is compared with other nonconformists: the eccentric, the confidence man, the master-thief, and the "wild man."

In trying to understand Grimmelshausen's work I got little help from the vast critical literature on this writer. It abounds with the most contradictory appraisals of his religious views, his humor, and his literary worth.

First of all, I felt it useful to account for the distinction between "high and low things" — to use Grimmelshausen's own phrase — in the life and literature of the Baroque era. Unlike the learned authors of that time, who wrote for polite society and sought recognition of their literary merits from their equally learned peers, Grimmelshausen in his popular tales shunned the pedantic dignity of high literature. He took pride in his "Simplician style," which he distinguished also from the moralizing style of edifying books. He told the truth laughingly in a language spoken by simple people, earthy, full of puns and proverbs, and by no means free of obscenities. His main works belong to "low literature." Chapter 13, which may be regarded as an essay in the sociology of literature, sketches the social conditions in which the German Baroque novel flourished and outlines the contrast between the high and low literature of the period.

The last three chapters in Part II are interpretations of Grimmelshausen's popular writings, each essay paying special attention in turn to one of the three main works in the so-called Simplician cycle of novels. For all its erudition the vast critical literature on Grimmelshausen has been devoted chiefly to restoring the original texts, to exploring the autobiographical aspects of his work, and to tracing painstakingly influences on his writings. Positivistic inclinations and religious prejudices can be detected in much of the critical literature. With a few exceptions, mainly Swiss and East German, the inquiries into the meaning of Grimmelshausen's work have been unimaginative and even parochial in character.

Nor have German critics, who are unfamiliar with recent American work on the tradition of presenting esoteric meaning in an exoteric garb, taken much pain to read between the lines of this writer, although he warned explicitly that only few readers would discover his intentions.

The more seriously I took this warning, the more clearly I saw that Grimmelshausen's humor in addition to being extremely entertaining has an irreverent function: it throws doubt not only on God's mercy but suggests that man in the misfortunes he suffers in peacetime as well as in war may be praying to God merely because he has been taught to do so.

The interpretations of Grimmelshausen, particularly in Chapters 14 and 16, will not be accepted by those critics who impute orthodoxy to his thought. But readers interested in the use of Aesopian language and in techniques of expressing heterodox thought allusively will perhaps be led to read or reread Grimmelshausen's work with an open mind.

War, sex, and religion are Grimmelshausen's main themes. While I started reading his works many years ago to learn about the total war he had witnessed, I found him also an instructor on the nature of Folly and a most accomplished conveyor of esoteric meaning in seemingly popular tales. This meaning is deeply disturbing. It would be unwarranted to suggest that according to Grimmelshausen God dies when man wages total war, but it is indeed possible to suggest that according to him man's folly comprises the ability to wage such war. And while peace, of course, is preferable to war, man's folly in peacetime is terrible enough because man must suffer its consequences without God's help.

CHAPTER TWELVE

The Fool and Social Order

The Many Faces of the Fool

PAUL LÉAUTAUD, a misanthrope clad in provocative rags, used to return every night from his place of work to his house in the suburbs of Paris to feed the animals in whose company he chose to live — at one time, 38 cats, 22 dogs, a goat, and a goose. There he wrote in the course of many years the nineteen volumes of his diary, using a steel pen by candlelight. Léautaud, who lived most of his life in the twentieth century, was an eccentric. His behavior (unlike his diary) offended no one of consequence.

Eccentrics are nonconformists, but as long as their unconventional behavior does not disturb the peace, neither police nor neighbors make life difficult for them. Exceptions occur in small towns where privacy is less respected than it is in large cities. In confining circumstances gossip and censure of harmless dissenters provide thrills of vicarious adventure and the comfort of vengeful righteousness. Even so, it is generally true that eccentrics are not treated like thieves or rebels, but rather as though they were simpletons falling lamentably below the average in intelligence, foresight, and prudence. If they are punished for their shortcomings, they rarely suffer anything

Presented at the annual meeting of the American Sociological Society, San Francisco, California, August 1967.

more severe than social failure, perhaps isolation, and conde-
scension or ridicule. With these inconveniences the eccentric,
like the simpleton, is usually permitted to go his way and make
a fool of himself.

Except when smiling indulgently at a "foolish child," we
speak today of "fools" and "folly" in a slightly pejorative sense.
No longer do we hear the faintest echo of the bells which used
to tingle on the fool's cap. Nor do we associate with the fool
his traditional symbol, the stick that evolved from the wooden
sword the comic actor used to brandish in antiquity.

The fool in the more colorful sense of the word once played
a prominent role on the social scene. His heyday in art and
literature was the period from the middle of the fifteenth to
the middle of the seventeenth century. *The Praise of Folly* by
Erasmus was published in 1511, in chronological time only a
few years later than Sebastian Brant's *Ship of Fools,* from which
it is removed in spirit almost as far as is reason from faith.
Brant's book is a satirical condemnation of men in all walks of
life for their failure to behave like good Christians. Brant, also
an author of hymns, censured man for neglecting his true
self-interest in salvation. He thought men were fools because
of such neglect. Erasmus kept an ironic balance between
Christian doctrine and the skeptical view of human nature that
he owed to Lucian rather than to the Scriptures. He did not
moralize. When Stultitia praised the follies of man it was clear
enough that some fools were happy not because God loved
them, but because they followed their natural inclinations.
From the end of the period in which the fool was socially
prominent, we have Velázquez' great paintings: "Aesop";
"Pernia," the buffoon of Philip IV; the so-called "Don Juan
of Austria" and portraits of other physical "abnormities."[1]
Velázquez' paintings remind us that fools throughout history
have often been physically deformed or mentally defective.

But the history of the fool is by no means confined to two
centuries. It extends back through the Middle Ages to antiquity

[1] Cf. E. Tietze-Conrat, *Dwarfs and Jesters in Art* (New York: Phaidon
Publishers, Inc., 1957).

and, more dimly, forward to our age. One of the famous mythical buffoons, Si-Djoha, who lived in the company of Timur Lenk, the conqueror, whom he entertained as a court jester, is proof of the fact that the popular imagination of the Arabs in the Middle Ages was no less preoccupied than was that of the Christians in the West with the juxtaposition of great folly and fearful power. One of the jests ascribed to Si-Djoha illustrates the point. His master, appalled by a glimpse he had caught of himself in a mirror, sobbed for two hours and so, dutifully or sympathetically, did his retinue. When the great man ceased weeping he noticed that Si-Djoha continued to sob. He explained to his astonished master, "If you saw yourself in the glass for a short moment and wept for two hours, is it surprising that I weep longer since I see you the whole day?"[2] Truly, only a fool speaks to a mighty man in this way, and such a fool may be a Christian as well as a Moslem, or, indeed, neither.

The more recent history of the fool is somewhat harder to trace. A learned student of folly has referred to Don Quixote as the last fool,[3] but then there is Dostoyevsky's *Idiot* and Jaroslav Hasek's *The Good Soldier Schweik*. Nor have the professional jesters completely vanished. There are the circus clowns for the children. There are comedians who pretend to be stupid so that their clever audiences will laugh. In every carnival, an atrophied off-shoot of the Saturnalia, we meet harlequins, whether they know something of the Commedia dell' Arte or not. And there are Will Rogers and Charlie Chaplin and Art Buchwald, none of them a Falstaff, but all of them distantly related to the great fools of the past.

It is not easy to describe the fool. It is a genus with many different species, and the most casual inspection of the historical

[2] Quoted by Enid Welsford, *The Fool. His Social and Literary History* (New York: Farrar and Rinehart, 1935), p. 30. *The Jests of Si-Djoha* is an anonymous collection of anecdotes about an unhistorical figure "known to us only by a reference in a tenth century work." The jests reached the West first by word of mouth.

[3] Walter Kaiser, *Praisers of Folly* (Cambridge: Harvard University Press, 1964), pp. 277 ff.

record reveals changes, ambiguities, contradictions, and paradoxes in the way human folly has been described. Furthermore,
however described, folly, too, seems to change her features
with the observer's perspective, so that her true face eludes us.
An evil woman like Goneril in *King Lear* says of those who
respect authority and old age that they are foolish,[4] although
in all her infamy she herself plays a role on what her father
regards as "this great stage of fools."[5] Thus, unbeknownst to
her, it is she who is foolish when viewed by someone who can
remove the masks from the players on that stage. In general,
to the fool the world is replete with folly, while the world considers the fool and not itself foolish.

The wilder paradoxes concerning folly originated in Christian
rather than pre-Christian teaching. Their source is Paul, not
Socrates. The latter was aware of the limits of his knowledge,
but he never said that knowledge or the search for knowledge
was folly. Nor did he urge the wise man to "become a fool that
he may be wise."[6] Finally, Socrates never spoke of "the foolishness of God," as did Paul.[7]

The lower classes are less intelligent than the upper classes.
In addressing primarily the lower classes, Jesus and his
apostles endowed foolishness with great virtue, presenting it as
a condition favored by God. The Christian fool, a sheep, follows the shepherd. As Erasmus put it through the mouth of
Stultitia,

> The Christian religion on the whole seems to have some kinship
> with folly, while it has none at all with wisdom. If you want proof
> of this, observe first that children, old people, women and fools
> take more delight than anyone else in holy and religious things;
> and that they are therefore ever nearest the altars, led no doubt
> solely by instinct. Next, you will notice that the founders of
> religion have prized simplicity exceedingly, and have been the
> bitterest foes of learning. Finally, no people seem to act more
> foolishly than those who have been truly possessed with Christian

[4] Shakespeare, *King Lear,* IV.2.50–62.
[5] Shakespeare, *King Lear,* IV.6.188.
[6] I Corinthians, III.18.
[7] I Corinthians, I.25.

piety. They give away whatever is theirs; they overlook injuries, allow themselves to be cheated, make no distinction between friends and enemies, shun pleasure, and feast on hunger, vigils, tears, labors, and scorn. They disdain life, and utterly prefer death; in short, they seem to have become altogether indifferent to ordinary interests, quite as if their souls lived elsewhere and not in their bodies. What is this, if not to be mad?[8]

Every fool, whether he follows Christ or nature, whether his name is Eulenspiegel or King Lear, calls into question the moral order around him. The fool looks at the world with sad or merry detachment, if not with hidden contempt. He does not share the ambitions and aspirations of those who seek success and try to avoid failure. He does not obey the law, but instead always conjures up "another order of things," or a reversal of the existing order, or plain misrule.

According to Erasmus, "another order of things would suddenly arise" "if someone should unmask the actors in the middle of a scene on the stage and show their real faces to the audience."[9] Like Lucian before him and Shakespeare later, Erasmus likened life to "a kind of stage play through which men pass in various disguises."[10] The fool shows the world without disguises. He does so in various roles. As a satirist he is an "Undeceiver-General,"[11] who proves that the appearance of moral conduct is but a sham covering up an evil, sinful reality. As a tragic fool he speaks almost in riddles, yet still clearly enough to suggest that man receives no help from God. While the divine voice of thunder on the heath where King Lear is left in his agony is incomprehensible, the fool and King Lear, having turned fool himself, speak the truth:

Fool: He that has a little tiny wit,
      With hey, ho, the wind and the rain,

---

[8] Erasmus, *The Praise of Folly*, Leonard F. Dean translator (New York: University Classics, Hendricks House, Farrar, Straus, 1946), p. 127.
[9] Erasmus, *op. cit.*, p. 66.
[10] *Ibid.*
[11] Francisco de Quevedo, *Visions*, Sir Roger L'Estrange, translator (Fontwell Sussex: The Centaur Press, 1963), pp. 69 ff.

> Must make content with his fortunes fit
> For the rain it raineth every day.
>
> Lear: True, my good boy.[12]

In his comic role, the fool is man undisguised, following his instincts, enjoying himself outside the pale of the social order. Through his antics and impudent speech he reminds those who observe the law that behind the masks of respectability lie the delights of nature. He, for one, has broken the shell of conventions that encrusts the natural life of the appetites. He loves life so much that he prefers discretion to valor, like Falstaff, and when buried, the ropes holding his coffin may break, so that, like Eulenspiegel, he remains standing upright in his grave.

We shall not pursue the subject of Christian folly nor, in particular, pay attention to the "holy fool," who avails himself of the fool's license for the sake of God and teaches His word through folly in parables.[13] Instead, we shall turn to the fools who follow their natural inclinations and care about preachers as little as about guardians of the law.

The Fool and Reality

Let us begin with the observation that a child may resemble a fool (as may a man who has drunk too much wine), especially by speaking the truth in circumstances in which the adult person soberly hides it or lies. The child crying out, while no one else dares to speak up, that the Emperor is naked, does not act in defiance of authority and convention, but in ignorance of them. We rightly ascribe the child's affront to lack of experience and redouble our effort to teach him the ways of responsible adults. As yet, he does not know any better; only in time will he learn from his parents and teachers when it is proper to hide the truth and when it is prudent to lie. He will learn how to dissemble not only in order to avoid in adulthood

---

[12] Shakespeare, *King Lear*, III.2.74–78.
[13] Cf. the important study of St. Simeon and St. Andreas by Erich Bens, "Heilige Narrheit," *Kyrios*, Vol. 3 (1938).

the consequences of candor that will be painful to him, but also in order not to offend others by telling a truth that hurts them. For in the adult world, the truth may be hidden for many different reasons: fear, trickery, pride, guilt, awe, courtesy. The child is deficient in all these regards. In his ignorance he is reckless and discourteous. He has yet to learn when to feel guilty. Though not unselfish, he lacks intelligence in pursuing his ends, and while he may tremble in the dark, he is not awed by God's power.

The fool behaves like an untutored child. The fool is the man who does not lie; indeed, inability to lie is as good a criterion of folly as any. "You are incomparable," Radomski says to Prince Myshkin, "that is, a man who does not lie at every step and who, perhaps, never lies. . ."[14] Similarly, Stultitia claims that she is not "two-tongued," and Falstaff that he is no "double-man," like the "wise" in this world.[15] By contrast, Gregory the Great observed polemically, "The wisdom of the world is, to conceal the truth of one's heart by trickery, to veil one's meaning in words, to make those things which are false appear to be true, to present the truth as falsehood."[16] Like the child, the fool speaks the truth and is permitted to do so because he is considered exempt from the responsibilities of other mortals who do lie, as everyone knows. Whatever he says can be discounted, if need be, and laughed at for its absurdity, or it may be taken in awe as something enigmatic and supernaturally inspired.

Ignorance or innocence which leads the child and the fool to violate the conventions of adult society may extend beyond the sphere of propriety to the perception of reality. A celebrated illustration of a fool's misconception of reality is to be found in Cervantes' *Don Quixote*. I am not referring to the general madness of the melancholy knight who mistakes windmills

[14] Dostoyevsky, *The Idiot*, III. Ch. 4.

[15] Cf. Walter Kaiser, *op. cit.*, pp. 222–223.

[16] Migne, *Patrologia Latina*, Vol. 75, Col. 947, quoted by Barbara Swain, *Fools and Folly during the Middle Ages and the Renaissance* (New York: Columbia University Press, 1932), pp. 198–199, note 32.

for villains and discovers great beauty in the ordinary face of a country wench, but specifically to a particular scene in the second part of the novel.[17] In this scene, Sancho Panza, himself a fool, indulges the spleen of his master, another kind of fool, by telling him that the three country girls approaching on their donkeys are illustrious ladies. Don Quixote, however, recognizes them for what they are, three ugly, peevish peasant maids. Thus, Sancho Panza, instead of asserting reality against his master's madness, as he usually does, plays a mad fool himself in order to indulge the spleen of his master, while Don Quixote for once seems to be free of his madness. But this reversal of roles turns out to be but an ingenious surprise that Cervantes springs on the reader in order to disclose the depth of the hidalgo's folly. Don Quixote kneels in front of the three girls, exclaiming in an exquisite bravura piece of chivalric eloquence that "some wicked enchanter spread clouds and cataracts over my eyes, changing, and to them only, thy peerless beauty into that of a poor rustic." Thus, the foolish knight recognizes reality for what it is, but instead of accepting it as such, avers that his senses are in error because he has been bewitched. After Dulcinea, who for contrast speaks the language of low comedy, has fallen off her donkey and jumped back on it like a tomboy, Don Quixote says to Sancho Panza, "See how I am persecuted by enchanters! Mark how far their malice extends, even to depriving me of the pleasure of seeing my mistress in her own proper form."[18]

On a less sophisticated level of folly we encounter simpler misconceptions of reality, for example, that of the child trying to grab the moon in his picture book, or the young fool in literature whose innocence and naïveté charm us: in German he is referred to as "*der reine Tor*," "the pure fool." Young Parzival, just taught by his mother that the difference between God and the Devil can be likened to that between light and

[17] Cf. Erich Auerbach, *Mimesis* (Garden City, New York: Doubleday Anchor Books, 1957), Ch. 14.

[18] Cervantes, *Don Quixote,* Charles Jarvis, translator (New York: John Wurtele Lovell, n.d.), Pt. II, Ch. 10, pp. 439–440.

darkness, encounters four knights in a forest. Not ever having seen a knight, but observing the shining armors, "the lad thought for sure that each one was a god."[19] Similarly, several centuries later, young Simplicius in Grimmelshausen's main novel is being raised in the house of a crude and ignorant peasant at the time of the Thirty Years War. The peasant warns him to beware of wolves when watching the sheep. When the boy, who has never seen either wolves or horses, meets some marauding soldiers on horseback, he thinks, in his folly, that each soldier and his horse are but one creature, a wolf.[20] It has been suggested that in telling this tale Grimmelshausen may have been influenced by the story of Parzival,[21] but while this may be so, it does not necessarily follow that the seventeenth century satirist shared Wolfram's intention to depict the pure fool's closeness to God.[22]

Fools—Thieves—Confidence Men

When we turn from the folly of children to adult folly, we face a bewildering variety of fools: buffoons and jesters at court, harlequins improvising their repartee on the stage, and jugglers in the market place; boys masked as bishops in church; slow-witted peasants and village idiots; physically stunted parasites, and entertainers of nimble wit or with a penchant for practical jokes, kept by lords and ladies for their amusement;

[19] Wolfram von Eschenbach, *Parzival*, 120, Helen M. Mustard and Charles E. Passage, translators (New York: Vintage Books, Alfred A. Knopf, Inc., 1961), p. 68.

[20] *Grimmelshausens Simplicissimus Teutsch*, J. H. Scholte, editor (Tübingen: Max Niemeyer Verlag, 1954), I, Ch. 3, p. 16.

[21] The first critic to suggest in considerable detail that *Parzival* had influenced *Simplicissimus* was Theodor Echtermeyer, *Hallesche Jahrbücher* (1838), p. 431, but Echtermeyer viewed *Simplicissimus* as a satire of *Parzival*, whereas Werner Welzig, *Beispielhafte Figuren. Tor, Abenteurer und Einsiedler bei Grimmelshausen* (Graz, Köln: Hermann Böhlaus Nachf., 1963), considers the young Simplicius as well as Parzival to be a "pure (Christian) fool."

[22] Cf. Paul Gutzwiller, *Der Narr bei Grimmelshausen* (Bern: Francke Verlag, 1959); cf. also Chs. 14 and 16 below.

mad men and epileptics, who in ages less enlightened than ours evoked awe since thy were thought to be supernaturally inspired, like poets or prophets; etc.[23] Folly in literature is no less varied. All literary fools point to forms of foolishness in life. Whether they are the creation of an individual mind or, in myth and folklore, of collective imagination, they present reality transmuted and sublimated.

In life, as in literature, folly is either natural or studied. Man can be a fool because nature was niggardly when he was born, or he may be endowed with the gift of playing a fool for gain and fun. In literature, the fool and the license he enjoys, offer an opportunity for impudently critical comment on worldly and divine authorities.

Natural fools are men deficient in intelligence because of poor native endowment or because of inadequate education. In epochs in which the distinction between the subhuman and human element in society was drawn with less compunction than we are prone to feel in our age, with its well-advanced humanitarianism and technology, both the antics of the feeble-minded, like those of the physically stunted, and the stupidity of the lower classes were a source of laughter. The more rigidly stratified and the less enlightened society is, the more it appears to men at the top that the unworthy, the ugly, and the comical are concentrated at the bottom. The Christian preference for the lowly lent poignancy to such discrimination, while it offered solace to the downtrodden by substituting, in Bertolt Brecht's cynical words from *Mahagonny,* "the just distribution of the other-worldly goods" for "the unjust distribution of worldly goods."

In light of the promise of life after death, the teaching that Christian folly was superior to worldly wisdom implied a radical criticism of the social order. Christian teaching tried to impose an ascetic discipline upon life prior to death. It

[23] Cf. T. K. Oesterreich, *Possession, Demoniacal and Other* (English translation, New York: R. R. Smith, 1930) and E. R. Dodds, *The Greeks and the Irrational* (Berkeley and Los Angeles: University of California Press, 1951), Ch. 3, "The Blessings of Madness."

presented the physical nature of man as corrupt and demanded that the pain that stems from the rule of men over men be cheerfully accepted like death.

Subsequently, the studied fool in literature was able to perform two major functions. First, by showing folly out-witting worldly wisdom, the fool could serve as an instrument of vicarious social revenge. If the privileged tended to associate low rank with the comical, it is not surprising that the under-privileged savored the pleasure of seeing the powerful and the wise subdued by a fool. Second, folly could become the ad-vocate of nature against all order. The fool could insist, with cheerful irresponsibility or in a melancholy cast, on the merely conventional character of all discipline, whether such discipline claimed political or religious sanction. Since the fool had been endowed by Christian teaching with the special virtue of having access to the truth, the fool as a champion of nature could be used for throwing doubt not only upon worldly wisdom, but upon Christian teaching itself.

The literary paradigm of the triumph of folly over reason is to be found in the debates of a fifteenth century figure, the shrewd, misshapen peasant Marcolf, with wise King Solomon, whom he unfailingly outwits. Perhaps this contest was not only between the respectable, moral platitudes of a King and the common sense of a physically deformed rustic, but on a deeper level between divine reason and the power of an ugly, satanic mind. In any event, Marcolf's foolishness is both a parody and sarcastic refutation of Solomon's wisdom. At every stage of the contest the fool triumphs over the sage, the lout over the lord, turpitude over splendor. In order to win his case in this drama of social revenge, Marcolf frequently resorts to mischievous pranks. For example, once he gains entry to the palace by releasing a hare so that the King's watchdogs chase the hare instead of guarding the gate. In another episode, Solomon refuses to join Marcolf in his vilification of women. Marcolf predicts that the King will do so in due course. He then spreads the false rumor that Solomon has ordered each man to take seven wives, whereupon the women raise such a clamor that the King, like Marcolf, vents his spleen against them. Finally, the King, unable any longer to endure Marcolf's resourceful insults, angrily orders him to go out of sight: ". . . let me never look you between the eyes again." Whereupon Marcolf crawls into an oven to lie there in such a posture that the King cannot see Marcolf's eyes, but only his backside. The coarseness of this insult is characteristic of the elementary revenge that throughout the history of the comical imagination nature delights in taking on nurture, *physis* on *nomos,* the bodily functions on the spiritual and — the underprivileged on those who are privileged. The King, so blatantly insulted by the lout, orders his servants to execute Marcolf, permitting him only to choose the tree from which he is to hang. The story ends, "So Marcolf and the servants travelled through the Valley of Hosaffat, and over the hill of Olivet, and from thence to Jericho, and over the River Jordan, and through all Arabia, and over the Grand Desert to the Red Sea, but they never found the tree on which Marcolf chose to be hanged."[24] As to King Solomon, he appeared as late as the eighteenth century, as a subject of laughter in Punch-and-Judy shows.[25] Later, Til Eulenspiegel and the antiheroes of the picaresque novel were to make fools of their adversaries by similar pranks.

No sphere of life is safe from the cheerful anarchism of the fool in literature. All conventions seem to be more vulnerable than they would be if all men were serious. The fool makes light of the meaning of words as well as of the social necessity of work, and of the distinction between mine and thine no less than of that between noble and base. Nor is the sacred exempt from the fool's laughter.

Consider the havoc the fool creates by his treatment of speech. Inadvertent rather than willful perversion of the conventional meaning of words occurs in medieval tales of the stupid peasant who gives foolish answers because he is unable

---

24 Quoted by Enid Welsford, *op. cit.,* p. 37.
25 Barbara Swain, *op. cit.,* p. 34.

to understand educated speech. The same device is used, however, by the studied fool, who outwits convention as a critic
rather than violates it as an ignoramus. Thus, when Solomon
says that he never again wants to look Marcolf between the
eyes, and later that he be hanged from a tree of his choosing,
the fool complies with the literal meaning of the commands,
thereby defying the obvious sense that the King intended.

In the jest book *A Hundred Merry Tales* (1526), a penitent
is enjoined by his confessor to say daily for his penance, "The
Lamb of God have mercy on me." A year later he tells his
confessor that he has done his penance, having said that morning and so daily, "The Sheep of God have mercy on me." It is
twelve months since he has been enjoined to do penance, and
the lamb, he avers, has become a sheep.[26] This is funny, but we
cannot be quite sure whether it is funny because the penitent
was stupid or because the sacred symbol of the Lamb has been
ridiculed.

Similarly, Til Eulenspiegel executed orders given to him in
their literal sense to the exasperation and detriment of the
masters for whom he works. At night he sifts flour upon the
earth of the garden since the baker who refused to give him a
candle ordered him to sift "by the moonlight." While serving a
tailor, he sews a seam under a barrel, because the master told
him to sew so that nobody could see the seam. Another time
he ruins the leather of a shoemaker by cutting all leather to fit
the left foot, because he had not been told to use for a model
"the last pair" of shoes, but merely "the last one," which
Eulenspiegel willfully misunderstands to mean the last shoe.
Once, being told to leave the house of a blacksmith, who over-
works his servants, he knocks a hole in the roof from the inside
and departs. From a hostess at an inn he demands payment
after treating himself to a sumptuous dinner because she told
him that he could eat and drink "for money." Again and again,

[26] *A Hundred Merry Tales and Other English Jestbooks of the Fifteenth and Sixteenth Centuries*, P. M. Zall, editor (Lincoln, Nebraska:
Bison Books, University of Nebraska Press, 1963), 67th Tale, p. 124.

he dupes and harms the conformists who behold the damage
and can only say, like the shoemaker, "I meant not that," or
"Ye do after my saying and not after my meaning."[27]

We still laugh about these stories, as people have done ever
since they heard such jokes for the first time. Let us note that
the good soldier Schweik often outwits his superior officers
in World War I by availing himself of ambiguities of meaning
in much the same way in which Marcolf duped King Solomon,
and Eulenspiegel the tailor.

As to work, without which society crumbles, fools are known
to shun it. Carefree and easy as they are, they like the fruits of
labor, but not labor itself. All lower-class fools steal their food
and drink always preferring wine to water and meat to bread.
All picaros are thieves, revenging themselves on the stinginess
of their masters or simply disrespecting private property. They
are parasites taking what they need from the owners. Fools
and picaros are natural consumers. They ridicule industry and
thrift like all other traits of socially useful respectability. In one
of José Rubén Romero's stories in *The Futile Life of Pito Perez*
— the Mexican latecomer to the guild of picaros and an em-
bittered fool — Pito takes charge of his uncle's store during his
absence and sells his goods on credit "without recording any
of the sales" in order not be become "addicted to the greedy,
petty habits of businessmen." Pito, "drunk either because of
the godly art of giving or because of the liquor" he is consuming "so devoutly and abundantly," merely watches "as
those earthly goods disappear."[28]

The disrespect for the institution of private property that the
fool displays by theft (or by not paying his debts or by willful
destruction) brings to mind two other socially deviant types
that have captured popular and literary imagination, the master
thief and the confidence man. In some respects they resemble
the fool.

As early as 1834 Søren Kierkegaard reflected upon the idea

---

[27] In the English version, "Howleglas" (1528), *op. cit.*, pp. 198–199.
[28] José Rubén Romero, *The Futile Life of Pito Perez*, William O. Cord,
translator (Englewood Cliffs, N.J.: Prentice-Hall, Inc., 1967).

of a master thief; he abstracted it from the ventures commonly ascribed to different thieves in the tales of various nations. He pointed out that villainy and thievishness were by no means the only basic traits of the master thief. Instead, he also possessed admirable skills and was kind, amiable, and often generous, stealing from the rich to help the poor. "Often, we must think of him," Kierkegaard said, "as of a person that is discontented with reality and expresses his discontentment by infringing upon the rights of others, thereby seeking an opportunity for deriding, and quarreling with, the authorities." Comparing the master thief with the head of a band of robbers, Kierkegaard observed that the latter seeks relaxation from the dangers and drudgery of his profession in gay social abandon, whereas the master thief represents "something more profound, a certain melancholy trait, reserve, a dark view of the conditions of life, inner dissatisfaction."[29] Kierkegaard was of the opinion that the matter thief resembled in certain respects Til Eulenspiegel, whom he regarded as the satyr of the North.[30] Indeed, the fool, too, is often melancholy at heart and, more than that, cruel and bitter. He, too, is a solitary figure rather than the member or head of a group. But the redistribution of values in favor of the poor, through which the generous master thief gains fame among the people, is no concern of the fool's. The fool is a natural anarchist, not a seeker of justice.

Nor does the confidence man right any wrongs. Though he usually operates on a grander scale than the master thief and excels him in fastidiousness, he, too, fills his pocket (whereas the fool fills his stomach). But he does share with the fool rather than the thief an outstanding ability to hoodwink other people. The confidence man exploits gullibility by misrepresentation and impersonation, his most astounding skill. Thomas Mann's Felix Krull exercises it while still a boy. He dissembles the symptoms of severe illness in order to stay away from

[29] Søren Kierkegaard, *Die Tagebücher*, Theodor Haecker, translator from the Danish (Innsbruck: Brenner-Verlag, 1923), pp. 4–6 (diary entry under date of September 11, 1834).
[30] *Op. cit.*, p. 10 (March 16, 1835).

school. He enjoys the applause of the crowd as another young Paganini, although he uses a bow greased with vaseline when pretending to play the violin in an orchestra. Similarly, before he is grown up he derives enjoyment from dressing up in various costumes, to represent a Roman flute player, a Spanish bullfighter, a youthful abbé, an Austrian officer, a German mountaineer, a Florentine dandy of the late middle ages, etc., looking in each disguise, "better and more natural than the last."[31] Like all fools, Felix Krull dislikes regular work, is fond of sleep, and believes that for him "the satisfaction of love is twice as sweet and twice as penetrating as with the average man."[32]

Anyone who has searched his heart or has read Thomas Mann's *Confessions of Felix Krull* is aware of the fact that a confidence man can make us laugh (so long as we do not become his victim). When laughing at him, we admire not only his incredible skill but also his success in exposing the foibles of society. Perhaps we secretly rejoice at the fact that those superior in wealth have been defrauded by one who is superior in intelligence and, by imposture, their equal in manners. At the same time we experience a feeling of reserve toward a man capable of impersonating others so perfectly as to throw doubt on his identity. We sense something pathological about the confidence man that is absent from the vitality of the fool and the dexterity of the master thief. If Kierkegaard was right in suggesting that the master thief takes a melancholy view of life, we have it on Thomas Mann's authority that the confidence man is depressed after his exploits.

Herman Melville, too, wrote a novel about an impostor who, like Felix Krull, is an expert impersonator; the subtitle of Melville's novel *The Confidence Man* is "His Masquerade." But Melville's confidence man is no fool. Thomas Mann made fun

---

[31] Thomas Mann, *Confessions of Felix Krull, Confidence Man,* Denver Lindley, translator from the German (New York: Alfred A. Knopf, Inc., 1955, paperback edition published by The New American Library, 1963), pp. 19–20.

[32] *Op. cit.,* p. 41.

of the style of the old Goethe, of the German Novel of Education, and of the values of middle class civilization generally, depicted so vividly and with so much empathy in some of Mann's earlier works. Except for religion, Felix Krull plays havoc with nearly everything that is respectable in the society in which he moves. In contrast, Melville's primary concern was with gullibility and doubt. Many of Melville's images are emblematic, and there are innumerable allusions to the Scriptures in his work. A good case has been made that his confidence man personifies — God.[33]

Whereas Thomas Mann, in *Felix Krull*, satirized among other things the social convention of modern bourgeois society, Melville in *The Confidence Man* took issue with God and Christ. His was not a funny book. Early in the novel, an Ahab-like character, the skeptic with the wooden leg, by profession a customhouse officer like Melville, warns the passengers on the river boat *Fidèle* not to trust the confidence man. In his first disguise as a poor Negro, the latter tries to arouse and exploit feelings of charity among the passengers. A heated exchange ensues between a Methodist minister and the customhouse officer. The latter derides the "game of charity" which the impostor plays: "charity is one thing, and truth is another." The Methodist, a "resolute champion" of the "church militant," grabs the exasperating skeptic by the collar of his coat and shakes him furiously for scorning faith and charity and for "his evil heart of unbelief." It is with the help of the Methodist minister that the confidence man wins his contest with the skeptic, since enough gullible and charitable passengers are aboard the *Fidèle* for him to prevail. The skeptic exclaims in vain, "You fools . . . you flock of fools, under this captain of fools [the minister], on this ship of fools."[34]

On Sebastian Brant's *Ship of Fools*, too, all men are foolish, because in medieval perspective, all men are sinners and fail to

[33] Lawrence Thompson, *Melville's Quarrel with God* (Princeton, N.J.: Princeton University Press, 1952).

[34] Herman Melville, *The Confidence-Man: His Masquerade* (New York: Grove Press, 1949), pp. 23–26.

conduct themselves as good Christians should, *sub specie aeternitatis*. Like Brant's ship, Melville's *Fidèle* transports men of all professions, ages, races, and nationalities. No doubt, the passengers represent mankind. Save for the skeptics, all of them are fools, but not because they are sinners, but because they are gullible victims of the malign impostor who seeks to gain their faith. In Melville's book, it is God who fools men. Or to put it less radically, Melville's *Confidence Man* is a fierce, though masked, attack on religion, while *Confessions of Felix Krull* merrily unmasks the pretensions of society.

Apart from disregarding the intended meaning of words and from preferring theft to work, the fool makes light of the moral order in many other ways. Order depends on law, and there can be no survival of the commonweal unless men with a sense of honor defend it. Men of honor are capable of choosing death in preference to the disgrace of cowardice or disloyalty. To the fool, however, the highest good is not honor, but life. If the fool is a knave in the eyes of honorable men, the latter are stupid in the eyes of the fool, because they do not seem to value life highly. The fool's indifference toward the honorable is most memorably expressed in Falstaff's "catechism" setting forth his belief that life is preferable to honor.

> What is honour? A word. What is that word honour? Air. A trim reckoning. Who hath it? he that died a'Wednesday. Does he feel it? No. Doth he hear it? No. It is insensible, then? Yea. To the dead. But will it not live with the living? No. Why? Detraction will not suffer it, therefore, I'll none of it: honour is a mere scutcheon, and so ends my catechism.[35]

In accordance with this catechism, Falstaff cunningly disgraces himself on the field of battle, first by playing dead, and then, in an extraordinarily bold mockery of honor, by wounding a dead enemy, the reckless and rash Hotspur. Finally Falstaff claims the distinction of having conquered Hotspur, trying to deprive Prince Hall, the true victor, of this honor. Before stabbing the dead man in the thigh, Falstaff repeats his credo:

[35] I *Henry IV*, V.1.136–143.

... to die is to be a counterfeit; for he is but the counterfeit of a man who hath not the life of a man; but to counterfeit dying, when a man thereby liveth, is to be no counterfeit, but the true and perfect image of life indeed. The better part of valor is discretion; in the which better part I have saved my life.[36]

It is in this final scene that Falstaff transcends for the second time in the play the comic qualities of his ancient forebear, Plautus' *Miles Gloriosus*. The Latin soldier is vain and lecherous, a braggart who falls prey to the extravagant flattery of his slaves and to the roguery of a courtesan's feigned love for him. Falstaff has many similar traits, and "the fat rogue," "Sir John Paunch," a "sweet creature of bombast," is made a laughing stock by Prince Hal, who disabuses him to his face without restraint:

Wherein is he good but to taste sack and drink it? Wherein neat and cleanly but to carve a capon and eat it? Wherein cunning but in craft? Wherein crafty but in villany? Wherein villanous but in all things? Wherein worthy but in nothing?[37]

But Falstaff is far more than a comic character. He denies order and the moral law; and if the sun is taken for the symbol of God, he challenges the divine order itself. In the first scene in which he appears he presents himself as a man not knowing "the time of day," a "squire of the night's body," a "gentleman of the shade," a "minion of the moon," not governed like the earth by the sun, but "as the sea is, by our noble and chaste mistress the moon, under whose countenance we steal."[38]

Shakespeare here echoed the saying to be found in Ecclesiasticus,[39] that a fool's discourse "changeth as the moon," and in the Latin of the Vulgate godliness is likened to the sun. As Erasmus had pointed out, "The moon is always understood to symbolize human nature, and the sun, the source of all light, to symbolize God."[40] In *Henry IV*, however, the sun is rather

[36] I *Henry IV*, V.4.116–122.
[37] I *Henry IV*, II.4.507–512.
[38] I *Henry IV*, I.2.31–33.
[39] Ecclesiasticus, XXVII.12.
[40] Erasmus, *op. cit.*, p. 118.

the symbol of noble majesty; the sun is associated with Prince Hal, the *cortegiano*,[41] who in the second part of the play inherits crown and scepter.

The last scene, then, in which Falstaff, the coward, pretends to be dead in order to save his life and then "rises" again to stab the corpse of Hotspur, provides more than comic relief: it shows the triumph of folly as a minion of the moon over a man who talked grandiloquently about honor. Were it not for Prince Hal, who knows that he, and not Falstaff, has conquered Hotspur, the scene would present natural disorder with the fool prevailing. In the second part of *Henry IV*, Falstaff comes to grief and dies. He must finally face the reckoning. Political order is re-established by Prince Hal, in his youth himself given to folly, but now a noble ruler preventing the lasting triumph of folly.[42]

If the meaning of ordinary speech is twisted by fools, neither is God's word sacred to them. Religious doctrine and rites, nay, religion itself, may be drawn into the madness of folly. The fool values life, his life and this life, more than anything else, not excluding the blessings of eternal life. To him, the only thing that is certain about life after death is death itself. In pictorial representations of the medieval Dance of Death, the powerful and learned are treated like the humble, and Death often wears the cap and bells of the jester, fooling all living souls. Nor does the fool have edifying thoughts about the creation of gods and men. Concerning that creation, he believes, as Stultitia puts it, that "the job is done by that foolish, even ridiculous part which cannot be named without laughter."[43] To the fool, then, there is nothing miraculous about creation. In general, fools play off the world of the senses against speculation and spirituality. To the senses, the physical functions of the body are undeniably real, a source of natural, ungodly pleasure and pain

[41] On Prince Hal as a perfect courtier in Castiglione's sense, cf. E. M. W. Tillyard, *Shakespeare's History Plays* (New York: The Macmillan Company, 1946), pp. 276–281.

[42] E. M. W. Tillyard, *op. cit.*, pp. 264 ff.; Walter Kaiser, *op. cit.*, pp. 195 ff.

[43] Erasmus, *op. cit.*, p. 49.

and the fountainhead of knowledge about life and death — inferior to, but firmer than, theology. Such common sense always existed along with Christian faith and doctrine. It found expression in proverbs and, intermingled with pre-Christian superstitition, in folk tales, in puns, the lowest form of humor, and in obscene jokes. The folk-fool and the picaro are never shocked by obscenity, and they do not hesitate to use it against theological speculation. Thus, the "trail of written remains" that the "ungodly" have left behind them "throughout the centuries"[44] includes "low" literature as well as the writings of ancient philosophers and historians which Melville's confidence man mentions: "the immorality of Ovid, Horace, Anacreon, and the rest, and the dangerous theology of Aeschylus and others . . . [and] views so injurious to human nature as in Thucidides, Juvenal, Lucian, but more particularly, Tacitus." The confidence man refers to such writings as "that mass of unsuspected heresy on every vital topic which for centuries must have simmered unsurmised in the heart of Christendom."[45]

The Fool as Social Critic

Many foolish pranks actually are crimes. Marcolf insults King Solomon. Eulenspiegel willfully damages the house of the blacksmith. Falstaff commits many unlawful acts. Simplicissimus steals sausages from a parson's smoke room: all picaros are thieves. Schweik steals dogs and is a malingerer, and although Pito Perez "never killed anyone" he knows quite a few jails "from personal experience." Fools never commit murder, but they do violate laws and conventions that we, as conformists, try to uphold. Why then do we laugh? Why are we amused by something that if done by anyone but a fool would endanger our way of life and make us turn to the authorities for protection?

Is it that the fool satisfies feelings of envy? In many of his

---

[44] Barbara Swain in commenting upon the creed of the ungodly in the *Book of Wisdom, op. cit.,* p. 47.

[45] Herman Melville, *op. cit.,* p. 39.

pranks he makes sport of the possessions of others — whether material or otherwise — that the envious do not want to acquire but have a consuming desire to see destroyed. Is it for this reason that the notorious meanness and cruelty of many fools and picaros does not diminish their popularity? The master thief who robs the rich and is generous towards the poor appeals to some sense of justice that is absent in envy, because envy is no wish for the transfer of fame, fortune, or power from the haves to the have-nots: it merely wants the haves to become have-nots.[46]

It may be noted in passing that envy is a solitary passion. If we feel it, we try to hide it, whereas we like to profess our sense of justice. Thus, laughing about foolish pranks we may be happy that misfortune befell the fooled objects of envy and at the same time enjoy the release from the shamefulness of this feeling. But there is more than that to our laughter at folly. Envy remains within the social order, as it were, whereas in laughing at great fools we rejoice at their ingenious disrespect for the rules we are forced to live by.

The social order is a mold into which nature has been pressed with a crippling effect. The licentious fool disregards this order as though this was the easiest and most natural thing to do. In the process he not only exposes hypocrisy and dissimulation and pricks the bubble of pretension, but he also robs the social order of its claim to sanctity and permanence. The fool does so without pleading a cause; he is no rebel wanting to do away with rulers, nor does he seek to establish a better rule. He is simply unruly. He seems to make no sense, but he acts as though in the light of nature everything that we think makes sense is in fact nonsense. When laughing at the fool we share this carefree disregard of the rules that we sometimes wish, and almost never dare, to break. If we never felt that order fettered our natural appetites, we would not laugh, but

---

[46] Cf. Helmut Schoeck, *Der Neid. Eine Theorie der Gesellschaft* (Freiburg-München: Verlag Karl Alber, 1966).

punish the fool who indulges his appetites and permits us to indulge vicariously our own. Through laughter we become the fool's passive accomplices.

In some sense, then, the fool resembles the figure of the wild man to be found in almost every phase of Western civilization; as Papagano he still delights us, and those who do not like Mozart can turn to Tarzan for a wild man in our age. Richard Bernheimer defined the persisent psychological urge to which "the notion of the wild man must respond" "as the need to give external expression and symbolically valid form to the impulses of reckless physical self-assertion which are hidden in all of us, but are normally kept under control."[47] The fool, like the wild man, seems to live beyond the pale of the social order and to assert *physis* against *nomos*. But there is an important difference between the two figures. The wild man is a subhuman creature, dressed either in pastoral green, as in Pieter Brueghel's picture of the battle of Carneval and Lent, or in furs like an animal. In various folk customs and fairy tales, the bear is a substitute for, or a companion of, the wild man.[48]

Even the innocent child ignorantly growing up in the woods, like Parzival or Simplicius, has been related by Bernheimer to the lore of the wild man rather than to that of the pure fool; but this can be done only by neglecting the career of the pure fool, in the light of which innocence is a necessary precondition of his rare perfection in maturity. Something childlike is in fact forever preserved in Parzival, as in all great fools.[49]

A fool never resorts to brute force in acts of physical self-assertion. Never does he abduct a maiden, as the wild man

[47] Richard Bernheimer, *Wild Men in the Middle Ages,* A Study in Art, Sentiment, and Demonology (Cambridge, Mass.: Harvard University Press, 1952), p. 3.

[48] Richard Bernheimer, who thoroughly discusses this aspect of the wild man, overlooked Grimmelshausen's fairy tale, "Der erste Bernhäuter," later included (with adaptations) in Grimm's collection of fairy tales.

[49] In Dostoyevsky's *Idiot* several characters remark that Prince Myshkin is a child and will still be a child when he reaches high age.

does. Fools outwit rather than out-club civilized men, and socially they are not creatures of the woods, but of the court or the town. They are not subhuman, related to demons and beasts; they are not wilder than ordinary men. They excel by confronting civilized life with foolishly truthful reflection rather than with brute force.

The fool lifts constraints, invalidates social values, and upsets the social order. His triumph is complete when folly manages to reverse the social order for a while. In the Roman Saturnalia the slaves became masters of the house, and in the medieval Festival of Fools, buffoonery and obscenity were put into the service of burlesquing Christian worship and morality. According to a letter written in 1445 by Charles VII, King of France, the Bishop of Troyes, his loyal councilor, had complained that although in 1431 the Council of Basel had

> . . . expressly forbidden to ministers and attendants of the Church to participate in a certain mockery and scandalous festival that is called the Festival of Fools, which is usual during the Christmas octave and holidays in not a few churches, cathedrals, and other chapter-houses, wherein said churchmen commit irreverences and mockeries toward God the Creator and His holy and divine services, to the grievous discredit and disrepute of the ecclesiastical calling at large, nevertheless, said churchmen in all churches and holy places during divine service, as well as outside, continue to utter great insolences, mockeries, and irreverences, with public spectacle and masquerades, using indecent attire unbecoming their state and profession, such as the raiment and garb of clowns, soldiers, and other similar occupations, some wearing female raiment, masks, false faces. . . .[50]

The Festival of Fools can be traced back to the ninth century, when Byzantine courtiers made fun of the divine mysteries. Not much later, on certain days, Western vicars and subdeacons began to mock the Magnificat at Vespers and even the Mass in the cathedral towns of France. For several centuries the Festival of Fools served as a safety valve for releasing the

---

[50] Quoted by Vilfredo Pareto, *The Mind and Society* (New York: Harcourt, Brace and Company, 1935), Vol. I, § 737, p. 446. Cf. also Barbara Swain, *op. cit.*, Chs. 4 and 5; Enid Welsford, *op. cit.*, Ch. 9.

tensions imposed by church discipline. As a doctor of Auxerre explained it, "wine barrels break if their bungholes are not occasionally opened to let in the air, and the clergy being 'nothing but old wine-casks badly put together would certainly burst if the wine of wisdom were allowed to boil by continued devotion to the Divine Service.' "[51] Despite repeated prohibitions, the mad and impious excesses of the Festival of Fools, recognized at the time as a relic of pagan rites,[52] died out only in the sixteenth century.

The Festivals had their secular counterpart in the fool societies that flourished in the towns, law courts, and universities of Europe from the fifteenth century to the end of the seventeenth century. The most famous of them, the *Enfants-sans-souci*, with young carefree and poor Parisians as members, was led by an annually elected *Prince-des-Sots* (to whom François Villon made a bequest). The fool society of Dijon had hundreds of members in the middle of the sixteenth century, most of them drawn from the third estate, but others also from the nobility and the clergy. While the Festival of Fools offered an opportunity for temporary reversals of the ecclesiastical order and of moral judgments, the fool societies with their *Princes-des-Sots and Mères-Sottes* were more permanent, legally recognized institutions dedicated to scandal, music, and satire. The members of these fool societies wore the traditional garments of imbeciles so that they could not be blamed for social and moral criticisms they advanced under the traditional license of folly. Different from both the village fool and the court fool, different also from the ecclesiastical fools, the fool societies were urban institutions, that sprang up in conjunction with the growth of towns and guilds and with the spread of secular education in the late Middle Ages.

It is perhaps not quite correct to say that the rulers of the fool societies were the middlemen "who conveyed the cap and bells from the shaven heads of the half-witted into the

[51] Quoted by Enid Welsford, *op. cit.*, p. 202.
[52] E. K. Chambers, *The Medieval Stage* (Oxford: Clarendon Press, 1903), Vol. 1, p. 292, note 2.

creative imagination of the philosopher, the satirist, and the comic poet."[53] Certainly, philosophers and satirists had known, long before the rise of fool societies, that it is possible and prudent to say the truth laughingly. Erasmus, to whom the sage-fool owes so much, studied ancient literature as well as the Scriptures. He was familiar with both Lucian and the northern mysticism of the *devotio moderna*. Without such learning the sophisticated irony of Stultitia would not have been possible.[54] Finally, not only the imagination of the comic poet but that of the tragic poet as well created great fools.

King Lear is the most eminent example of the foolish reversal of political order as a means of presenting the truth about the human condition in a profoundly melancholy cast. On the heath, Lear is deprived of reason as well as majesty. He has become a fool akin to the jester in his company. The King is destitute, like the beggar he meets, and in agony, like Gloucester, the great blinded lord, led by the beggar. Lear's prayer to "sweet heaven" that he may be spared madness has met with no answer except that the voice of God can be heard as thunder; but thunder is void of meaning. Lear, the outcast, has become a fool of inspired madness. In addressing Gloucester he says:

> . . . thy name is Gloucester.
> Thou must be patient; we came crying hither . . .

And his words are reinforced by Edgar:

> Men must endure
> Their going hence, even as their coming hither.[55]

When the political order is completely reversed, it is the tragic fool who recognizes the truth: patience, endurance, resignation, rather than salvation, are man's lot. As Enid Welsford put it, "Patience, here, seems to imply an unflinching, clearsighted, recognition of the fact of pain, and the complete

[53] Enid Welsford, *op. cit.*, p. 217.
[54] Cf. Walter Kaiser, *op. cit.*, pp. 1–100.
[55] Shakespeare, *King Lear*, IV.6.182 and V.3.9–100.

abandonment of any claim to justice or gratitude either from Gods or men."[56] Lear is a "fool of fortune," not of God.

The Fool and Modernity

As an important figure on the social scene, the fool could not withstand modernity. The claims of modern science and the spread of Enlightenment lumped the sage-fool in literature with other pale and somewhat embarrassing achievements of the past — pale, because no fool ever promised future glories to man, as did science; embarrassing, because science is serious and folly is not. Modern man credits scientific knowledge with the power to subdue nature, hopes to extend human life ever more and to bring about an affluent, just, and peaceful social order. He does not hesitate to speak of the abolition of war, of human engineering, or of social inventions, and he is concerned with sharpening his sight when forecasting political "futures."

The fool would have included all these hopes and preoccupations in a catalogue of human follies. While asserting *physis* against *nomos,* no fool ever believed that nature could be conquered by man, and those who used to laugh about folly did not dream of it either. Modern enlightened man retaliated by discarding the fool's comments on human affairs as fatuous nonsense. Enlightened man scorns the classical fool. In Nicholas Breton's words, he is but "the shame of nature, the trouble of wit, the charge of charity, and the loss of liberality."[57]

We still speak of folly and fools, but in literature as in everyday speech, "fools" and "folly" have been attenuated in meaning, and sapped of deeper significance. With a few exceptions — Charlie Chaplin among them — fools now satisfy tastes unaccustomed to excellence. The obscenities that the old fool indulged in are still abroad, but they have been lifted from richer textures of life and literature and relegated to the bar-

[56] Enid Welsford, *op. cit.,* p. 266.
[57] Nicholas Breton, "The Good and the Bad, *Archaica,* 2 vols., Sir E. Brydges, editor (London: 1815), Vol. 1, p. 24, quoted by Barbara Swain, *op. cit.,* p. 185.

racks, to cheap picture postcards (as George Orwell has shown[58]), and to similar forms of lowbrow *l'art pour l'art*. In life we treat a fool like an eccentric and we would indeed be eccentrics ourselves were we to believe that in madness (not caused by drugs) man is inspired.

Let me conclude these comments by observing, foolishly perhaps, that in our time, the role of the Undeceiver-General is played by the psychoanalyst, and that many sad fools have become his patients. By the same token, the fool societies of our time are composed of "hippies," while the descendant of the court fool is a professional comedian appearing on the television screen, telling jokes that more often than not originated in the mind of a ghost writer not sage enough to play the fool and not sad or bold enough to plumb the depth of irreverent humor.

[58] George Orwell, "The Art of Donald McGill," *A Collection of Essays* (Garden City, N.Y.: Doubleday Anchor Books, 1941), pp. 111 ff.

CHAPTER THIRTEEN

Court and Tavern in the German Baroque Novel

THE THIRTY YEARS WAR crippled German political and cultural life for several generations. During the war Germany lost probably one-third of her population. In 1648, when the Peace of Westphalia was concluded, she was left with about thirteen and a half million inhabitants. Only a very small fraction — perhaps five per cent — of this staggering loss had resulted from violence in battle. The relatively low rate of battle casualties — 1000 to 1500 per year on the average — was testimony to the inefficiency of firearms. Bullets weighed ten to the pound, their penetrating power was low, and many of them missed their aim. This state of technology sustained the belief, so widely held in the seventeenth century and indeed well into the eighteenth century, that invulnerability could be acquired by magic and overcome only by magic bullets (or weapons other than firearms). Famous generals employed workers to manufacture such bullets of silver or glass.[1]

As was true of war until the second half of the nineteenth

From "A Woman Named Courage," Ch. 8 of *The Arts in Society*, Robert N. Wilson, editor (Englewood Cliffs, New Jersey: Prentice-Hall, Inc., 1964).

[1] A. T. S. Goodrick in his introduction to his (incomplete) English translation of *The Adventurous Simplicissimus*, published in a limited edition (London, 1912) and reprinted in a paperbound edition (Lincoln: University of Nebraska Press, 1962), p. xvi.

century, the biggest toll in lives was taken by epidemic diseases. In the Thirty Years War other contributing factors to the awesome loss in life were local famines and marauding bands, many of which were composed of deserters from the armies.

While the long war was a total war in its time, its destructive power was shallow, making some rapid recovery possible. Stone and brick buildings survived even in those cities which were sacked, and wooden houses were quickly rebuilt. But owing to the shortage of capital and the low degree of administrative efficiency, demobilizing the troops was a painful process taking several years. Many mutinies occurred. In certain districts soldiers formed outlaw bands so that "for many years after the war merchants preferred to travel in great companies and well guarded."[2]

While the war had led to some mixture of races, it had failed to open new routes of social advancement. "The social hierarchy emerged from the war as rigid as before."[3] The war produced a landless aristocracy, strengthened the impatience of the peasant in relation to the rest of society, and contributed to the further decline of the burgher. When peace finally came, the privileged classes attempted to fortify their social position. The landed gentry succeeded in having feudal restrictions reimposed, so that in many districts peasants were no longer allowed to leave their village or to pursue any home industry. Many experienced middle-class secretaries and councilors were replaced in the service of princes "by a swarm of young place-hunters of noble birth whom the peace had deprived of their proper employment, and whose pride was only equalled by their incapacity."[4]

The influence of the commercial class had been declining prior to the outbreak of the Thirty Years War, and the outcome of the war weakened its position further. When peace was

[2] C. V. Wedgwood. *The Thirty Years War* (New Haven: Yale University Press, 1949), p. 509.

[3] *Ibid.*, p. 517.

[4] A. T. S. Goodrick, *op. cit.*, p. x.

concluded, industry and trade were hampered by innumerable tolls and taxes, a bewildering variety of weights and measures, and a multiplicity of laws regarding trade. For example, goods shipped from Strasbourg to the frontier of Holland had to pass no less than thirty different customs stations.[5] For a long time to come the middle class in Germany was to be composed of dependent officials rather than of entrepreneurs and merchants.

As Miss Wedgwood has pointed out, "the breakdown of social order, the perpetual changing of authority and religion in so many districts, contributed to the disintegration of society which was more fundamentally serious than the immediate damages of war."[6] The common people lived in fear of the devil and of witches, and not only the common people listened eagerly to reports of apocalyptic visions of the end of the world.[7] Many of these beliefs were taken seriously by both Christian and Jewish theologians; nor were the ties between science and magic as yet entirely cut.

Germany as a whole was divided into three hundred principalities. She had neither a political nor a cultural center like Paris. At the court in Vienna, Latin and Italian were spoken, and Vienna, like Munich, was a site of Jesuit, rather than German, culture. Political life in Germany was provincial in character. Absolutism lacked the scope and luster that it attained in contemporary France. The German courts enjoyed the ephemeral splendor and celebration of power rather than its substance. Nor did Germany have the salon as a social institution in which *bienséance* was developed and pedantry shunned. Instead, bombastic dignity was valued more than true elegance; heroic gestures, like all theatricality — whether in fireworks or opera, in masquerades, or in public displays —

---

[5] Robert Ergang, *The Myth of the All-Destructive Fury of the Thirty Years' War* (Pocono Pines, Pa.: The Craftsmen, 1956), p. 33.

[6] C. V. Wedgwood, *op. cit.*, p. 516.

[7] Cf. *Selbstzeugnisse aus dem Dreissigjährigen Krieg und dem Barock*, Marianne Beyer-Fröhlich, editor (Leipzig: Philip Reclam Jun., 1930); Abba Hillel Silver, *A History of Messianic Speculation in Israel* (Boston: Beacon Press, 1959), Ch. 7, and preface.

were applauded. And all this rarefied, illusory, expensive culture was entirely removed from the mainstream of society. The distance from the courts to the people was farther than that from the monarch to Heaven.

German literature was dependent upon achievements in Italy, Holland, England, and, above all, France and Spain. Especially the German novel — whether heroic, pastoral, picaresque, historical-political, or comical — consisted almost exclusively of translations, adaptations, and imitations of foreign works. There was a deep gulf between the educated minority and the uneducated mass of society. Since the authors valued scholarship, they did not write for wide public approval.

Popularity meant for an author that he had failed to produce a work of art. Poets excluded from their collected works songs that had had the misfortune of reaching the common people. The poets were ashamed of having written such poetry.[8] Similarly, in serious baroque music popular taste was given no consideration. Complaints that the common people failed to understand the elaborate church music of the age were disregarded by the composers. In his *Psalmodia Christiana* (1665), H. Mithobius took note that the common people were unable to follow "all tricks and artifices of the musician," but in his view it was sufficient for them to know that they were listening to a sacred tune. Instead of suggesting that contrapuntal complexity be abandoned to bring the music within the grasp of the untrained, Mithobius held that "God cannot be praised artificially enough" and that the people should rise to an understanding of music by "exercise."[9]

The historical-political novel was fully intelligible only to the aristocracy, because only they could understand the many allusions it contained to contemporary events and personages.

---

[8] Martha Lenschau, *Grimmelshausens Sprichwörter und Redensarten* (Frankfurt am Main: M. Diesterweg, 1924), p. 11.

[9] Quoted by Manfred F. Bukofzer, *Music in the Baroque Era* (New York: W. W. Norton & Company, 1947), p. 411.

It was not rooted in the life and imagination of the people,[10] but written for a socially exclusive audience whose life and manners it idealized. Anton Ulrich, Duke of Brunswick, anonymous author of *The Syrian Aramena* (1669–1673) and *The Roman Octavia* (1676), was one of the foremost writers in this genre. Goethe thought highly of his style, and some German critics regard him still today as the greatest German baroque novelist.[11]

Anton Ulrich's *Aramena* contains a long *Voransprache*, a preface addressing "the noble reader," in which the social theory of what we shall call the conventional novel is fully developed. Claiming that the historical-political novel, like Barclay's *Argenis* (originally written in Latin), d'Urfé's *Astrée*, or the Duke's *Aramena*, contain more truth than do historical yearbooks, the author of the preface proudly presents the conventional novel as a mirror of princes. "Such novels are real schools for the court and the nobility, which ennoble the soul, the mind, and the manners and teach refined, courteous speech."[12] Similarly, the publisher (Esaias Fellgiebel) of some of Daniel Casper von Lohenstein's tragedies recommended the author's novel *Arminius and Thusnelda* (1689) to "princes, noblemen and persons in the service of the state in peace time as well as war": they would be both pleased and instructed by it.[13] Lohenstein, a patrician, wrote

---

[10] Richard Alewyn, *Johann Beer, Studien zum Roman des 17. Jahrhunderts* (Leipzig: Mayer and Müller, G.m.b.H., 1932), p. 122.

[11] Especially Günther Müller in many of his works, such as his "Barockromane und Barockroman," *Literaturwissenschaftliches Jahrbuch der Görresgesellschaft* (*Barock*, Vol. 4), Günther Müller, editor (Freiburg: Görres-Gesellschaft, 1929), pp. 1–19.

[12] Anton Ulrich von Braunschweig, in the preface to *Die durchleuchtige Syrerinn Aramena* (Nürnberg: Johann Hofmann, 1678–1680). On Anton Ulrich and La Calprenède's influence on him, cf. the excellent dissertation by Carola Paulsen, *"Die durchleuchtigste Syrerin Aramena" des Herzogs Anton Ulrich von Braunschweig und "La Cléopatre" des Gautier Coste de La Calprenède. Ein Vergleich* (Bonn: typed).

[13] Daniel Casper von Lohenstein, *Römische Trauerspiele*, Klaus Günther Just, editor (Stuttgart: Anton Hiersemann, 1955), p. 143.

for noblemen who, different from the country squires, were educated to assume positions in the higher bureaucracy of the absolutist states.[14]

The conventional novel dealt with matters of state in an exemplary and representative fashion. Its main characters were members of ruling houses, and since the interest of state coincided with the fate of the ruling families, their affairs of the heart and their intrigues had political significance. Of *Aramena* it was said in the preface that "it had grown at the court and not in the dust of the schools. It is not covered with the dust of the vulgar, but speaks of the history of princes with great politeness and in quite princely a fashion." The alleged purpose of the novel was to rid the aristocracy of its common opinions and to ennoble their minds through examples of virtue and true wisdom. In order to accomplish this aim, the august characters were placed in situations of conflict in which reason gained the ascendancy over passion, the interest of state triumphed over love, and constancy and dignity prevailed.

In all conventional novels of the period history was merely a façade for staging the moral problems of contemporary aristocratic life. Whether Roman, as in La Calprenède's *Cléopatre* or Anton Ulrich's *Octavia;* Teutonic, as in La Calprenède's *Faramong,* Lohenstein's *Arminius,* and Buchholtz's *Herkules;* or Asiatic, as in La Calprenède's *Gassandre,* Anton Ulrich's *Aramena,* and Zigler's *Asiatische Banise,* history was always a fountainhead of virtue and wisdom. Since nothing new happened in history, lessons for modern use could be gleaned from ancient events.[15]

The conventional novel also offered models of polite conversation on a variety of topics, which permits insight into the manners at court. For example, Anton Ulrich's *Aramena* con-

---

[14] Paul Hankamer, *Deutsche Gegenreformation und deutsches Barock,* 2nd ed. (Stuttgart: I. B. Metzler, 1947), p. 441.

[15] Max Wehrli, *Das barocke Geschichtsbild in Lohenstein's Arminius.* Wege zur Dichtung. Zürcher Schriften zur Literaturwissenschaft, Emil Ermatinger, editor (Frauenfeld/Leipzig: Huber & Co., 1938), xxxi.

tains a conversation on the question of whether it is possible for a disappointed lover to love a second time, and in Lohenstein's *Arminius* a discussion is held in the company of distinguished ladies on whether it is a lesser misfortune to be blinded or to be castrated.[16]

All conventional novels demonstrate through the behavior of the main characters the importance of dissimulation in guarding oneself against false friends, rivals, and evil intrigues. Dissimulation is associated not only with the pervasive distrust which governs all human relations in high places, including those among lovers and friends, but also with the demands of dignity and courtesy. In the conventional novel, as in life at court, the distance between two persons is never closed.[17] Even friends and lovers remain ultimately strangers, who at the slightest turn of fortune are at once inclined to believe that they have been mutually betrayed or deceived.[18] Never is unshakable confidence placed blindly in a friend or a lover. In these circumstances the ability to suppress emotion is both necessary for insuring survival in an intensely dangerous milieu and praiseworthy as a sign of dignity that no misfortune can undermine. Lohenstein in his *Arminius* repeats almost verbatim a rule of conduct contained in Gracian's *Art of Worldly Wisdom* (which he translated into German) to the effect that neither fortune nor misfortune should affect the facial expression of the hero. The hero's perfection becomes visible when he receives the news of being condemned to death, and neither his voice nor the expression of his smiling mouth changes: he continues playing chess.[19]

In this moral climate silence is often pregnant with meaning. Anton Ulrich at one time explains a moment of silence

[16] Cited by Max Wehrli, *op. cit.,* p. 77.

[17] Günther Müller, "Höfische Kultur der Barockzeit," in H. Naumann and G. Müller, *Höfische Kultur* (Halle: Max Niemeyer, 1929), p. 135.

[18] Cf. Clemens Lugowski, *Wirklichkeit und Dichtung* (Frankfurt am Main: M. Diesterweg, 1936); and Herbert Singer, "Joseph in Aegypten," *Euphorion,* Vol. 48 (1954), p. 267.

[19] Cf. Luise Laporte, *Lohenstein's "Arminius"* (Berlin: Germanische Studien, 48, 1927), p. 41.

as the result of both grief and the desire not to annoy society by complaints. The personal and the intimate are suppressed. Everything is representational and public. Even Zesen, whose ethos is more bourgeois than that of Anton Ulrich, says in his *Assenat* of Joseph and his bride that it would be unseemly to divulge their conversation.[20] In the conventional novel only the villains display unbridled passion. Heroes and heroines attain mastery over nature by silence, dissimulation, patience, and stoical equanimity.

The authors of the historical political novel were ". . . mostly either distinguished members of the titled nobility and other aristocrats or people acquainted with such persons."[21] For poets and writers who were not of aristocratic descent few avenues to social recognition were open. Perhaps the most important one was membership in a language society where intellectually distinguished commoners met aristocrats with an interest in literature.[22] Another way of attaining social distinction was through panegyrical poetry and prose praising other authors and, above all, some personage at the summit of political power.[23]

---

[20] H. H. Borcherdt, *Geschichte des Romans und der Novelle in Deutschland* (Leipzig: Weber, 1926), p. 219.

[21] Anton Ulrich, preface cited in footnote 12.

[22] One of the most influential societies of this kind, the Fruchtbringende Gesellschaft, was founded by Prince Ludwig of Anhalt-Göthen in 1617. It existed until 1680. According to a contemporary source, until 1662 its members consisted of one king, three electors in the German Empire, forty-nine dukes, four margraves, ten landgraves, eight Pfalzgrafen, nineteen princes, sixty counts, thirty-five barons, and six hundred "noblemen, scholars, and other distinguished persons of bourgeois standing, who had acquired great merit in Germany through the sword as well as the pen." (Neumark [anonymous], *Der neusprossende Teutsche Palmbaum* . . . (Weimar: 1668), p. 34, cited by Ernst Manheim, *Die Träger der öffentlichen Meinung* (Brünn: Rudolf M. Rohrer, 1933), p. 81, note 2). On the language societies in general, cf. Karl Viëtor, *Probleme der deutschen Barockliteratur* (Leipzig: Weber, 1928), pp. 63–72. On Grimmelshausen's relation to them, cf. Felix Scholz, "Grimmelshausen's Verhältnis zu den Sprachgesellschaften und sein 'Teutscher Michel'," *Euphorion*, Ergänzungsheft, No. 17 (1924), pp. 79–96.

[23] Curt von Faber du Faur, "Monarch, Patron, and Poet," *The Germanic Review*, Vol. 21 (1949), pp. 249–264.

The most eminent examples of popular novels in the seventeenth century are Grimmelshausen's so-called "Simplician" writings. They comprise *The Adventurous Simplicissimus,* published in 1669, and three sequels, *Courage, the Adventuress* (1670), *The Strange Skipinthefield* (1670), and *The Enchanted Bird's-Nest,* Part I (1672) and Part II (1675). In addition, Grimmelshausen was the author of a number of other writings in which Simplicissimus, the main character in the cycle of novels, reappears as the fictitious author as well as adventurer and critic of life.

Grimmelshausen remained throughout his life a child of the lower middle class. He was at home in taverns rather than at court. He knew beggars and soldiers but no great merchants or important officials; he was familiar with peasants and lowly people in small towns and villages, with camp followers and jugglers, but only with a few members of the aristocracy. His relations with polite society were tenuous; nor did he belong to any literary clique or society. His wide knowledge was acquired autodidactically, mainly with the help of compendiums. He did not travel abroad and did not speak any foreign language.

The kind of people Grimmelshausen knew best appear in his Simplician tales. The relation of these tales to the conventional novel resembles that of comedy to tragedy. Martin Opitz' description of comedy fits the Simplician writings well, though not perfectly. In his *Book on German Poetry,* he said that "comedy consists of low (*schlecht*) things and persons; it deals with weddings, festivities, gambling, fraud and roguery of knaves and vainglorious soldiers, with love affairs, the frivolity of youth, the miserliness of the aged, with procuring and other matters that occur every day among common people."[24]

Grimmelshausen's main characters in the Simplician writings are not heroes. They are socially undistinguished — soldiers, camp followers, highwaymen, and the like. Their actions have

[24] Martin Opitz, *Buch von der deutschen Poeterei* (1624), Wilhelm Braune, editor (Tübingen: Max Niemeyer, 1954), p. 20.

no political consequences whatever. In their adventures they are ensnared by the physical needs of the body, by passion, and by evil. They do not love but fear their neighbors, much as the courtier in the conventional novel fears his rival, and they see the hand of the devil in everything unexpected that happens. They are concerned not with dignity but with survival. Affairs of state are of no interest to them.

The difference between the Simplician writings and the conventional novels of the baroque era is also manifest in the use of style and language. Grimmelshausen conceived of "high and low things" as opposites, but he contrasted the Simplician or comical (*lustig*) style not with the style of the conventional baroque novel but with the theological style, that is, with the form and content of sermons and serious devotional books.

The Simplician writings abound with proverbial expressions and colloquialisms of the lower classes, whereas the language of high or learned society is formal and precludes proverbs; even Grimmelshausen's own two conventional novels are virtually free of proverbs. The liberal use of proverbs is one of the many features which Grimmelshausen's Simplician writings have in common with the popular literature of the chap books. There are also the same descriptive chapter headings and the "oral style" of delivery, originally born of the custom of having the chap book read out loud. The oral style is most evident when the narrator, who tells his tale in the first person, interrupts himself to inform the reader directly that he should listen to the next adventure. This device, which Grimmelshausen employs very frequently in *Courage, the Adventuress,* creates an illusion of the almost physical presence of listeners sitting around the storyteller.

Scatological imagery is quite prominent in Grimmelshausen's writings. In order not to misinterpret this aspect of his work, it must first be understood that the inclusion of such material violated no moral taboo. Scatological topics were vulgar and hence comical. They appear not only in many chap books, but also in comedies of the period written by distinguished poets like Gryphius[25] and seen by the same audience that attended performances of tragic plays by the same authors. All satirical, comical, and picaresque writings emphasize the physical functions of man and abound with such imagery. Examples can be found in ample profusion in Quevedo's *Buscon,* if not in Alemán's *Guzman,* in Sorel's *Francion,* and in English tales of roguery.

In Grimmelshausen, and in the picaresque novel as well, scatological incidents furnish the most powerful scenes of humiliation. It seems that they do more than merely ridicule social distinction by pointing to common human frailties and natural functions that all men share alike. The victim in such scatological scenes is frequently reduced to a primitive state of helplessness. He is dragged through excrements, and in this regard the fiercely aggressive function of seventeenth century comical literature leaves nothing to the imagination. Everything is presented in the most blatant directness to the senses: excrement is smelled, felt, heard, and even tasted. When it is felt, it is often by the face, as if the noblest part of the human body is the preferred target of degradation.[26]

It is only in a social environment in which the demands of Christian morality do not interdict erotic pleasures that these scatological interests recede. Most writers who deal with erotic subjects do not indulge in descriptions of vomiting,

---

[25] Andreas Gryphius, *Horribilicribrifax,* in *Die deutsche Barock-komödie,* W. Flemming, editor (Leipzig: Philip Reclam, jun., 1931). On the use of scatological humor, in Gryphius, cf. also the introduction by W. Flemming, p. 18.

[26] See, for example, *Grimmelshausens Courasche,* J. H. Scholte, editor (Halle: Max Niemeyer, 1923), Ch. 17; *Des wunderbarlichen Vogelnests zweiter Teil,* in *Grimmelshausens Werke, H. H. Borcherdt,* editor (Berlin, Leipzig, Vienna, Stuttgart: Deutsches Verlagshaus Bong & Co., 1921), Vol. 3, Ch. 7; cf. also Francisco de Quevedo, *The Life and Adventures of Don Pablos the Sharper,* Mack Hendricks Singleton and others, translators, in *Masterpieces of the Spanish Golden Age,* Angel Flores, editor (New York: Holt, Rinehart & Winston, Inc., 1957), p. 112; and Gryphius, *op. cit.*

flatulence, and soiling oneself or others. For example, the Renaissance novella, which explored the erotic sphere freely, shunned, on the whole, the scatological realm.[27]

Grimmelshausen's novels seem to be filled with Christian condemnation of sex as sin. His description of sexual adventures and, more broadly, of all natural functions of the body fit the image of man as an animal that but for the power and grace of God would be devoid of spiritual life. At the same time, this spiritual life has an ethereal and synthetic quality in the Simplician tales, as though it could well be a superstitious delusion, whereas these same tales make it quite clear that there is nothing illusory about eating, vomiting, flatulence, defecating, and fornication. The pain of childbirth is the reality which remains of the woman's belief that she will give birth to the Messiah; dreams of peace on earth vanish in an itch that is caused by vermin; theological discussions end abruptly with a narrow escape from death; beauty is disfigured by syphilis; plans for marriage are thwarted by sudden loss of testicles or by unexpected threats of murder.

Grimmelshausen was, of course, neither an atheist nor a torchbearer of enlightenment. In many regards, the spirit of his Simplician tales points back, rather than forward, to religious skepticism and political disaffection in earlier times. It is related in spirit to *Reynke de Voss*, which Goethe called an unholy Bible of the world, and to *Til Eulenspiegel*, who, asked by her on his death-bed for a last word of wisdom, gave his mother the most cynical advice that ever came from the mouth of a dying man.[28]

---

[27] In his comments on Johann Beer's *Das Narrenspital*, 1681 (Hamburg: Rowohlt, 1957), Richard Alewyn discusses the relationship between scatological humor "from the later Middle Ages to the end of the baroque" and "repressed sexuality" (p. 147). The "hero" in *Das Narrenspital* may claim unique distinction by an unsurpassed performance in breaking wind. The point on repressed sexuality as an explanation of scatological humor was also made previously by Richard Alewyn in *Johann Beer*, pp. 174–175.

[28] *"Die muter sprach ach lieber sun gib mir dein süss ler da ich dein bei gedenken mag. Ulenspiegel sagt ia liebe muter wan du wilt deins*

Grimmelshausen was cool toward the organized religion of the Christian churches and seems to have had nothing but smiles for various facets of Christian theological doctrine which conflicted with the observation of nature, with common sense, and self-interest. On a few matters of great relevance to Christian theological doctrine, Grimmelshausen's views bordered on blasphemy. This fact is concealed from plain sight by a cloak of orthodoxy.

Grimmelshausen often played with blasphemy in his Simplician writings, but the three most striking instances are: the central tale in *The Adventurous Simplicissimus* concerning the madman who calls himself Jove, who wants to punish the world and hopes to establish eternal peace; the story about the false Jewish Messiah in *The Enchanted Bird's-Nest,* Part II; and *The Story of Courage.*

If a moral doctrine were distilled from Grimmelshausen's Simplician tales, it would be rigorously Christian in character, but the moral rigor of the man was tempered by grim laughter and by the fascination that natural, rather than moral, behavior, exerted upon him. He wrote about man as he naturally is. Men of freer spirit, like Leibniz, found *The Adventurous Simplicissimus* delightful reading. He wrote to the Duchess

----

gemachs thun, so ker den ars von dem wind so gat dir der gestank nit in die nass." (*Til Ulenspiegel,* 1515, Herman Knust, editor(Halle: Max Niemeyer, 1884), p. 140.)

For the encounter with Jove see *Grimmelshausens Simplicissimus Teutsch,* J. H. Scholte, editor (Tübingen: Max Niemeyer, 1954), III, Chs. 3–6. The three most important discussions of this episode, which has been studied very carefully, are Julius Petersen, "Grimmelshausen's 'Teutscher Held'," *Euphorion,* Ergänzungsheft, No. 17 (1924), pp. 1–30; Günther Weydt, "Don Quijote Teutsch. Studien zur Herkunft des Simplicianischen Jupiter," *Euphorion,* Vol. 51 (1957), pp. 250–270; and Manfred Koschlig, "Das Lob des 'Francion' bei Grimmelshausen," *Jahrbuch der deutschen Schillergesellschaft,* Vol. 1 (Stuttgart: Alfred Kröner Verlag, 1957), pp. 30–73. Cf. also James Franklin Hyde, *The Religious Thought of Johann Jacob Christoffel von Grimmelshausen as Expressed in the Simplicianische Schriften* (Dissertation, Indiana University, 1960) [typescript]. On the story of the false messiah, cf. still Otto Weinreich, *Der Trug des Nektanebos* (Berlin and Leipzig: 1911); cf. also Ch. 16, below.

of Hannover that the work approached the genius of Charles
Sorel's *Histoire Comique de Francion*.[29] This is high praise indeed, both because of the intelligence of the critic and because
of the comparison he made.

[29] On *Simplicissimus* and *Courage* being read by the Duchess Sophie
of Hannover, cf. J. H. Scholte, *Der Simplicissimus und sein Dichter*
(Tübingen: Max Niemeyer, 1950), p. 144; the relevant passage in
Leibniz's letter to her (of April 1688) is quoted by Manfred Koschlig,
op. cit., pp. 33–34. Attacking the older view that Grimmelshausen's
Simplicissimus was influenced by Spanish picaresque models in German
translation, Koschlig tried to show the debt Grimmelshausen owed to
the comical novel by Charles Sorel. By contrast, Günther Weydt, in the
article cited in footnote 28, and before that in his essay "Zur Entstehung
barocker Erzählkunst. Harsdörffer und Grimmelshausen," *Wirkendes
Wort*, 1 (Sonderheft: 1952), proved Grimmelshausen's indirect indebted-
ness to Cervantes by way of various intermediaries, of whom Harsdörffer,
the industrious translator and adaptor of picaresque and other foreign
tales, was especially important as a literary source. Koschlig correctly
assesses the common function of Grimmelshausen's and Sorel's humor,
but seems to overstate the influence of Francion on the character of
Grimmelshausen's Jove. Koschlig also failed to comment on the significant differences between the French and the German work. Sorel dealt
with the upper classes as well as university life and the lowly elements
in society. Both the social scope of his observation was larger and the
fervor of his early nonconformism greater than Grimmelshausen's. Sorel
wanted to teach people "to live like Gods." (Charles Sorel, *Histoire
Comique de Francion*; 5e livre. Emile Roy, editor [Paris: Librairie
Hachette, 1926], II, p. 123.)

CHAPTER FOURTEEN

Simplicissimus, the Irreverent Fool

SOME great literary works enjoy immortal fame for reasons that have little to do with the deepest concern of their authors. *Don Quixote, Gulliver's Travels, Moby-Dick* are books of this kind, and so, perhaps, are *Til Eulenspiegel* and *Alice in Wonderland.* These writings capture the imagination of young readers because great adventures never fail to enchant them. As they grow older they forget much that it is useful to remember, but not the knight of the sad countenance fighting windmills, or Eulenspiegel with his fool's cap laughing on an uphill climb in joyous anticipation of his descent; they always recall Gulliver tied by the Lilliputians and the elusive terrible white whale, and the Mad Hatter. But later in life some of them reread the books of their youth and then, perhaps, they suspect design in Eulenspiegel's folly and method in Don Quixote's madness; perhaps they discover that Ahab's whale hunt is a struggle with God and *Gulliver's Travels* a comment on a philosophical subject; and even Lewis Carroll's whimsies may then hold more than mere enchantment. Grimmelshausen's main work, *The Adventurous Simplicissimus,* belongs in this class of writings. Anyone who has read it in his youth will not forget Simplicius Simplicissimus and his adventures — some of them buoyantly roguish and profoundly comical, others cruel and obscene, a few of them deeply moving, and some

From *Social Research,* Vol. 33 (Spring 1966).

mysterious like dreams. But what lies behind the adventures?

The book was first published in 1669, twenty-one years after the conclusion of the Thirty Years War, which provides the setting of the first five parts of the novel. In *Continuatio,* the last part, peace reigns, and so it does in the last two books of the Simplician cycle of novels, *The Enchanted Bird's-Nest,* Parts I and II, whereas the two other tales of the cycle, *Courage, the Adventuress* and *The Strange Skipinthefield,* are also war books.[1]

Grimmelshausen published all but three of his works under a pseudonym, using no less than eight different anagrams of his name for that purpose.[2] Two of the books published under his real name were "serious" conventional novels, more or

[1] There is no complete translation into English of *The Adventurous Simplicissimus.* The edition published under this title by University of Nebraska Press (Lincoln: 1962), with a preface by Eric Bentley, is a reprint of a translation by A. T. S. Goodrick, originally published in London, 1912. It is not based on the critical edition of the German text of the first five books, edited by J. H. Scholte (Halle: 1938; 3rd edition Tübingen: Max Niemeyer, 1954), and of *Continuatio des abentheurlichen Simplicissimi,* the sixth book, J. H. Scholte, editor (Halle: Max Niemeyer, 1939). The translation by Walter Wallich, *The Adventures of a Simpleton* (London: New English Library Ltd., 1962), omits even larger parts of the work. Even the best English renditions of the work by Hellmuth Weissenborn and Lesley Macdonald (London: Calder, 1965) and by George Schulz-Behrend (Indianapolis, New York, Kansas City: The Bobbs-Merrill Company, The Library of Liberal Arts, 1965) contain slight adaptations and deletions. The only other works of Grimmelshausen that are at present available in English can be found in H. J. C. von Grimmelshausen, *Courage, the Adventures and The False Messiah,* translation and introduction by Hans Speier (Princeton, N.J.: Princeton University Press, 1964); this is a complete translation of the second novel (the seventh book) in the Simplician cycle and of a novella to be found in Chapters 12–20 of *The Enchanted Bird's-Nest,* Part II, the last or tenth book of the cycle, published in 1675. Another translation of *Courage* by Robert L. Hiller and John C. Osborne has been published under the title *The Runagate Courage* (Lincoln: University of Nebraska Press, 1965).

[2] On Grimmelshausen's use of anagrams cf. Hans Speier, "A Woman Named Courage," *The Arts in Society,* Robert N. Wilson, editor (Englewood Cliffs, N.J.: Prentice-Hall, Inc., 1964), pp. 193 ff., esp. 214–218 and the literature cited there.

less satisfying the baroque taste for solemnity and learning. They are little read today and have indeed less literary merit than have other German novels of the period, especially those by Anton Ulrich, Duke of Brunswick; but like Grimmelshausen's "serious" works, Anton Ulrich's novels today rest also respectfully buried in the graveyard of scholarship. All of Grimmelshausen's so-called Simplician writings, however, still are vibrantly alive; they seem to belong to folk literature. They deal with common or vulgar, and hence comical, people — the kinds of people Grimmelshausen knew well. In the terrible war that brought the wolf packs to once cultivated fields in Germany and decimated the population, he served first as a simple soldier and then as a regimental clerk. When peace finally came he remained a simple man, an innkeeper and bailiff in a small town not very far from Strasbourg. Never in his life did he mingle with the great captains of war and state. Nor did he keep much company with the rich in the city or with high dignitaries of the churches; none of the famous and learned authors of his time seems to have been a friend of his.

Illustrious ladies and gentlemen and their concerns, the heroic affairs of state and of love, can be found only in the serious, historical-political novel and in solemn baroque tragedy. To the extent that socially prominent characters appear at all in the Simplician tales their morals and manners are almost invariably satirized. Grimmelshausen said that his popular works dealt with "the low things" in life, and were written in "the Simplician style"; he distinguished that style from "the theological style" of sermons and other edifying prose. According to his own words, the Simplician style is a way of writing that hints at the truth through laughter. In this style the truth is not being told directly, and solemn statements may therefore be suspected of not being true. Those familiar with the old tradition of laughingly telling the truth know that this kind of writing is salutary and sweet: salutary, since it drives melancholy thoughts away, and sweet because it offers the bitter truth to us as a sugar-coated pill.[3] In short, those who read *The Adventurous Simplicissimus* are well advised to heed Grimmelshausen's warning: "It happens sometimes that . . . behind the printed words that deal with insignificant things something else is hidden which evades discovery by many a reader."[4]

What is it that is hidden in the book? Before suggesting an answer, it must be said that some of the impressions derived from a first reading of the work may be misleading, as may also be some of the literary criticisms to which it has been subjected. Most critics now rightly agree that *The Adventurous Simplicissimus* is neither a "realistic" novel of the Thirty Years War nor a picaresque tale pure and simple, but most of them also hold the opinion that the truth of the book is the truth of the Gospel. As we shall see, this opinion is open to some doubt.

The Adventurous Simplicissimus is cast in autobiographical form, and various incidents in it reflect Grimmelshausen's own experiences in the Thirty Years War. The work is indeed one of the great books on war as a scourge of man;[5] the book can be compared to Jacques Callot's series of famous etchings, *Les misères de la guerre*. Both works abound with stark images of the ruin of town and countryside, the abject misery and unrestrained cruelty of soldiers and peasants alike, the degradation of men by sudden misfortune and windfalls of luck. Grimmelshausen presents all this as the story of a boy growing to manhood while caught in a maelstrom of violence, hunger, greed, and corruption. But for all the knowledge he had of total war in the seventeenth century, he saw war as the extreme form of the human condition: in peacetime as

---

[3] Cf. Ch. 16.

[4] *Grimmelshausens Simpliciana*, J. H. Scholte, editor (Halle: Max Niemeyer, 1943), p. 43.

[5] "There is a great literature of war, and very much of it speaks poignantly today. The *Simplicissimus* may well be the most poignant book in all this literature because its war, alas, is our war, our *kind* of war." (Eric Bentley, in his preface to *The Adventurous Simplicissimus* [Lincoln: 1962], p. vi.).

well man remains warlike because of the terror he strikes and fears. "Reality" may be said to be "distorted" in Grimmelshausen's Simplician tales. Not only that which is sinful according to Christian teaching occupies a prominent place in them, but also the filthy, the rapacious in sex, and especially the scatological. By contrast, large areas in the canvas of life are left blank. What Grimmelshausen says about government and work is stated mainly in allegorical form; on love between man and woman he is silent; on family life he says very little. By contrast he waxes eloquent on popular superstitions: the belief that some people are bulletproof, that possession of a mandrake root can bring wealth or a bird's-nest can make its owner invisible — on all this and the fear of the Devil, so widespread in seventeenth century Germany, Grimmelshausen is an invaluable source of information, but a realist in the modern sense he was not.[6]

Nor is *Simplicissimus* a picaresque tale pure and simple. Grimmelshausen was influenced by Spanish models in the picaresque tradition as well as by German satirists like Moscherosch, and perhaps more than has been realized until recently by Charles Sorel's *Histoire Comique de Francion*.[7] Grimmelshausen read many chap books of the preceding centuries; as the autodidact he was he used compendia of learning, contemporary compilations of history, books on astrology, and a great deal more. These "sources" have been most painstakingly investigated by several generations of scholars, and no end of the research is in sight. But his main work does not treat us to a string of self-contained adventures of a picaro, who throughout remains a solitary satirical figure without a moral history of his own. In *The Adventurous Simplicissimus* the picaresque form is modified by the introduction of secondary

---

[6] This point was made first by Richard Alewyn, *Johann Beer, Studien zum Roman des 17. Jahrhunderts* (Leipzig: Mayer und Miller, G.m.b.H., 1932), pp. 208 ff.

[7] Cf. especially Manfred Koschlig, "Das Lob des 'Francion' bei Grimmelshausen," in *Jahrbuch der deutschen Schillergesellschaft*, Vol. 1 (Stuttgart: Alfred Kröner Verlag, 1957), pp. 30–73; and Günther Weydt, "Don Quijote Teutsch," *Euphorion*, Vol. 51 (1957), pp. 250–270.

characters. Next to Simplicissimus himself, the two most important persons in the novel are Heartsbrother, his friend, an almost exemplary Christian, and Olivier, an unscrupulous highwayman and murderer, who in his youth read Aretino in church. Simplicissimus encounters both men repeatedly in his life; he may be said to occupy a middle position between them and thus between goodness and evil. He fails to be as good a Christian as Heartsbrother, but unlike Olivier, he is no devil in human form. Both Heartsbrother and Olivier die, whereas Simplicissimus, armed with common sense, prudence and laughter, lives forever, like a legend. Taken as the story of a moral struggle that is never completely won, *The Adventurous Simplicissimus* is structurally more closely knit than the usual picaresque tale.

Many scholars hold that Grimmelshausen wanted to depict man's struggle for salvation in this world of temptation and evil. They argue that Simplicius, an innocent peasant boy, turns into a venturesome young soldier who after a life full of error, folly, and sin finally learns that peace of mind can be attained only through the renunciation of pleasure and ambition, through remorse and trust in God.[8] Indeed, Simplicissimus eventually confesses his sins and becomes a Catholic; furthermore, after many fresh adventures he renounces the world twice, once at the end of the fifth book and again toward the end of the sixth book of the novel. Thus it seems clear beyond doubt that the author of *The Adventurous Simplicissimus* was a devout Christian believer, and that the hidden truth of his popular writings is revealed not only in the solemn admonitions against sin and vice, to which the reader is treated whenever he has been made to laugh about them, but also in the ending of the tale.

Beyond doubt? Neither Grimmelshausen's life nor, upon close reading, his literary work stills all doubt. Grimmelshau-

---

[8] According to the esthetic counterpart of this view Grimmelshausen moved from the old picaresque novel toward the modern Novel of Development, the first in German literature, adumbrating Goethe's *Wilhelm Meister*.

sen was born and reared a Protestant and turned Catholic most probably at the time of his marriage when he was twenty-eight years of age. His conversion does not necessarily reflect his religious belief, for in his time many men changed their religion for practical reasons. It is true, his works contain very many solemn Christian admonitions, but they are inserted between comical accounts of folly and vice, told with admirable zest and undeniable relish. There are also many sharp attacks on priests and parsons alike. Nor was Grimmelshausen an admirer of the monastic life: he compared it with life in prison; if he admired anything it was the communistically organized life of the Hutterites, an Anabaptist, heretical sect. Furthermore, no less than three times in the Simplician cycle of novels are the diversity of the Christian churches and the existence of other religions adduced as reasons for not choosing any of them through conversion. Not only Simplicius but also a Jew argues slyly that salvation of the soul is too precious to be risked by a choice that might be wrong, since each belief claims to be the only one that is right.

If all of this limits the reader's religious comfort he is bound to get even more upset by the disagreement among Grimmelshausen's critics. For a long time the author was regarded as a Protestant writer, for example by Jakob Grimm. More recently, the view has gained favor that he wrote from a Catholic standpoint.[9] But still other critics have detected irenical tendencies or even leanings toward Pelagianism in his work.[10] A few students have been unable to suppress their doubts that the serious Christian admonitions in his comical

[9] This view is very widely held by modern critics; cf., for example, J. H. Scholte, *Der Simplicissimus und sein Dichter* (Tübingen: Max Niemeyer, 1950); James Hyde, *The Religious Thought of Johann Jacob Christoffel von Grimmelshausen as Expressed in the Simplicianische Schriften* (Dissertation, Indiana University, 1960, typewritten); and Werner Welzig, *Beispielhafte Figuren Tor, Abenteurer und Einsiedler bei Grimmelshausen* (Graz and Köln; Hermann Böhlaus Nachf., 1963).

[10] Irenical tendencies: Friedrich Gundolf, "Grimmelshausen und der Simplicissimus," *Vierteljahrsschrift für Literaturwissenschaft und Geistesgeschichte*, Vol. 1 (1923), p. 254; on Pelagianism: Paul Gutzwiller, *Der Narr bei Grimmelshausen* (Bern: Francke Verlag, 1959) p. 109.

books, particularly in the last novels of the cycle, are to be taken seriously.[11] One Swiss scholar has recently referred to Grimmelshausen as a nihilist,[12] and no less than a hundred and thirty years ago at least two German critics viewed *The Adventurous Simplicissimus* as a satire of Parzival.[13]

Dissimulation

In order to find the way to "the truth" let us begin by mentioning two of Grimmelshausen's own statements about his book. First, in one of the poems prefacing his conventional novel *Dietwalt und Amelinde* the author says that *The Adventurous Simplicissimus* describes the world in a way that gives nature its due.[14] Similarly, in the main novel itself Simplicissimus is called "a natural man," incidentally by a character suffering from religious delusions.[15] Sometimes, when a particular story might offend readers of refined taste, Grimmelshausen concludes with the apologetic explanation that he wants his story to be "complete." It seems that "incompleteness" meant to him not telling what he considered to be the whole truth about man's nature. Now he depicts man not only as a being that is tempted to commit evil, sinful acts, but also as an animal subject to the weakness and urges of all animals. Man must eat and drink and therefore vomits, passes

---

[11] *Cf.* Hans Ehrenzeller, *Studien zur Romanvorrede* (Bern: Francke Verlag, 1955), p. 78, and Hildegard Wichert, *Johann Balthasar Schupp and the Baroque Satire in Germany* (New York: King's Crown Press, 1952).

[12] Paul Gutzwiller, *op. cit.,* p. 108.

[13] This view is usually attributed to George Gottfried Gervinus, *Geschichte der deutschen Dichtung* (1835–1842); *cf.* Carl Hammer, "'Simplicissimus' and the Literary Tradition," *Monatshefte,* Wisconsin, Vol. 40 (1948), p. 461; it was advanced much more fully by Theodor Echtermeyer, *Hallesche Jahrbücher* (1838), p. 431.

[14] Quoted by Manfred Koschlig, "'Edler Herr von Grimmelshausen,'" *Jahrbuch der deutschen Schillergesellschaft,* Vol. 4 (Stuttgart: Alfred Kröner Verlag, 1960), p. 217.

[15] *Grimmelshausens Simplicissimus Teutsch,* J. H. Scholte, editor (Tübingen: Max Niemeyer, 1954), hereafter cited as *Simplicissimus,* p. 210.

water, breaks wind, and defecates. These natural body functions occupy a prominent place in all chap books and picaresque tales and in the realistic novels of the period. They occur in baroque comedy as well. All this is vulgar, like our own barracks humor, and a source of raucous laughter. To modern sensibilities, the literary treatment of the scatological is offensive, especially if used, as it is by Grimmelshausen — and by Bandello, Charles Sorel, and others before him — for depicting revenge by humiliation rather than by violence. Indeed, scatological incidents are the stuff of humiliation. They reveal the frailty of good manners; they shatter pride and dignity; they afford an opportunity for degrading intellectual pretensions; and they lengthen the terrible distance between man and God. And yet, different from human degradation by torture and violence, which have their origins in man's power over man, the weakness of man manifesting itself in his dependence on bodily needs is merely "vulgar." There is really no sound reason for feeling more revolted by accounts of such vulgarity than by accounts of torture, say those contained in Dante's *Inferno*.

Secondly, the preparatory poem in *Dietwalt und Amelinde* urges the reader to acquaint himself with *Simplicissimus* because this story can show when it is safe to speak, when it is necessary to be silent, and how important it is to be on one's guard in the company of the powerful. Nothing in this advertisement refers to the religious career of Simplicissimus. Surprisingly, Grimmelshausen does not speak of his work as though it could lead the reader to Christian piety but rather as if he held it to be a guide to worldly conduct.

In this connection, it should be noted that early in the novel Simplicius, the young ignorant boy, receives his first solemn instruction from a hermit (who later turns out to be his father). The pious man may be expected to admonish the young simpleton to love his neighbor, avoid temptation and trust in God's mercy. Instead, he gives him this advice: know thyself; shun bad company; be steadfast. Surprisingly enough, there is nothing particularly Christian about these precepts: in baroque literature the "hermit" often is merely a mask for a "sage."

The Simplician world is corrupt and dangerous. He who wants to survive in it must dissemble, hide his true feelings, show false feelings, be evasive, and, if need be, lie. As the following instances show, distrust and dissimulation are as pervasive in Grimmelshausen's tales as they are in the serious novel of the period.

In his youth, Simplicius pretends to have lost his wits and plays a fool who tells his noble master and his distinguished guests the truth about their unchristian behavior. But the boy is troubled, since he has not really lost his mind. At this point a good parson says to him: "You must not worry about that. The foolish world wants to be deceived. If you are still in possession of your wits, use them to your advantage. You must imagine that, like Phoenix, you have gone from unreason through fire to reason and thus have been reborn into a new human existence."[16] It is generally acknowledged that the symbol of the Phoenix and the image of rebirth through the acquisition of worldly knowledge are of great importance to an understanding of *The Adventurous Simplicissimus*. A picture of the Phoenix appears as the only illustration in the first edition of the work, taking the place of the long preface customary in serious baroque literature. The place also contains a poem in which the parson's worldly advice, just cited, appears for the first time.

Simplicius treats this parson, too, with consummate dissimulation. When disagreeing with him, he adds, "I was smart enough not to say anything for if I am to confess the truth, by becoming a fool I became first of all prudent and more cautious in everything I said."[17] Dissimulation and the need for it stay with Simplicissimus throughout his life. Once, he reports that he feigns virtue in order to be loved more.[18] Later, when taken prisoner, he talks to the colonel under whose authority he

---

[16] *Simplicissimus,* p. 114.
[17] *Op. cit.,* p. 115.
[18] *Op. cit.,* p. 207.

lives "so cautiously that nobody could know his mind."[19] A Calvinist clergyman admonishes him not to fall prey to women, but the young lover hides his true heart behind clever lies.[20] When Simplicissimus meets the satanic Olivier, he calls him "brother," adding, "I called him that in order to be all the more protected from him."[21] Still later, Simplicissimus justifies his worldliness to Heartsbrother, his conscientious friend. "One must not provoke God," he says, "but come to terms with the times, and use the means that we cannot do without . . . St. Paul, the Apostle, too, . . . marvelously came to terms with his time and the customs in this world. . . ."[22] These examples can be multiplied from every book in the cycle. So can examples of distrust. The need for distrust and dissembling is well justified by a character in *The Strange Skipinthefield:* "He who is overwhelmed must accept the will and wishes of those in whose power he finds himself."[23]

Death

In the baroque period life was widely held to be a descent toward death. Poets rose to the height of their power when they lamented the transitoriness of human existence.

"Just as this light grows weak so in another day and year
I, you, and what we have or see will disappear."[24]

So wrote Andreas Gryphius. The poets found ever new images of decay. The young lover pleaded for the favor of his beloved by reminding her that she soon would be ugly, old and dead.

[19] *Op. cit.*, p. 260.
[20] *Op. cit.*, p. 264.
[21] *Op. cit.*, p. 337.
[22] *Op. cit.*, p. 375.
[23] *Grimmelshausens Springinsfeld,* J. H. Scholte, editor (Halle: Max Niemeyer Verlag, 1928), p. 20.
[24] Andreas Gryphius, *Werke,* Hermann Palm, editor (Hildesheim: Georg Olms Verlags-buchhandlung, 1961), Vol. 3, Sonnets IV, 3.

"Time will spare your beauty
No more than the roses,"

sang Weckherlin. And Logau:

"Your mouth, now coral glow,
Will mold.
Your hands will perish like the snow
And you'll be old."

Disappointed lovers, like Hofmannswaldau, avenged themselves by lyrical descriptions of their sweethearts' unenjoyed beauty ruined by age. One observer explained this sombre cult this way: "When we consider the innumerable corpses which both raging pestilence and martial arms have piled up not only in our Germany but in almost all of Europe, then we must confess that our roses have been transformed into thorns, our lilies into nettles, our paradises into graveyards, nay, our whole being into a picture of death."[25]

Grimmelshausen was not quite so mournful as were these poets. Except for the moving descriptions of the death of the hermit he depicts misfortune and death quite factually without the investment of as much emotion as was later to be expended on descriptions of inclement weather in nineteenth-century novels. He reports the death of great military leaders, the fall of cities, and defeat in battle with the detachment of a chronicler who wastes few words on common events.

Rather than with death he appears preoccupied with change and transformation. Everything in nature and society, he felt, will soon be different from what it happens to be at present. To express this feeling he adopted from Hans Sachs, the sixteenth-century poet, the allegorical figure of *Baldanders* — Soon-different — a kind of popular goddess Fortuna who governs the world. He even arranged for a meeting between Simplicissimus and Soon-different in which the latter offers to teach the great fool the art of understanding the speech

25 Quoted from Johann Peter Hallmann, *Leich-Reden* (1682) by Walter Benjamin, *Ursprung des deutschen Trauerspiels* (Berlin: E. Rowohlt, 1928), p. 231.

of inanimate objects. Soon-different does so by presenting to Simplicissimus a riddle in the form of apparent nonsense words, which the reader of the novel is expected to decipher himself. If he succeeds, instead of being consoled by a hint of God's wisdom, he is teased by another enigmatic message: "Why don't you imagine how all things fare, put this into the words of a discourse and believe that which resembles the truth; then you will have what your foolish curiosity desires."[26]

Grimmelshausen's seeming indifference toward disaster is most shocking when misfortune strikes the main characters of the narrative. For example, Simplicissimus mentions a battle in which "Count Götz lost his life and Heartsbrother his testicles; they were shot away; I got my share in the leg, but it was little more than a scratch. Then we returned to Vienna. . . ."[27] Heartsbrother, Simplicissimus' close friend, very soon thereafter becomes paralyzed. Simplicissimus dryly comments: "In this way, fortune changes unexpectedly. Shortly before Heartsbrother had decided to marry a young noblewoman . . . now he had to think of something else. For since he had lost that which he wanted to use in the production of offspring, and since he was threatened by his paralysis with a lingering illness, in which he needed good friends, he made his last will naming me as the only heir to his estate. . . ."[28] Thus, compassion for the suffering friend is smothered by onrushing fresh events and by the author's absorbing interest in the Change of Fortune.

If such a change crushes not your friend but an enemy, you rejoice; you shake with laughter; and it should be noted that Grimmelshausen's candor in depicting this natural joy is censored by Christian ethics. Perhaps the most striking example is Simplicissimus' reaction to the death of his second wife. It is true, she is a spendthrift, a very bad housekeeper, a drunkard, and an adulteress to boot. Nevertheless, we might

---

[26] Grimmelshausen, *Continuatio des abentheurlichen Simplicissimi,* p. 41.

[27] *Simplicissimus,* p. 385.

[28] *Ibid.*

expect her death to assuage his hostile feelings. Oh, no! She
dies unexpectedly, "which," says Simplicissimus, "so pleased
my heart that I almost got sick from laughing."[29] The impact
of this statement upon the reader is intensified by its explosive
brevity, a literary technique of which Grimmelshausen was an
unsurpassed master. Never did Grimmelshausen indicate any
deep belief that after death man's soul lives on, possibly in
heaven.

Friendship

In a life fraught with the ever-present danger of sudden
disaster, only very few avenues of escape are open. In Grimmelshausen's world man is not in the position of, say, a seventeenth-century French nobleman who could, if he renounced
his ambition, leave the court and join a salon in the city or
return to his country estate. No woman ever enters a convent.
Nor does Grimmelshausen regard the family as a place in
which respite from the struggles and dangers of this world
can be found. Love between man and woman offers no relief.
What remains when the pretty or designing words of love are
forgotten are lust, the fleeting satisfaction of animal appetites,
subjugation, cruelty, abuse, disease, filth. Women are "animals
with braids" or "veiled animals," and love very often is rape.
Even the word "love" is rare. Instead, Grimmelshausen frequently uses an expression known from bird snaring: "*mit der
Leimrute laufen*": "being in love" is "running about with twigs
smeared with bird lime."

Two kinds of human bonds, however, offer some protection
against disaster, that between an experienced older man, a preceptor, and a young man, following his guidance; and more
importantly in many regards, that of true friendship between
two men of equal age. Simplicius', the boy's, relation with the
hermit, and later with a pastor in Hanau, then the young man's
relation with the older Heartsbrother, and to a lesser extent
even with the strange man who in his moments of madness

[29] *Simplicissimus,* p. 404.

thinks he is Jove: all these bonds are fashioned after the
ancient image of an experienced guide who like Aeneas helps
a curious novice to discover the world. The model of such a
guide perhaps nearest to Grimmelshausen was Robertus in
Moscherosch's main work.

Important as such tutorial ties are for Simplicius' education
and survival, they do not have the weight of friendship. Grimmelshausen believed that nothing equaled it as a haven in this
evil, hazardous world and as solace for the anguished soul
of an active man. Only among friends is there no need for dissembling.

While heterosexual love in Grimmelshausen's world invariably enslaves the lover as well as the loved one, the friendship
between the younger Heartsbrother and the Simplicissimus
breaks out of the haunted circle of lust and danger. Simplicius
loves his friend "almost more than himself."[30] The two young
men swear a solemn oath of "eternal brotherhood,"[31] pledging
"never to abandon each other in good or bad fortune, in happi-
ness or misery" and "to love each other until death."[32] Simplicissimus speaks of his affection for Heartsbrother almost
like a modern romantic youth revealing the intoxicating effect
of his infatuation with a girl. He mentions a "sweet" quarrel
between himself and his friend; indeed, he says of himself and
his friend that they were "drunk with love." And Simplicius
finds simple and moving words about the death of his friend:
"While I could not change it, it changed me." "I shunned all
company and sought only solitude to follow my sad thoughts.
. . ."[33] He knew that in all his life he would never again find a
friend like him.

Paradoxically, for modern readers this exquisite emotion
is marred by the sober standard with which Grimmelshausen
and, presumably, his contemporary readers measured the
worth of friendship: friends are friends if they are unselfish

30 *Op. cit.*, p. 374.
31 *Op. cit.*, p. 158.
32 *Op. cit.*, p. 164.
33 *Op. cit.*, p. 394.

enough to share their possessions without regard to individual advantage and without fear of being robbed or murdered.

Grimmelshausen's literary critics have viewed Simplicissimus' friendship with Heartsbrother almost exclusively as an instrument of moral reform, but Heartsbrother's role as Simplicissimus' guide to Christian faith and morality is less impressive than it appears at first glance. To begin with, Simplicissimus reports that Heartsbrother's impaired health improves when he hears the news of Olivier's death. Since Heartsbrother has suffered much from the evil man, this is perhaps a natural, but certainly not a Christian, reaction. Next, the good Heartsbrother knows that Simplicissimus got rich by associating with Olivier, the robber and murderer. The money in his friend's possession is therefore tainted by heinous crimes. Simplicissimus himself says that one of the reasons why his friend first rejects his company on a pilgrimage and his offer of support is "revulsion" about the tainted money. But Heartsbrother never urges his friend to part with his illgotten wealth. Instead, he eventually accepts Simplicissimus' financial support as well as his company. Finally, when Simplicissimus later shows and offers to his friend the gold he has hidden on his person, Heartsbrother forgets all about the evil origin of the gold: he is overwhelmed by Simplicissimus' trust in him, and praises his friend for his lack of fear that he, the good and pious Christian, might rob him of the tainted money. Thus, Heartsbrother's praise of friendship appears like a subtle exercise in immorality. If we do not overlook this feature of the author's portrait of friendship, we are left with a startling choice. Either Grimmelshausen was a morally insensitive man in respect to friendship, or he wanted to render Heartsbrother's sterling character more natural and less incredible by providing it with a blemish; perhaps he believed that goodness can never reach the purity of evil.

Grimmelshausen's portrait of the relation between Simplicius and Heartsbrother presents a strange mixture of very ancient and startlingly modern traits of friendship. It brings to mind an observation in Lucian's dialogue on friendship that when life is fraught with dangers sworn brotherhood is "a necessary thing." But, different from brotherhood among the ancient Scyths, to which Lucian refers, friendship in seventeenth-century Germany was hardly an institution vital for the functioning of the social order. No matter how important the bond between Simplicius and Heartsbrother is for weathering the storms of adversity, as an escape from the world of struggle, from public, political life, it adumbrates a later cult, that of private, intimate friendship among the romantics.[34]

Historically, sworn brotherhood is a pre-Christian, heathen institution, that flourished in societies in which man did not turn the other cheek, but avenged insults and slew his enemies without scruples, sometimes while they were asleep. In such societies, one did not love one's neighbor, nor were all men equal as sinners. In Christian teaching the friend is replaced by the neighbor, a sinner like yourself, and by God Himself as the only being capable of helping you. "He that feareth the Lord directeth his friendship aright; for as he is, so is his neighbor also."[35] In the seventeenth century, Christian moralists of all faiths sternly insisted on the religious error of placing reliance on any man, however beloved he might be.

For example, the Catholic Abraham à Sancta Clara, in order to exhort man not to place his trust in any human being, took him through the various stages of life — birth, youth, manhood, and old age — always asking, "Who's there?" and always offering the reply, " 'A good friend,' says the guardian angel." At every age the guardian angel, and not any mortal, is the good friend.[36] Similarly, in 1657, the Protestant pastor Johann Balthasar Schupp in his book, *Der Freund in der Not* ("The Friend in Times of Affliction"), described the inconstancy of human affairs and repeatedly warned his son not to trust

---

[34] Grimmelshausen's most famous predecessor in substituting "modern" friendship as *"une force inexplicable et fatale"* for ancient, true and noble friendship was Montaigne; *cf. Essays* 1, 27.

[35] *Eccl.* VI. 17.

[36] Abraham à Sancta Clara, *Aus dem handschriftlichen Nachlass* (Vienna: Akademie der Wissenschaften, 1945), Vol. 3, pp. 67–73.

anyone, compatriot or stranger, nobleman or commoner, his own brother or his wife. "Do not rely on privileged people, on kings, princes, or other great masters," he said. "For they are men, and all men are liars." "When I ponder the course of human affairs, I see that one often is in greater danger among false friends than among true enemies." Schupp's teaching is more rigorous than that of Jesus Sirach. The German pastor despairs of finding any friend among men. The father's best advice to his son is not to trust any neighbor but "to see above all that you have God for a friend."[37] Grimmelshausen's portrait of friendship denies the soundness of such teaching.

Conversion and Renunciation

After many adventures as a soldier, as a kind of Robin Hood, as an obliging young man rendering amorous service to some ladies in Paris, as a quack, and in many other roles, Simplicissimus unexpectedly encounters a madman in a church who shocks him into awareness of his sinful conduct. He is overcome by fright, confesses, and becomes a Catholic. Curiously enough, this conversion has no effect on his life. Immediately following his religious shock, he turns to new rogueries as though nothing had happened, or rather, as though his conversion was but another adventure.

Finally, however, weary of his wasted life, he resolves to become a hermit. Again, this withdrawal from the world is not Grimmelshausen's answer to the question of how to find peace for the human soul, although most critics have so interpreted the author's intent. Having taken a most eloquent farewell from his sinful life, in words borrowed from Antonio de Guevara, a Spanish Catholic moralist, Simplicissimus concludes the Fifth Book with this comment on his new life as a hermit: ". . . but whether I shall persevere in it, like my blessed father, remains to be seen."[38] These words are not Guevara's

---

[37] Johann Balthaser Schupp, *Der Freund in der Not* (Halle: 1878), pp. 10, 12, 48.
[38] *Simplicissimus,* p. 463.

but Grimmelshausen's. Could the author have been more forthright? Could there be a clearer warning to read the remaining books of the cycle before drawing the conclusion that Guevara's famous "Adieu, World," the sonorous renunciation of mundane affairs, tells us something unequivocally important about Simplicissimus or Grimmelshausen? It appears that the author's intention still "remains to be seen."

In the first chapter of the next book Simplicissimus admits to "thousand-fold temptation" in the beautiful Black Forest where he lives as a hermit. Instead of fasting he enjoys his food. He delights in the noble sight of Strasbourg in the midst of the country below him. He can see the spire of its cathedral through a telescope that he has taken along, and at night, with the help of another instrument that magnifies sound, he listens to the barking of the dogs far away and to the stirring of the deer in the woods nearby. How this hermit loves the world! Indeed, soon he ceases to work and pray and resumes his life of worldly adventure.

Toward the end of the Sixth Book, however, we find him once more withdrawn from the world, this time not by an act of his own free will, but in consequence of a shipwreck. The chapters describing Simplicissimus' life on a remote island represent one of the first true Robinsonades in modern European literature. It struck André Gide's fancy and made him wonder whether Defoe had been familiar with it.[39] Grimmelshausen was inspired to incorporate the fantastic story in his novel by a satire, *The Isle of Pines,* published in London in 1668; its author was Henry Neville.

Neville described the aftermath of a shipwreck that had allegedly taken place in 1589. Five persons, George Pine, an accountant, the fourteen-year-old daughter of his principal and three maids, including a Negro girl, were washed ashore on an isle rich in fruit, fish and fowl, water and palm wine. The good accountant had his pleasure first with one of the maids,

---

[39] André Gide, *Journal, 1939–1949* (Paris: Bibliothèque de la Pléiade, 1954). p. 69.

then with the other, then with the daughter of his principal
and finally with the Negro girl. When the captain of a Dutch
ship landed on the deserted island seventy-eight years later
the population had grown to 1789 persons. The tremendous
success of Neville's satire in Western Europe had little to
do with popular interest in the idyllic rebirth of civilization on
a faraway island. J. H. Scholte dryly remarked on the success
of Neville's satire, "Simple souls probably liked the idyl of the
Robinsonade. More sophisticated minds will have enjoyed the
persiflage of the biblical notion of original mankind . . . 'Pines'
stands almost too clearly as an anagram for 'penis.' It does not
appear that all translators realized this realistic root of the
story of population growth."[40] Probably Grimmelshausen was
clearly aware of this allusion as was Dryden, in whose *The
Kind Keeper* Pleasance says, " 'Tis a likely proper fellow, and
looks as he could people a new Isle of Pines."

Although Grimmelshausen stayed away from the theme of
the natural growth of population, he made liberal use of
Neville's satire in describing the island on which Simplicissimus finds himself stranded after his shipwreck. This fact alone
might have cautioned the critics not to read too much religious
meaning into his second withdrawal from the world. It is true
that Simplicissimus adorns the island with wooden crosses
and pious signs bearing quotations from the Scriptures, but
compared with his adventures in the world that he has left all
his activities on the island have an air of unreality and, indeed,
of theatricality about them. As one critic has remarked, the
hermitages of Simplicissimus exhaust themselves in "a pose
affecting piety."[41] Furthermore, on his island Simplicius the
hermit again leads anything but an ascetic life. The exotic
food and drink which he enjoys make the reader's mouth
water. Grimmelshausen had no illusions about it. In a later
work he refers to the island as "Lubberland."[42]

[40] *Grimmelshausens Simpliciana*, J. H. Scholte, editor (Halle: Max
Niemeyer, 1943), pp. xviii, xx.

[41] Gutzwiller, *op. cit.*, p. 70.

[42] *Simpliciana*, p. 18.

After fifteen years of devout and comfortable life in his solitary paradise Simplicissimus is discovered by a Dutch captain who tries to persuade him to return to civilization. Simplicissimus declines. He paints a vivid picture of the sinful life that Europeans lead in peacetime as well as in war. He contrasts the idyllic solitude of his island with the turmoils of the wicked world. But then he adds whimsically, with a twinkle in his eye, that everything else aside, were he to return from the island to Europe he might drown on the voyage. Apparently nothing is dearer to him than his life — a subject for despair but also for never-ending laughter.

In the later novels of the Simplician cycle Simplicissimus reappears merely as a minor figure. In *The Strange Skipinthefield,* after his return from the island he plays the unaccustomed role of a stern Christian who lives in peace with himself, his old foster parents and his illegitimate son. He urges his old comrade Skipinthefield, now a beggar and cripple seventy years of age, to abandon recklessness and swearing, and to prepare his soul for the hour of reckoning. The old rascal dies a Christian on Simplicissimus' farm. In this novel Simplicissimus is also eager to prove that his son is not the son of Courage, but of her maid: we learn that in his younger days Simplicissimus knew both of them at the same time. There are two other enigmatic incidents involving Simplicissimus. In one of them we see him in a market place making money by turning poor and sour wine into good wine. And in a most remarkable conversation Simplicissimus argues that man ought to weep about his sins rather than laugh about his folly, since the Scriptures do not report that Christ had ever laughed.[43]

---

[43] Grimmelshausen probably took this argument, directly or indirectly, from Thomas More. "In the thirteenth chapter of his *Dialogue of Comfort against Tribulation* More says: 'And for to prove that this life is no laughing time, but rather the time of weeping, we find that our saviour himself wept twice or thrice, but never find we that he laughed so much as once. I will not swear that he never did, but at least wise he left us no example of it. But, on the other side, he left us example of weeping.' More must have known that exactly the opposite is true of Plato's—or Xenophon's—Socrates: Socrates left us no example of

This lecture is immediately followed by a joke so obscene that Simplicissimus' listeners shake with laughter. The only man in all of Grimmelshausen's writings of whom it is pointedly said that he does not like to be laughed at, is Jove, the madman who plays God.

Grimmelshausen was a great satirist who made people laugh at human folly committed in a wretched and exhilarating world in which everything will soon be different. And God? On his island Simplicissimus calls him "a dark light," an expression which a learned critic has taken as proof of Grimmelshausen's leaning toward Cusanus and his doctrine that opposites coincide. But the profoundly equivocal "dark light" — *das finstere Licht* — cannot be compared with the contrary image of radiant light that ever since St. Augustine and Dionysius the Areopagite has been the symbol of God in Christian writing. "He who knoweth the truth knoweth that Light: and who knoweth it, knoweth eternity."[44] Grimmelshausen's "dark light" has nothing in common with Dante's Light Eternal that loves and smiles[45] or with Gryphius' image: "God, light dwelling in the light" — *Gott, der licht in licht wohnhafftig.*[46] Andreas Gryphius was a deeply religious man. Was Grimmelshausen? Was he a believer? Or was the hidden "truth" of his work that God is wrapped in darkness? He surely believed in the fickleness of fortune, in transformation, in chance. We cannot be certain that he believed in God. His genius, sustained by folklore and proverbs, created an image of himself which to this day has remained ambiguous: Simplicissimus, the most simple man, a fool who likes food and undiluted wine and adventure; a natural man pitting his wits against misfortune,

---

weeping, but on the other side, he left us example of laughing. The relation of weeping and laughing is similar to that of tragedy and comedy. We may therefore say that the Socratic conversation and hence the Platonic dialogue is slightly more akin to comedy than to tragedy." Leo Strauss, *The City and Man*, (Chicago: Rand McNally and Company, 1964), p. 61.

[44] St. Augustine, *Confessions*, Bk. VII, Cap. X.

[45] Dante, *Paradiso*, XXXII, 124–126.

[46] Gryphius, Sonnets III, 3; *op. cit.*, p. 99.

bored by theological disputations, but always ready to tell a good story. He spoke the language of the common people, but for that was no less admired by duchesses like Sophie of Hanover, and philosophers like Leibniz. His heart was heavy from the cruelty of life, but lightened by folly and by the song of the nightingale. Grimmelshausen's laughter reverberates through the centuries — lusty, grim, and sometimes blasphemous.

Grimmelshausen explicitly said that anyone who failed to read all ten books of the Simplician cycle of novels could not hope to grasp the truth hidden in Simplicissimus. The last great novella of the cycle, and probably the last story the author ever wrote, almost certainly is a satire of the Christian belief in the immaculate conception of the Virgin Mary.[47]

[47] Translated into English under the title, *The False Messiah. Cf.* footnote 1. This novella is discussed in Chapter 16.

CHAPTER FIFTEEN

Courage, the Adventuress

THE FIRST of four sequels to *The Adventurous Simplicissimus* in Grimmelshausen's so-called Simplician cycle of novels consists of the confessions of a camp follower in the Thirty Years War. This book, *Courage, the Adventuress*, was published in 1670.

Courage, a woman more adventurous, more evil, and considerably more interesting than Defoe's Moll Flanders or Brecht's Mother Courage, is introduced to the reader first in a minor episode of *The Adventurous Simplicissimus*, when the hero, at a watering place in the Black Forest, meets a lady who pretends to be a noblewoman. He is attracted by her, but soon she strikes him as "more mobile than noble,"[1] since for due payment she readily grants him the favors he seeks. Finally he

Condensed from "A Woman Named Courage," Ch. 8 of *The Arts in Society*, Robert N. Wilson, editor (Englewood Cliffs, New Jersey: Prentice-Hall, Inc., 1964). A shortened version of "A Woman Named Courage" appeared in the "Introduction" to my translation of Grimmelshausen's *Courage, the Adventuress and The False Messiah*, Princeton University Press, Princeton, New Jersey, 1964. In a personal communication dated August 22, 1964, Eric Bentley took exception to my comments on the meaning of the name Courage in Bertolt Brecht's play *Mother Courage*. In response to this criticism, the passage dealing with the name of Brecht's famous character (p. 274 below) has been slightly enlarged.

[1] *Grimmelshausens Simplicissimus Teutsch*, J. H. Scholte, editor (Tübingen: Max Niemeyer, 1954), Vol. 5, Ch. 6 (hereinafter cited as *Simplicissimus*).

leaves her to marry a young peasant girl. Not long thereafter he finds a newborn son of his abandoned on his doorstep.

Courage, the Adventuress, is the autobiography of the wily harlot whom Simplicissimus met at the watering place. She discloses her whole adventurous and dissolute life allegedly for the sole purpose of taking revenge on her lover, for she has never forgiven him (although her name was not mentioned in his tale). The original German title of her story begins with the words *"Trutz Simplex . . ."* ("To Spite Simplex . . ."), Simplex being a short colloquial version of the name Simplicius Simplicissimus.

The Wild Virago

On the title page of *Courage, the Adventuress,* Grimmelshausen indicates that in this novel the reader will find the account of a descending life. As a young woman, Courage is the wife of a cavalry captain, then she marries a captain of foot soldiers, then a lieutenant, thereafter she becomes a sutler woman, next the wife of a musketeer, and finally a gypsy.

Different from the heroes of the picaresque novel, who proceed from one adventure to the next without change in character, Courage does change under the influence of experiences. In the early part of the novel she is not the evil woman into which she later turns. To be sure, in part it is her native endowment that makes her a lustful creature, envious, greedy, and vindictive, but in part the evil in her emerges from senseless misfortune and in response to the cruelty of men.

Courage's exploits equal or excel those of men. In battle she is more valiant than her male companions, on a marauding expedition more daring, as a thief more resourceful and cunning. In most of her enterprises she is mistress, rather than helper; often she directs men to assist her. Her vitality is inexhaustible. When at the end of her career she has reached the status of an outcast, she remains a queen, if only of the gypsies, aged, but still beautiful in appearance, her spirit unbroken and her skill unrivaled.

Whenever she fights men, whether with her fists as a young girl, with sword and pistol in battle later, with a cudgel after one of her many wedding nights, with a knife in the woods, or with wit, false tears, and pretty words — she almost always wins. Almost without exception men who oppose her are beaten up or humiliated, taken prisoner, killed, duped, or exploited by her. Courage is as much an Amazon as a harlot.

Indeed, she has many of the qualities of the heroines in the idealistic novels of the baroque era. Like them, she is a manlike, vigorous creature, a virago in the sense in which Pope still used this word:

> To arms! to arms! the fierce virago cries,
> And swift as lightening to the combate flies.

The virago was an ideal of the Renaissance, fashioned after illustrious ancient models. Viragos appear not only in Ariosto's and Bojardo's heroic poetry, but also in life: women like Caterina Sforza — *"prima donna d'Italia"* to her contemporaries — or Isabella d'Este, the wife of Marchese Francesco Gonzaga, were admired for both their beauty and their courage in meeting the formidable risks of their careers.[2] The third book of Castiglione's *Cortegiano* contains the portrait of the perfect lady at court and the Renaissance tribute to the civilizing influence that women exerted on men, but it also presents many great ladies in contemporary Italy, as well as in antiquity, who showed "virtue and prowess" in "the stormes of fortune."[3]

In the German idealistic novel of the seventeenth century, this Renaissance ideal is still potent: many heroines are Amazons.[4] Even the middle-class Protestant, Andreas Heinrich Buchholtz, shows Valisca, his heroine, to be the equal of man in the fields of science and music, as well as in battle. Disguised

[2] Jacob Burckhardt, *Die Kultur der Renaissance in Italien,* 14th ed., Walter Goetz, editor (Leipzig: Kröner Verlag, 1925), p. 271.

[3] Baldassare Castiglione, *The Book of the Courtier,* Done into English by Sir Thomas Hoby, anno. 1561, Everyman's Library, p. 218.

[4] For the following discussion, cf. Antoine Claire Jungkunz, *Menschendarstellung im deutschen höfischen Roman des Barock* (Berlin: Germanische Studien, 1937), pp. 42, 78–90, 189, 220.

as a beautiful young man on a journey to Prague, she "does miracles" fighting off the highwaymen who assault her. At the Persian court, again in men's clothing, she shines in the arts of fencing and shooting with bow and arrow. She cruelly kills three Persian servants, defends her honor against the attack of a lover by thrusting her "breadknife" into his heart, and slays robbers with lightning speed. She fights gloriously as a general in battle, her beautiful hair falling down to her shoulders, a precious sword and a quiver of arrows at her side. In Buchholtz's novel, not only is Valisca a virago, but also Herkules himself has female qualities: for all his manliness, he is beautiful like a young girl, dances daintily, and sometimes fights clad in the garb of an Amazon.

Viragos appear also in the novels of Anton Ulrich and D. C. von Lohenstein. Anton Ulrich's Aramena is a royal personage and hence, on the whole, dignified rather than heroic: the wisest and most learned men seek her company even in her childhood in order to converse with her "about the most difficult things." And yet, the author shows her also as a warrior going to battle, with an expression "as majestic as benevolent, and as sensible as pious." At one time, she goes to the field leading a group of her female court attendants, "a marvelous host of the most beautiful ladies in the world."

But the most extraordinary viragos were created by Lohenstein. His princesses, Thusnelda, Ismene, and Erato are all fighting, duelling Amazons. Lohenstein uses the generally favored technique of showing an unidentified cavalier triumphant in extreme danger, without revealing at first that it is a woman who behaves so heroically. Then he lets the reader share the thrill of the loving hero at discovering that it is a beautiful woman, an Amazon, that has aroused his admiration.

"Amazon" is a word reserved in all these books for use in bestowing the highest possible praise upon a woman. Lohenstein gave this description of Thusnelda through the eyes of Marbod, who loves her:

The day before Marbod had looked admiringly at Thusnelda only [!] as a woman, but this day he saw her on horseback as a valiant heroine. He had honored her as a half-divine being, now he was compelled to worship her as a goddess, for she sat astride her horse as a true amazon; in the race and in the shooting contest she did better than all, and she slew twice as much game as anyone else. For no stag was too swift for her, no bear too cruel, no lynx too terrible.[5]

Anton Ulrich's second great novel, *Die Römische Oktavia,* H. A. von Zigler's *Asiatische Banise,* and Philipp von Zesen's novels do not present anything comparable: the Amazon motif recedes in these works. So it does in the writings of Johann Beer, whose realistic tales abandon the heroic, idealistic mood and discover new subjects of everyday life for literary treatment. But even in Beer's works Amazons do reappear, though with less bombast and fanfare. For example, in one of Beer's major works "a strange cavalier," his visor closed, suddenly appears to help the noble friends who fight the villain and his evil companions. The stranger wounds and captures the wicked man, and when the friends, rejoicing about their victory, want to thank the stranger, he lifts his visor. Then, the friends all grow pale. They behold "the beautiful Amalia, disguised in knightly armor." Needless to say, beautiful Amalia is loved by one of the cavaliers whose valor she excelled so impressively in the fight.[6]

If the modern reader is amused by all of this theatrical display of heroism, just as he might be amused by the theatricality of the heroes and heroines in distress — when they pray with tears streaming down their cheeks or lift their eyes up to the Heavenly Father in martyrdom — he is in a mood which Grimmelshausen seems to have shared. For Courage is at least as much a caricature and mockery of the Amazons to be found in the conventional baroque novel as she is a picaresque character. Her relation to the ideal virago resembles that of Don Quixote to the knightly code. Like the once much-admired ladies who populate the idealistic novel, Courage is an Amazon, but as a

[5] Quoted in *op. cit.,* p. 88.

[6] Johann Beer, *Kurtzweilige Sommer-Täge,* 1683, Wolfgang Schmidt, editor (Halle: Max Niemeyer, 1958), p. 116.

counter-heroine. She displays the qualities of a wild virago, in the modern sense of that term, while still retaining all the physical features of the ideal, in particular radiant beauty, physical prowess, and manlike energy. Like the Amazons in the conventional novel, she is also highly intelligent and indestructible in trial and misfortune. But in three respects she is a counter-heroine.

First, despite her noble, if somewhat tainted, origin, she moves in a socially undistinguished milieu, resembling in this regard all of Grimmelshausen's main characters. She is never at court, and when she meets an ambassador, spends some short time at a nobleman's castle, or lives for a while like a woman of means in town, it is for her sexual enjoyment and the amassing of a fortune.

Second, it is not virtues that are put to test after test in Courage's life, as is true of the heroic careers in the conventional novel. If anything is tried, it is her ability to survive as a victim of a blind and impenetrable destiny. A plaything of senseless fate, which tosses her up and down in quick and violent motion. Courage is flung back and forth from the heights of prosperity to the depths of poverty, from health and beauty to disfiguring illness, from safety and comfort to hunger and humiliation. Thus, in Chapter 11 of her story, we find her happily married and prosperous; then her husband is killed in the war — an event told in one sentence. In the next chapter she is captured by the enemy, and a fiendish, revengeful officer thrusts her into an abyss of rape and sadistic torture. At the end of this chapter a very young nobleman rescues her, and she is treated like a little princess in his castle, but before long, some servants of the young nobleman's parents abduct her under false pretenses. Expecting to be married by her noble lover in Hamburg, she is abandoned and threatened with murder. In the meantime, all her savings, too, have been lost. So again, within the confines of a single chapter, the princess turns into a woman forced to earn her living at night. Pitting her wit and vitality against misfortune, she becomes in the end an outcast, because neither man nor woman can win in a world which is more surely of the devil than of God: God is silent. But she survives and, like Simplicissimus, lives forever.

Finally, by all ordinary standards of Christian morality, which Grimmelshausen himself reasserts continuously, if only in the interstices of his tale, Courage is corrupt and wicked, whereas the heroines of the idealistic novel remain of untarnished virtue, no matter how often and how cruelly this virtue is put into thrilling jeopardy. Courage does not want to be virtuous. She has wild, insatiable appetites for men and riches, but no conscience. Her moral character owes nothing either to religious teaching or to Descartes' theory of passion, but almost everything to Galen's views of the human temperaments. "I cannot take out my gall," she says, "as the butcher turns the pig's stomach inside out to cleanse it." She is full of lust and avarice and envy, and most easily aroused to fierce anger; she is evil, although it should be stressed that she never inflicts pain on others without provocation. But she is natural, and this cannot be said of the heroines whose Christian conscience she in fact defies and denies with every fiber of her existence.

Revenge

It was not Grimmelshausen's main intention in *Courage, the Adventuress*, to parody the conventional literary motif of the Amazon. While he succeeded in doing that, he had a still more important purpose in mind. Nor did he primarily want to show the corrupting influence of a long war on human character,[7] since the fact that life is corrupt had more weight with him than the fact that war is corrupting. Grimmelshausen stated his intention clearly through the mouth of Courage in the grand opening chapter of the novel. There Courage explains why she

[7] This is G. Weydt's view of Grimmelshausen in his monograph, "Der deutsche Roman vom 15. bis 17. Jahrhundert," *Deutsche Philologie im Aufriss*, 2nd ed., Wolfgang Stammler, editor (Berlin: E. Schmidt, 1952), Vol. 2, p. 1256. This study is perhaps the best modern introduction to the history of the picaresque novel and Grimmelshausen's place in it.

has decided to tell the story of her shameful, adventurous life. The sole motive of her confession, she says, is revenge. She wants to avenge herself on Simplicissimus, one of her many lovers, who had spoken ill of her. She laughs derisively at the idea that her monstrous confession might be taken as an act of penitence: her vengefulness involves not only Simplicissimus, but God himself. She defies both.

Her soul is entirely untroubled by the dissolute life she has led. If she confesses anything it is her godlessness. She fears God as little as men. She loves life and is not afraid of death. Thoughts of punishment and damnation, of divine justice and hell-fire, never curb her worldly passion. She loves money but not her neighbors, and she says so. Her life is exuberantly evil. Nature has made her so, and neither the magistrate nor the priests, neither man nor God, is able to change it. By telling her story in order to avenge herself, she makes a mockery of the act of confession in the Christian sense.

Courage's spite and revengefulness are aroused by small provocations. At one time she avenges herself on a young woman merely because in church a gallant pays more attention to this lady than to her. At another time she believes that someone has played a practical joke on her, and her fury knows no bounds. When her competitors make some gains which she thinks would be hers, if it were not for them, she must "repay" them. When she fears that one of her lovers may be influenced by his drinking companions to get hold of her money and wrest from her the power that she wields over him, she bides her time to rid herself of him and gives him a magical bauble as a good-bye present that nearly sends him straight into hell.

She knows herself perfectly well: "I stole not from necessity or want, but mostly in order to avenge myself on those I found hateful."[8] And again, "My heart was vengeful and unrelenting whenever I felt that the least offense or wrong had been done to me."[9] The intensity of her feeling is conveyed by Grimmels-

---

[8] *Grimmelshausens Courasche*, J. H. Scholte, editor (Halle: Max Niemeyer, 1923), Ch. 20 (hereafter cited as *Courage*).
[9] *Ibid.*

hausen not only by a whole series of rogueries in which revenge is the main motive but also, with startling force, by Courage's observation that her heart is like her body: when hurt, it takes a long time to heal.

Nor is the motive of revenge merely a trait of Courage's character. It reappears in other characters of the novel and in other works of Grimmelshausen. One of the officers whom Courage has taken prisoner happens to capture her some time later in battle. Not because he is attracted to her, but merely in order to avenge his humiliation of having been captured by her, a woman, he abuses her sexually and encourages other men to do the same. He acts in furious rage rather than under the impulse of unbridled sexual desires, and so his hatred and inability to forget the injury that was once inflicted upon him lead to the most brutally sadistic scene of the novel.

There are many other incidents in the Simplician writings which suggest Grimmelshausen's preoccupation with brutal revenge. The young Simplicius almost becomes the victim of a terribly vengeful man who is his master. Disguised as a girl, he arouses the sexual appetites of three persons at once, his master, his master's wife, and his master's servant. When the master believes that the servant is more successful in his advances than he has been, he immediately calls Simplicius "a bloody whore" and turns "her" over to the stable boys for sexual abuse. The master acts according to a maxim whose truth seems to have been so self-evident to Grimmelshausen, and possibly to many of his readers, that he treated it casually, like a proverb. As Simplicissimus puts it, when he is disappointed by the character of his second wife, "since I found myself so betrayed, I thought to betray the traitress."[10]

The Strange Skipinthefield, the eighth book of the Simplician cycle of novels, is written so that Simplicissimus and his old comrade will get even again with the spiteful harlot, and *The Enchanted Bird's-Nest,* Part II, the last book of the cycle, contains a novella on the theme of revenge.

[10] *Simplicissimus,* V, Ch. 8.

Grimmelshausen's interest in the subject is so intense and abiding that one begins to wonder whether he himself was a vengeful man. Given the sorry state of information on the author's life, it is impossible to be sure. Furthermore, we do not know how much to attribute to the torture of Grimmelshausen's soul and how much to the tradition which required of him as a satirical writer that he present and condemn pride and envy and anger as well as all other vices. So we are left with a surmise.

It seems that Grimmelshausen was proud of his aristocratic origin and struggled, not too successfully, for recognition as an author among members of the higher aristocracy. He never stooped to the obsequious deference that other writers paid their betters for patronage. It is almost certain that he took literary revenge on a wealthy physician in the vicious portrait he painted of Dr. Canard in *The Adventurous Simplicissimus*. He seems to have resented the criticism of literati who, more erudite than himself, found his work wanting in style and taste. Grimmelshausen struck back at them in his works and seems to have avoided their company.

There is, finally, another seemingly trivial point that needs to be made in this connection. It is known that Grimmelshausen was derisively called "the red steward" (*"der rote Schaffner"*) by a colleague in the employ of the Schauenburg family. Grimmelshausen had red hair, which according to a very old and widespread superstition was regarded as a sign of evil character. Since superstition holds especially the lower classes of society in its grip, it is likely that Grimmelshausen was exposed to the full force of this prejudice in the army camps and taverns, the countryside and villages, where he spent most of his life.

Already Martial had said that Zoilus was to be avoided because of the red color of his hair; the Latin satirist held red hair to be as bad a portent as a club foot.[11] In Christian civiliza-

---

[11] *Crine ruber, niger ore, brevis pede, lumine laesus, rem magnam praestas, Zoile, si bonus es.* Of red hair, swarthy of face, short of foot, of

tion, red hair was ascribed to Judas and the devil. In German proverbs the red-haired are knaves marked by God.[12] A Russian proverb says, "There never has been a red-haired saint,"[13] and a Spanish proverb, "Red hair on the head — treachery in the soul."[14] Commenting on this proverb, Werner Krauss mentions a sixteenth-century collection of anecdotes which contains the story of a man who was flogged because of a miscarriage of justice. When the judge noticed the error he remarked, "If he has not committed his crime, he is going to do so, since he has red hair."[15]

In Quevedo's *Historia de la vida del Buscon*, 1626, the despicable Cabra, a clergyman who is "generous only in height," has red hair, and the author adds significantly, "Need anything further be said?"[16] In Philips von Zesen's *Simson*, 1679, the hero's evil father-in-law has red hair,[17] and in H. A. von Zigler's *Die asiatische Banise*, 1668, Prince Balacin says of reddish hair that it betrays not infrequently evil intentions.[18]

Perhaps, it is not only a literary curiosity, but a psychologically significant fact, that Grimmelshausen wrote a grimly humorous pamphlet in defense of red beards, *Bart-Krieg* ("The War of Beards").[19] It contains further evidence, drawn from

---

eye blear, you show yourself to be a portent, Zoilus, if you are virtuous. (Martial, *Epigrams*, Vol. 2, XII. 45. [Loeb Classical Library, p. 356].)

[12] Friedrich Seiler, *Deutsche Sprichwörterkunde* (Munich: C. H. Becksche Verlagsbuchhandlung, 1922), pp. 401–402.

[13] Andrew Guerschron, *Certain Aspects of Russian Proverbs* (London: F. Muller Ltd., 1941), p. 155; see also Iwan Klimenko, *Das russische Sprichwort* (Bern: A. Francke, 1946), p. 27.

[14] Werner Krauss, *Die Welt im spanischen Sprichwort* (Wiesbaden: Limes Verlag, 1946), p. 45.

[15] *Ibid.*, p. 53.

[16] Francisco de Quevedo, *op. cit.*, p. 94.

[17] Cf. Jungkunz, *op. cit.*, p. 37.

[18] *Ibid.*, p. 75.

[19] The title of Grimmelshausen's pamphlet is "Bart-Krieg." Grimmelshausen's authorship of this pamphlet was proved only in 1940 by Manfred Koeschlig, "Der Bart-Krieg—Ein Werk Grimmelshausens," *Neophilologus*, Vol. 34 (1938–1939), pp. 42 ff. "Der Bart-Krieg" is included in *Grimmelshausens Simpliciana*, J. H. Scholte, editor (Halle: Max Niemeyer, 1943), pp. 128–148.

proverbs and other sources, on the prejudice from which he seems to have suffered, and an attack on the "physiognomists" who infer moral qualities from physical characteristics. As was his habit, Grimmelshausen took much of his historical material — for example, on Martial — and some of his arguments from Garzoni, but this makes the choice of subject no less significant.

At least one perceptive literary historian, Walther Muschg, has suggested that Grimmelshausen must have regarded his red hair as a misfortune, since he wrote his "The War of Beards" in defense of the red-haired.[20] Muschg has mentioned in this connection a number of writers who may have felt their physical deformity as a stigma; their work may have been influenced by the cripple's hatred of the healthy and by feelings fluctuating between "horror of themselves, extreme sensitivity and cynical conceit." He points out that "many great satirists and polemicists had such a stigma."[21] Excluding from Muschg's list those writers who were repulsively ugly, there remain the cripples: Aesop, Thomas Murner, Scarron, Pope, Lichtenberg, Gottfried Keller, Kierkegaard. The name of Quevedo may be added: he was lame.

The Naming of Courage

Many characters appearing in Grimmelshausen's novels have significant names that are changed often. The development of Simplicissimus toward manhood is marked by various names, each appropriate to the respective stage of his career: "boy," Simplicius, "the Calf," Simplicius Simplicissimus, the Huntsman, Beau Alman; in the end he remains forever Simplicissimus, the most simple man. The meaning of the name Heartsbrother, Simplicissimus' friend, is apparent.

The extraordinary marriage contract between Courage and the musketeer who later is named "Skipinthefield" contains the stipulation that her husband answer forever to a name to be

[20] Walther Muschg, *Tragische Literaturgeschichte* (Bern: A. Francke, 1948), pp. 265–266.
[21] *Ibid.*

derived from the first command she gives him. Courage orders him to "skip into the field" so that in his absence she can enjoy herself with another man.[22]

These and other instances of significant names in Grimmelshausen's work are well known, but the shocking double meaning of two names has been overlooked. One occurs in the story of the false Jewish Messiah, Grimmelshausen's greatest novella (see p. 307 below),[23] the other in the story of Courage.

In *Courage, the Adventuress,* Libuschka (the young girl), while dressed like a boy, is called Janco. In her adolescence she acquires the name Courage. Grimmelshausen's account of the naming of the great harlot is both daring and masterful. While Janco, the girl in boy's clothing, is a captain's servant, she gets into a fight with another boy at the sutler's. "When we were in the thick of it," she says, "this fellow grabbed me between the legs, because he wanted to get hold of my tool that I did not have." She prevails over him. Later in his quarters the captain asks Janco, whom he still takes for a boy, why she had beaten up her opponent so terribly. She replies, "Because he tried to grasp my courage which no other man has ever touched with his hand."[24] Then she confides in the young captain that she is a girl who disguised herself as a boy merely to escape abuse by the soldiers. She begs him to protect her honor, and he promises to do so but to her delight does not keep his word.

When the captain understands the meaning of the word "courage," with which the girl had "so colorfully described the emblem of her sex," he cannot help laughing at her and calls her Courage. Try as she will to rid herself of that name, it clings to her forever. Perhaps an important detail should be added here. In the story of her life the reminiscing woman explains that she used the word "courage" in her talk with the captain for reasons of seemliness: she wanted to avoid using a lewd

[22] *Courage,* Ch. 15.

[23] This novella is part of *Des wunderbarlichen Vogelnests zweiter Teil,* in *Grimmelshausens Werke,* H. H. Borcherdt, editor (Berlin, Leipzig, Vienna, Stuttgart: Deutsches Verlagshaus Bong & Co., 1921), hereafter cited as *Bird's-Nest II,* taking up nine of its twenty-seven chapters.

[24] *Courage,* Ch. 3.

word that would have hinted without sense of shame at her *female* sex organ. The name "Courage," then, stands for what Grimmelshausen regarded as the physiological site of vitality, bravery, and godlessness.

Grimmelshausen's choice of Courage as a picaresque character for one of his main works invites some further speculation. Today, it is considered unlikely that *Courage, the Adventuress* owes much to Francisco de Ubeda's *Picara Justina* (1603), although Grimmelshausen may have been familiar with the longwinded German translation of that work. Ubeda's novel was an avowed imitation of *The Celestina* (1449)[25] and other picaresque Spanish tales, whereas Grimmelshausen's *Courage*, like *The Celestina*, is a masterpiece in its own right. Even if there were close dependence on *Picara Justina*, however, the question would still remain why Grimmelshausen's imagination was captured by a female picaro. Why did he, despite all his ostensible contempt for love and women, create such an extraordinarily vivid picture of a manly woman whose beauty and vitality excelled the evil in her? No one who has read the sequel to *The Adventurous Simplicissimus* will escape the conclusion that Grimmelshausen was fascinated by Courage. He admired her.[26] While condemning sex in all his writings, in this novel he managed to present at the same time the portrait of an irresistible woman, who after she has been abused by men, reacts with lusty sexual abandon and revenge and yet remains human and powerful.

[25] There are several English translations of *Tragi-Comedia de Calisto y Melibar,* popularly known as *The Celestina* (after the character of the procuress in the play), including one by Lesley Byrd Simpson (Berkeley and Los Angeles: University of California Press, 1955, paperbound edition, 1959).

[26] The point that Grimmelshausen admired Courage is also made by Siegfried Streller, *Grimmelshausens Simplicianische Schriften* ([East] Berlin: Rütten & Loening, 1957), p. 195. Streller speaks of Grimmelshausen's "unconfessed sympathies for this hated and loved character" and refers to the magnificent description of Courage (then already sixty-six years old) by the Swiss clerk in *Grimmelshausens Springinsfield,* J. H. Scholte, editor (Halle: Max Niemeyer, 1928), Ch. 4 (hereafter cited as *Skipinthefield*).

Let us pursue this subject one step further. Courage is a tomboy in her youth and by force of circumstances passes for a boy. Later she repeatedly speaks of her burning desire to wear men's clothing and to be in every way like a man. As a grown woman she remains barren, and she behaves like a man not only in battle and as a forager, but also in some of her marriages. At one time she establishes superiority over her husband after the wedding night in a physical fight with him. In her relations with Skipinthefield, the social sex roles are completely and formally reversed.

It is striking that both Simplicius and Courage have their first sexual experiences in homosexual situations. It also appears that Grimmelshausen had a keen interest in hermaphrodites and in the changing of sex. References to hermaphrodites occur in several of his works.[27]

Finally, there is a most curious description of Skipinthefield's distress shortly before the blasphemous marriage arrangement is made. Tortured by his love for Courage, Skipinthefield enters the woman's tent under the pretense of wanting a pot of wine. Grimmelshausen describes his appearance as seen through Courage's eyes as follows: "He looked so pale and disconsolate then as though he had just gotten a child without having or knowing its father, and without having either milk or meal-pap for it."[28] This sentence is strangely ambiguous. The musketeer cannot be imagined to have given birth to a child, but if his appearance resembled that of a *father* who is pale and disconsolate merely because he has no means of feeding his newborn child, why does Grimmelshausen associate the misery of the man with the absence of a father, rather than a mother? It is just possible that the ambiguity is intended to suggest Courage's feeling toward the musketeer, who is so weakened

[27] *Bird's-Nest II*, Ch. 18. Cf. also the story of Aemilia, who after twelve years of marriage changes her sex and becomes Aemilius (Grimmelshausen's *Ewigwährender Kalender*, Engelbert Hegaur, editor [Munich: Albert Langen Verlag, 1925], pp. 396–397).

[28] Er "sahe so bleich und trostloss aus/ als wann er kürtzlich ein Kind bekommen/ und keinen Vatter/ Meel noch Milch darzu gehabt oder gewüst hätte." (*Courage,* Ch. 15).

by his love that he appears contemptibly womanish to her. Or else we are left with the possibility that the sentence contains a slip of the pen. (Taken as such, it does not carry the weight of the curious birth certificate of Herman Melville's son, on which the writer entered his name and, by mistake, that of his own mother as parents of the child,[29] but the description of the poor musketeer's condition remains strangely ambiguous.)

Along with everything else that has been said, the strange sentence might lend support to the suggestion that Grimmelshausen had ambivalent feelings toward women and sex. Perhaps he felt even dimly anxious or uncertain about his own sexual wishes. In his fantasies, "the red steward" may have come close to identifying himself with this golden haired Amazon who defied God.[30]

But these are speculations. There are few baroque authors who do not invite similar speculations. In many conventional baroque novels, as in comedy and farce, disguise and confusion of the sexes are common. Homosexual allusions are far more prominent in Callot's engravings than in Grimmelshausen's Simplician writings, and other writers of the period were intrigued by homosexuality as well.

Harsdörffer shared Grimmelshausen's interest in hermaphrodites. The Catholic convert Anton Ulrich was much concerned with incest as an involvement that puts virtue to a thrilling test. In one of Lohenstein's tragedies a corpse is unearthed and covered with passionate kisses. About Buchholtz it has been said that while "the Christian element, which he strongly emphasizes is for him identical with the world of superintendents and *Konsistorialräte* from which he sprang," his scenes of martyrdom are so depicted that before the imagination of this

---

[29] Henry A. Murray in his introduction to Herman Melville's *Pierre* (New York: Farrar, Strauss & Cudahy, Inc., 1949), note, p. xxxvii.

[30] Courage has blond hair (*Skipinthefield*, Ch. 4). So do the heroines in the conventional baroque novels, even if they are of Roman or oriental descent. This shade of hair, also to be found on women painted by Rubens, signifies the purity of the heroine, a convention that dates back to the Greek erotic novel and to Greek and Roman lyrical poetry. (Cf. Jungkunz, *op. cit.*, p. 33.)

conciliatory and mild man "the fantasy of the Marquis de Sade fades into paleness.[31] Buchholtz presented the relations between man and woman so crudely that only a few years after the publication of his novels he had to be defended against the accusation of pornography.[32]

Grimmelshausen and Bertolt Brecht

To the modern reader Bertolt Brecht's *Mother Courage and Her Children,* written in 1939 and first published in English in 1941, is better known than Grimmelshausen's Simplician novels, from which Brecht took the milieu of the Thirty Years War for his play and the name of its main character. But Brecht's play has very little to do with *Courage, the Adventuress* or, for that matter, with *The Adventurous Simplicissimus.*

In Brecht's play the main character is Anna Fierling, a mother of three illegitimate children whom she loses one by one in the cruel war. The name Courage clings to her because she keeps trying to make a miserable living by pulling her cart and selling her wares to the soldiers, although misfortune after misfortune befalls her. In a sense, her name is that of all those downtrodden but undaunted who go on living despite their misery. "The way you run your business and always come through," says the chaplain in the play, "is highly commendable, Mother Courage — I see how you got your name." To which Mother Courage replies,

> The poor need courage. Why? They're lost. That they even get up in the morning is something — in *their* plight. Or that they plow a field — in war time. Even their bringing children into the world shows they have courage, for they have no prospects. They have to hang each other one by one and slaughter each other in the lump, so if they want to look each other in the face once in a while, well, it takes courage. That they put up with an

[31] Curt von Faber du Faur, *German Baroque Literature. A Catalogue of the Collection in the Yale University Library* (New Haven: Yale University Press, 1958), p. 213.

[32] Paul Hankamer, *Deutsche Gegenreformation und deutsches Barock,* 2nd ed. (Stuttgart: I. B. Metzler, 1947), p. 418.

Emperor and a Pope, that takes an unnatural amount of courage, for they cost you your life.[33]

If courage is viewed as a martial virtue, Mother Courage is an ironical name; but since otherwise anyone who stands up to adversity and risks his life in his fight for a livelihood may indeed be called brave, Anna Fierling justly answers to the name Mother Courage. In the first scene of the play she says that she is called Courage because once she drove her cart with fifty loaves of bread through gunfire because she feared to lose her possessions.

Mother Courage was to teach the spectator that a woman who carries on her trade despite the loss of her three children and continues to try in this way to profit from war deserves no sympathy. Brecht wanted the spectator to be indignant about Mother Courage rather than feel compassion for her suffering.[34] He blamed lack of political comprehension on the part of his audiences, both in Zurich, where his play was first performed in 1946, and in East Berlin in 1949, for the misunderstanding of his propaganda. In his *Versuche* he noted that unlike his audiences he was not interested in the "moving vitality of the mother-animal," and had only scorn for those who took pity on Mother Courage as a modern Niobe.[35] He wanted her to be understood as "a hyena of the battlefield." The success the play had must therefore be attributed to a misunderstanding on the part of the audience and to the author's failure to express his intention clearly: the play aroused sentiments among the spectators which he condemned (although he might have shared them).

Communist authorities in the Soviet Zone of Germany proposed to Brecht that he add a speech by Mother Courage to the play in which she would admit her error and announce her res-

[33] Bertolt Brecht, *Mother Courage and Her Children: A Chronicle of the Thirty Years' War* (New York: Grove Press, Inc., 1963), pp. 75–76. English version by Eric Bentley. Copyright 1955, 1959, 1961, 1962, 1963, by Eric Bentley.
[34] Martin Esslin, *Brecht* (Frankfurt am Main and Bonn: Athenäum Verlag, 1962), pp. 312ff.
[35] *Op. cit.*, p. 314.

olution to fight all warmongers from now on. Brecht did not make these changes, but he made others in order to stress what he considered to be the negative qualities of Mother Courage's character; nevertheless, he failed.

Grimmelshausen and Brecht only seem to talk about the same historic events in their works. Grimmelshausen knew the Thirty Years War from his own experience. *The Adventurous Simplicissimus* was published more than twenty years after the long war had run its course. Brecht wrote *Mother Courage* about twenty years after the end of World War I in which he had taken part as a medic in 1918. His experiences at the age of twenty in an army hospital in Augsburg shocked him deeply and inspired some of his most powerful antiwar ballads in the early twenties. Two decades later, in *Mother Courage,* Brecht expressed no more and no less than the views of war held by young German left-wing intellectuals in the early years of the Weimar Republic.

This is particularly true of the notion that the underprivileged are exploited by the military class and that the members of that class prefer war to peace. For example, in the opening scene of the play the sergeant utters opinions that sound distinctly, if anachronistically, like the militaristic views attributed by the political left to the Prussian officers' corps in the Kaiser Reich. "Peace, that is merely a mess, war makes for order."[36] Similarly, later in the play, the chaplain speaks of the "final victory," the *"Endsieg,"*[37] a word that in German has the ring of World War I political usage.

Brecht presented the wretched life of Mother Courage and her three children in a setting that was historically remote and hence seemingly timeless, but the author's sentiments remained confined to the radicalism of his early manhood in Germany.

[36] *"Frieden, das ist nur Schlamperei, erst der Krieg schafft Ordnung."* (Bertolt Brecht, *Mutter Courage und ihre Kinder* [1939, but first published in German only in 1949]. Paper bound edition [Berlin: Suhrkamp Verlag, 1960], p. 7). Mr. Bentley translates, "You know what the trouble with peace is? No organization. And when do you get organization? In a war." (*Op. cit.*, p. 13.)

[37] Bertolt Brecht, *op. cit.*, p. 77.

Grimmelshausen, who knew more than Brecht about the brutalities and miseries of war from his own experience as a soldier, wrote about the Thirty Years War, the total war of his lifetime, in the natural, coarse tongue of the common people. Brecht's simple people speak a language of contrived simplicity. *Courage, the Adventuress,* as well as *The Adventurous Simplicissimus* reach beyond the specific events of the war, because Grimmelshausen held all war to be a poignant expression of the human condition, rather than a state of affairs for which a particular social class was responsible.

Grimmelshausen can be cited in support of the orthodox opinion that war is a scourge sent by God to punish sin, but he knew that in war the innocent suffer with the guilty. The dynastic interests in the Thirty Years War did not concern him. In his view, it was "an internal war and a conflict between brothers";[38] even many years after the Peace of Westphalia was concluded he seems to have been of the opinion that the rivalry among the Christian churches stood in the way of lasting peace. This is at least the argument which Simplicissimus offers to the mad character who thinks of himself as Jove and has come to establish eternal peace.

Grimmelshausen presented many of his general views on war, as on other subjects, in the form of proverbs. This includes the saying, "Young soldiers — old beggars," also to be found in *The Pentameron;*[39] it is the main lesson contained in the life of *The Strange Skipinthefield.* Again, "boys who fail to obey father and mother follow the drummer, if not the hangman";[40] an elaboration of this theme is *Der stolze Melcher (The Proud Melchior),* one of Grimmelshausen's last writings, in which he equated turning soldier with joining a gang of loud-mouthed, hard-drinking gamblers, robbers, and seducers of maidens. Grimmelshausen was of the opinion that war attracts especially

[38] *Simplicissimus,* I, Ch. 18.
[39] *Simplicissimus,* III, Ch. 19. Basile, *The Pentameron,* Sir Richard Burton, translator (London: William Kimber, 1952), p. 96.
[40] *Simplicissimi Galgenmännlin,* in *Werke,* H. H. Borcherdt, editor, Vol. 4, p. 305.

the rotten elements in society. They drift into the armies. "Oh, Jove," says Simplicissimus, "if you send a war, all the evil fellows and daredevils will join it and torment the peace-loving, pious people."[41]

"In war," Courage observes, "most people become worse rather than better,"[42] and she attributes this fact to the company which soldiers and camp followers keep. The point is worth noting. Grimmelshausen was not of the opinion that any abstract conditions account for human vice and depravity. It is quite concretely the example given by other men — what they do to you and others — that is corrupting. Such corruption — by bad example, by temptation, and as in the case of Courage, by humiliation — cannot occur without corruptibility, a general quality of human nature. Precisely for this reason man should avoid bad company. "Avoid bad company" is one of the three pieces of advice given by the hermit to his son Simplicius, the young, ignorant boy. War, to Grimmelshausen, meant above all, a tempting opportunity for young people to keep especially bad company.

Grimmelshausen depicted the disorder and corruption of the world, in peacetime as well as in war. He showed man in his blindness, his cruelty, and his suffering, and as a liar to both others and himself. He plumbed the depths of man's terror in this world.

41 *Simplicissimus,* III, Ch. 3.
42 *Courage,* Ch. 9.

CHAPTER SIXTEEN

Grimmelshausen's Laughter

. . . multi nomine divorum thalamos iniere pudicos.

(Ovid, *Metamorphoses*)

LITERARY HISTORIANS have produced a small library of books on Johann Jacob Christoffel von Grimmelshausen, Germany's greatest seventeenth-century writer, but they have paid little attention to his story *The False Messiah* which takes up nine of the twenty-seven chapters in the author's last work, *Des wunderbarlichen Vogelnests zweiter Teil* ("The Enchanted Bird's-Nest, Part II"), published in 1675. Grimmelshausen did not give any separate title to this story. At least once, in 1920, it was published separately under the title, *Die Judennovelle;* for reasons that will become evident, *The False Messiah* is a more appropriate title. The story is a novella of great distinction, a tale of considerable interest to students of seventeenth-century beliefs and superstitions, and an imaginative treatment of an ancient irreverent dream of man.

The False Messiah deals with a subject of universal interest which appears in the literature of many languages — European and non-European, ancient and modern. The subject is a battle between nature and religion, or to put it more specifically,

From *Ancients and Moderns,* Joseph Cropsey, editor (New York: Basic Books Publishing Co., Inc., 1964). A shortened version of this essay appeared in the "Introduction" to my translation of Grimmelshausen's *Courage, the Adventuress and The False Messiah* (Princeton, New Jersey: Princeton University Press, 1964).

between unbridled sexual appetite and religious beliefs. This battle, which nature wins by resorting to an outrageous ruse, can also be described as a confrontation of two different kinds of folly. The folly of superstition consists in embracing false beliefs that sustain false fears and vain hopes and thus stand in the way of good sense and true faith. All great fools bear witness to the folly of unbridled appetites: Rabelais' Panurge, Shakespeare's Falstaff, Grimmelshausen's Simplicissimus (in his youth), and many others. All of them enjoy food and wine and sleep.[1] So, characteristically, do all picaros; in *Lazarillo de Tormes,* loaves of bread are the face of God, and it is said that the dead are taken to the house "where they neither eat nor drink."[2] Nor are fools in the habit of otherwise defying nature. Indeed, many of the great fools in literature boast of their amorous exploits in contrast to Christian moralists who, particularly in the seventeenth century, found passionate love "to be nothing but folly."[3]

The main reason for the neglect of *The False Messiah* by literary historians has been their preoccupation with Grimmelshausen's main work, *Der abentheurliche Simplicissimus* (*The Adventurous Simplicissimus*), published in 1669 and republished very many times to this day. *The Enchanted Bird's-Nest* leaves no memory of a unique character in the reader's mind, as do the life of Simplicissimus and two other novels of the Simplician cycle — *Die Landstörzerin Courasche* (*Courage, The Adventuress*), and *Der Seltzame Springinsfeld* (*The*

---

[1] Cf. Walter Kaiser, *Praisers of Folly: Erasmus, Rabelais, Shakespeare* (Cambridge: Harvard University Press, 1963).

[2] "The Life and Adventures of Lazarillo de Tormes," in Mendoza, *Lazarillo de Tormes,* Thomas Roscoe, translator, and Mateo Alemán, *Guzman d'Alfarasche,* 2 vols. (London: J. C. Nimmo and Bain, n. d.), Vol. 1, p. 59.

[3] Francisco de Quevedo, *Visions,* Sir Roger L'Estrange, translator and J. M. Cohen, author of introduction (Fontwell, Sussex: The Centaur Press, 1963), p. 67. (These words are the conclusion of Vision IV, "Of Loving Fools.") Quevedo, who was born in Madrid in 1580 and wrote his powerful picaresque novel *La vida del Buscon* and his *Sueños* or *Visions* while still in his twenties, was translated into German before he was translated into English. H. M. Moscherosch was the author of the German adaptation of the *Sueños.*

Strange Skipinthefield), both published in 1670. Once a reader has encountered Simplicissimus, the simplest man, and Courage, the blasphemous, lusty camp follower, they live in his memory as vividly as Til Eulenspiegel and Celestina; and even Skipinthefield, the happy-go-lucky soldier who loses a leg — begging, swearing, and playing the fiddle — is not easily forgotten.

Like the first three novels of the Simplician cycle, the last two, parts I and II of *The Enchanted Bird's-Nest*, consist in the main of a series of adventurous tales told by picaresque antiheroes; but the two narrators of *The Bird's-Nest* — a young halberdier in the first part and a merchant in the second — who relate their experiences and are the main characters in these books — do not claim the same attention as do Simplicissimus, Courage, and Skipinthefield. Grimmelshausen attributed great importance to the significance of names. The main characters in all his other Simplician novels carry names that signify their nature, or rather the specific roles in the human comedy which Grimmelshausen has assigned them. When these roles change, so do their names. In the light of these precedents, it is not unimportant that the young halberdier and the merchant remain nameless. The center of the last two books of the Simplician cycle is, as the titles indicate, a bird's-nest rather than a particular picaro or a picara. Before turning to the story of *The False Messiah*, let us look at this magical object.

Invisibility and Omniscience

In many different lands we encounter the belief that certain plants, stones, and other objects, such as rings, have the power to make their owner invisible. When leaves or twigs of such plants or stones are carried by a siskin, a raven, or some other bird into its nest, the nest itself assumes magical potency and becomes invisible.

Invisibility is always closely associated with the divine and its opposite, the satanic, just as there is a close relationship between soul and shadow, shadow and mirror, mirror and truth. Casting no shadow is a sign of noncorporeality, a quality of saints according to the Persians, of Mohammed according to Arabic tales, of God, and in certain countries, of the Devil. Similarly, in the folklore of many lands, people who are allied to, or have studied with, the Devil cast no shadow; they have lost their souls.

Though the magical object and the person who carries it are invisible, their shadows and their reflections are not. The mirror image of the magically invisible person can be seen in water or in a looking-glass. This notion may derive either from the belief in the purifying power of water and its equivalent, the mirror, or from the identification of the mirror image with the noncorporeal soul of the subject. In various languages, the word for shadow also means mirror image.

Often the mirror is believed to show everything that is hidden and mysterious and to be a magical instrument for seeing that which is beyond the natural power of the eye to perceive.[4] Thus, in Rembrandt's famous etching, Dr. Faustus watches the appearance of the sign of the Holy Spirit in a looking-glass. It has been suggested that Rembrandt's inspiration for this etching may have come from I Corinthians 13:12, in which Paul compares man's knowledge with looking into a mirror.[5] What he sees is enigmatic, in need of interpretation. "*Vidimus nunc per speculum in aenigmate*: For now we see through a glass, darkly."

Probably Grimmelshausen was in some regards a superstitious man himself, but in any event, he was too good a storyteller not to use for dramatic effect superstitions that could be counted on to keep his readers spellbound. In following this practice, he gave voice to hopes and fears among the people of his time; even today his works can be studied with great benefit as source books of beliefs current in the second half

---

[4] See Hanns Bächthold-Stäubli, "Spiegel," *Handwörterbuch des deutschen Aberglaubens* (Berlin: 1938–1941), Vol. 9, pp. 547–577.

[5] Martin Bojanowski, "Der Spiegel in Rembrandts Faustradierung," *Deutsche Vierteljahrsschrift für Literaturwissenschaft*, Vol. 18 (1940), pp. 467–469.

of the seventeenth century, particularly in the lower and middle regions of society. For example, in Grimmelshausen's time and still, in fact, in the eighteenth century, not only uneducated peasants and lowly soldiers, but also high ranking personages believed that certain people were invulnerable except to specially made bullets. Each of Grimmelshausen's popular works casts some light on the nature of these superstitions: in *The False Messiah*, a whole chapter is devoted to them. But the man who wrote so much about invulnerability also remarked that the best way of ensuring it was to avoid standing in the way of a bullet. Similarly, in several of his works, again including *The False Messiah*, the magic power of a mandrake root is mentioned — as it is in Shakespeare — in deference to reader interest; yet Grimmelshausen also wrote a short treatise describing and not fully accepting this superstition.

In three books of the Simplician cycle, various aspects of the belief in invisibility are preserved for students of folklore, and much of what is now known about the superstition in Germany is derived from Grimmelshausen: the discovery of the nest through its reflection in the waters of a brook;[6] the protection of the hidden magic stone by folding the nest into a handkerchief;[7] the appearance of the second invisible owner — the halberdier — as a mirror image in the looking-glass of a lady;[8] and the final destruction of the nest by a priest who drops it from a bridge into the Rhine River.[9] But Grimmelshausen wrote neither for folklorists nor merely for readers wishing to be entertained. As we shall see, he used the fantastic notion of invisibility to convey his ideas on man's relation to nature

[6] *Grimmelshausens Springinsfeld* (hereafter cited as *Skipinthefield*), J. H. Scholte, editor (Halle: Max Niemeyer, 1928), Ch. 13.

[7] *Grimmelshausens Wunderbarliches Vogelnest. Erster Teil* (hereafter cited as *Bird's-Nest I*), J. H. Scholte, editor (Halle: Max Niemeyer, 1931), p. 4; and *Des wunderbarlichen Vogelnests zweiter Teil* (hereafter cited as *Bird's-Nest II*), in *Grimmelshausens Werke*, Hans Heinrich Borcherdt, editor (Berlin, Leipzig, Vienna, Stuttgart: Deutsches Verlagshaus Bong & Co., 1921), Vol. 3, Ch. 3.

[8] *Bird's-Nest I*, p. 63.

[9] *Bird's-Nest II*, Ch. 27.

and God. In his hands, the miraculous nest turned into a device for exploring beliefs more momentous than the attribution of magical properties to stones, nests, and mirrors.

The first part of *The Enchanted Bird's-Nest* consists of a series of incidents in which the young halberdier observes people from all walks of life. His invisibility enables him to see them when they think they are unobserved. A nobleman and a young lady, both of them impoverished, try to trick each other into marriage by pretending to be rich; an old grandmother instructs a young beggar on how to profit from charity by pretending to share whatever faith prevails in the place where he happens to be: "Lutheran or Catholic or Calvinist"; a rich peasant opposes the marriage of his daughter because he resents the cost of the wedding, whereupon the daughter secretly admits her lover to her bed; a young wife of an old steward laments the news that her sick husband will not recover just after she has confided to her mother that she wished him dead; an innkeeper dilutes his wine with water; a parson tries to seduce the wife of a parishioner; a monastery is riddled by evil intrigues;[10] two students of theology and law, while disputing the beliefs of the Pre-Adamites, are held up by a highwayman and found to be less well prepared to face death than they are to discuss heresy.

Folly, hypocrisy, and sin pass before the eyes of the halberdier. He is in the position of the dreamer who in Francisco de Quevedo's fifth *Vision,* "Of the World," is led by an old man called "The Undeceiver-General" to "The Hypocrites' Walk," there to behold "the difference between things themselves and their appearances."[11] It is important to note, however, that Grimmelshausen's social panorama, besides being more varied than Quevedo's, serves a more radical purpose than that of the Spanish satirist. The halberdier and the merchant do not merely have satirical dreams; both of them can make themselves invisible at will, and since invisibility

[10] In *Bird's-Nest I,* p. 111, Simplicissimus compares life at court and life in a monastery with life in prison.
[11] Francisco de Quevedo, *Visions,* pp. 69 ff.

is a divine-satanic quality, the two parts of *The Enchanted Bird's-Nest* are books involving God and the Devil. Like God, the halberdier is omniscient about the human heart. He learns secrets kept from ordinary mortals by simulation and dissimulation. He is able to unmask the people who hide their true faces and he sees them in their nakedness.

Perhaps Grimmelshausen was not only interested in fantasies of a god-like man who discovers hidden truths, but also fascinated by the art of secret discovery itself; several episodes in his works seem to suggest such a fascination. As a soldier and also as a hermit at his retreat in the Black Forest, Simplicissimus uses spy glasses and special hearing devices to overcome the limits which distance sets to the unaided senses. Various comic scenes also occur in which a person overhears the sexual activities of lovers who think that they are alone; both Simplicissimus and the halberdier have such experiences. In *The False Messiah*, invisibility serves various purposes. Among others, it allows the distrustful merchant secretly to test his friend's honesty, and gives him the pleasure of seeing a beautiful girl without his being seen.

In the age of enlightenment, not many years after Grimmelshausen's death in 1676, concern with such practical interests became a fashionable subject. In 1692, Christian Thomasius offered to Frederick III, Elector of Brandenburg, "the new invention of a science, well founded and highly necessary for the commonweal, of how to recognize in ordinary conversation the secrets hidden in the hearts of other people, even against their will."[12] Thomasius explained that a single word inadvertently dropped in conversation at dinner or at the gambling table, a glance, a fleeting expression — any of these might be a clue to the true intention that a man tried to hide. Sometimes the dissembler was bound to be careless, and an astute observer would in the end distinguish the affected

---

[12] Christian Thomasius, "Erfindung einer Wissenschaft anderer Menschen Gemüt zu erkennen," in *Aus der Frühzeit der deutschen Aufklärung*, F. Brüggeman, editor (Weimar and Leipzig: Philipp Reclam jun., 1928), pp. 60 ff.

from the natural. Even the most careful dissembler would fail;
he could not conceal minor excesses of his passion, either because he simply did not regard them as excessive or because
most persons reputed to be sensible and wise did not bother
to conceal them.

Julius Bernhardt von Rohr, in a conduct book full of advice,
elaborated this psychology of unmasking in convenient, if
pedantic, detail.[13] He not only described ways of recognizing
the true character of rivals in the service of a prince, but also
addressed himself to such subjects as the choice of a marriage
partner, the upbringing of children, and the management of
servants. "Where there are two sisters," he said, "prefer the
company of the one whom you esteem less. Then you will have
a better opportunity to get to know the other, because she has
no reason for dissembling."[14] Von Rohr suggested occasionally
leaving children alone in order to observe their play and thus
explore their inclinations when they think themselves unobserved, "for in your or the preceptor's presence they will
dissemble and give no free rein to their nature."[15] As to the
treatment of domestics, von Rohr advised against announcing
the day of one's return from a journey, so as "to fall upon them
unexpectedly."[16] Von Rohr presented a long list of techniques
of detecting the true nature of another person:[17] pretending to
love his suspected passion; arousing his passions through in-
toxication, gambling, or the company of women; talking about
one's own views in order to induce him to be candid; pretending to be well aware of everything one wants to find out; observing the person's wishes, his dress, the company he keeps,
the books he reads, the games he likes, his reactions to winning
and losing, the appearance of his children and servants, his
working, leisure time, and eating habits; talking with third

---

[13] Julius Bernhardt von Rohr, *Einleitung zu der Klugheit zu leben,* 3rd
ed. (Leipzig: 1730).
[14] *Ibid.,* p. 310.
[15] *Ibid.,* p. 334.
[16] *Ibid.,* p. 358.
[17] *Ibid.,* pp. 505 ff.

persons about him with due regard to whether they are his friends or his enemies, whether they usually talk much or little, whether or not they benefit from the person they talk about, and so on.

Evidently, all these techniques are grounded in the belief that everyone hides his true self either defensively in fear of others who are more powerful than himself or aggressively in the endeavor to attain his own ends and satisfy his passions at the expense of others. In such endeavor, man pretends to be free of the passions that propel him, but cannot help betraying himself by inadvertently offering certain clues to the skillful observer. As Thomasius pointed out, great statesmen like Richelieu and Mazarin possessed such skill, and, indeed, without it no prince could ever choose his advisors wisely, no minister could recognize worthy clients, and no client could succeed in dealing with his patron.

Thomasius was careful to explain that his new science was of no avail when used against men who were "to a high degree true Christians," because in order to explore their hearts "a supernatural and divine science was required."[18] He also warned that no knowledge of others could be attained without self-knowledge. He might have added that many older conduct books written for aspiring courtiers by clerics and disappointed men of affairs contained everything that could possibly be said about dissimulation. This literature flourished in the area of absolutism. The conduct books were founded on political experience at the courts where success and security depended on the favor of the prince. Such favor was not always predictable; many sought it, but only one could grant it. And it was always granted to the disappointment of others who had sought the same favor. As Guevara said in his *Institutiones Vitae Aulicae*, "A courtier must fear everyone and be on guard against him. Is there anyone who loves another person at court so much as not to wish him dead or at least to try to become his equal, no matter how close he is to him through

---

[18] Christian Thomasius, *op. cit.*, p. 78.

family bonds or confidence?"[19] In the serious novels of the baroque era, reserve and distrust between lovers, as well as rivals, are prominent and pervasive, and in conduct books, like du Refuge's *Traité de la Cour* (1623) and *The Instructions of Cardinal Sermonetta to His Cousin Petro Caetano* (1633), reserve and distrust are recommended as "a counterpoison" against the secret malice and evil designs of others.

Grimmelshausen's Simplician writings are closer to the worldly spirit of this literature than is generally recognized. Dissimulation and distrust are as prominent in his writings as they are in the conventional novels of the period. A few incidents, chosen at random, illustrate the starkness of evil and intensity of distrust that prevail in Grimmelshausen's world.

When Simplicius, the child, emerges from the woods where he has lived with a hermit, he comes to Hanau, entering "the world" for the first time. At once the governor of Hanau takes him for a spy, "as everyone is in the habit of suspecting evil."[20] The boy is turned over to the gaoler and hangman to be tortured. At one point in his military career, Simplicissimus has a chance of becoming the leader of a squadron. In this situation, his "worst enemies" are those close to him. His captain wants him dead to acquire his fine horse. He is hated by another officer, who wants one of his own relatives to get the command. Simplicissimus must be on guard against a certain lieutenant whom he had observed in a moment of fear and weakness. The petty officers envy the hero because he might be preferred to them. And "the worst of it was that not a single soul told me how everyone felt toward me."[21] Later, when the old foster-father of Simplicissimus comes home to tell a strange tale of his son's miraculous disappearance in the Mummelsee, there were some, says Simplicissimus, who "had they not known of my physical strength would have believed

[19] Antonio de Guevara, *Institutiones Vitae Aulicae Oder Hofschul*, Aegidius Albertinus, German translator (Munich: 1602), p. 4.

[20] *Grimmelshausens Simplicissimus Teutsch* (hereafter cited as *Simplicissimus*), J. H. Scholte, editor (Tübingen: Max Niemeyer, 1954), p. 55.

[21] *Simplicissimus*, p. 236.

that my foster-father had murdered me so that he, an avaricious old man, would be rid of me and be the sole master of my farm."[22]

The Enchanted Bird's-Nest does not teach the reader any techniques of detecting hidden malice and evil intent. Instead, the book presents a general view of life according to which appearances cannot be trusted, because behind the façade of reasonableness, politeness and morally impeccable behavior lie boundless folly and evil. Folly and evil are rooted in the passions.

Grimmelshausen accounted for the formation of character in various ways. Courage, the most lusty woman in the Simplician writings, says of herself that she became what she is because of her bile and her phlegm. If we take her words as an indication of Grimmelshausen's own views, he agreed with Galen's theory of the temperaments. In addition, Courage becomes more evil as she grows older in consequence of terrible mistreatment by men whose animal appetites she arouses by her extraordinary beauty. No doubt Grimmelshausen regarded sexual desire as a major source of evil as well as of folly. Finally, he observed through the mouth of Courage that war made people worse rather than better. Needless to say, Grimmelshausen explicitly denied that in peacetime people were good; he considered "the environment" in which people lived as a possible source of their corruption only because he meant by "environment" the company a person kept; in war soldiers keep company with soldiers, and this in his view meant that they almost invariably kept very bad company, since only the worst elements in society were attracted to soldiering. According to Grimmelshausen, another main source of folly and evil was wealth, especially in the form of money. Grimmelshausen had nothing to say about getting rich through work; the peasants are the main producers of goods consumed in society. Many ways of getting wealthy are evil, including maurading in war, gambling, robbery, murder, fraud, flattery,

[22] *Ibid.*, p. 414.

magic; envy is aroused by money, and money makes both misers and spendthrifts. Often wealth is a consequence of power, rather than power being a consequence of wealth, and then the powerful make the life of their subjects bitter by squeezing them dry. The most evil man in the Simplician writings is Olivier, a ruthless, conscienceless murderer. In the account he gives of his upbringing, he places much stress on the bad company he kept in his youth and on the corrupting influence that an evil tutor exerted upon him. Similarly, when Simplicissimus recalls the early days of his life, he compares his mind with a *tabula rasa* and with a field that is fertile by nature but incapable of bearing fruit withoult cultivation. He refers to Aristotle, Averroës, and Cicero as authorities in support of the view that the human mind or soul — terms that are used interchangeably — needs impression and exercise for its perfection. What rules should govern the conduct of a wise man? According to Grimmelshausen, the wise man knows himself, avoids bad company, and is steadfast.[23]

Invisibility and Omnipotence

In the first part of *The Enchanted Bird's-Nest*, the world is like a puppet show which only the halberdier understands, because with the help of the nest he observes both the play and the strings of passion that make man move on the stage of the world. Like God, however, the halberdier is not only omniscient, but also omnipotent; he pulls the strings whenever he disapproves of the play. The halberdier helps the poor, throws the wanton parson onto a heap of manure, boxes the ears of Calvinist peasants in a tavern when they make fun of Catholic rites, saves the students from being robbed and slain, prevents a shepherd from committing sodomy, and acts in many other ways sometimes like an avenging angel and sometimes like a guardian angel. Is he an agent of the Al-

[23] *Simplicissimus*, p. 35.

mighty, or does he do what God fails to do? Nothing in the novel suggests that Grimmelshausen regarded him as anything but an ordinary man who had magically acquired complete knowledge of man. The halberdier is a simple fellow with some charmingly mischievous traits. In particular, he does not do any work, but with the help of his nest steals food and wine to his heart's delight; and on one occasion, after a dedication festival of a church, he deflowers a willing young girl.

Twice the halberdier is indeed taken for an angel: by the shepherd whom he saves from committing sodomy and suicide and by a poor laborer's family, whose abject misery he relieves without betraying his presence by giving stolen food to the starving children and two gold coins to their parents. The second incident, a very rare indication of Grimmelshausen's own feelings of compassion, occurs the day after the halberdier's reflection appears in the looking-glass of a vain, wealthy lady, striking her with fear that she is looking at the Devil himself.

Now comparing the lady's terror with the poor family's belief in angelic assistance, the halberdier becomes pensive. "Why are human judgments," he asks, "generally so false?"[24] He concludes that errors in opinion result from the emotions of the person who passes judgment. The lady in front of the mirror was told by her conscience that her vanity was sinful folly; and it is for this reason that she believed the mirror image to be that of the Devil. The poor family bewailed their misery and prayed to God for help. To whom were they to attribute the miraculous presents "but to the one to whom they had complained of their misery"?[25] Did Grimmelshausen want to suggest that God helped the poor as little as he did the sodomitical shepherd? He certainly suggests that the gratitude of the poor for God's charity was as misplaced as was the fear of Satan which gripped the rich lady in front of the

[24] *Bird's-Nest I,* p. 73.
[25] *Ibid.,* p. 74.

mirror. Or as the halberdier puts it, "Although each party in his judgment about me had completely contradicted the other, both of them were equally deceived by opinion; and this taught me how little confidence we may have in our own notions."[26]

This is an extraordinary statement. It is the only passage in the Simplician cycle where Grimmelshausen has applied the word "Wahn" (opinion or delusion)[27] to the belief in divine help as well as to the belief in the machinations of the devil. The passage is also important because it is immediately followed by the halberdier's remark, "Small wonder, therefore, that old Simplicissimus put on all the engravings to be found in the story of his life: 'Opinions Deceive' ('Der Wahn betreugt')."[28] Like so many other words and phrases in Grimmelshausen's work, "Opinions Deceive," the famous Simplician adage, has various meanings. It certainly implies that appearances cannot be trusted because of man's proneness to simulate and dissimulate. "The world is full of masks," reads one line of the poem that appears on the frontispiece of *The Enchanted Bird's-Nest*. Ony those who see through man's dissembling will not be deceived. "Opinion" or "delusion" in a more specific application, however, denotes man's notions about God and Satan, and these opinions or delusions seem to be a special kind of folly, influenced, as are all judgments, by emotions.

The halberdier finally decides to part with the bird's-nest.

---

26 "Ob nun gleich beyde Theil von mir so unterschiedlich geurtheilt/ dass sie auch nicht unterschiedlicher hätten urthlen können/ so hat doch der Wahn alle beyde betrogen/ und mich gelernet/ wie wenig unserm eignen Beduncken zutrauen und zu glauben sey." (*Bird's-Nest I*, p. 74.)

27 The word "Wahn" is used by Grimmelshausen to denote either "blind judgment" (e.g., "das blinde Urtheil oder der Menschen Wahn;" *Bird's-Nest I*, p. 73) or "opinion" (e.g., "Verbleibe dennoch bey meinem gefasten Wahn. . . ." *Bird's-Nest I*, p. 106). On the relation between baroque "Wahn" and "*opinio*" according to the Stoics, cf. Werner Welzig, *Beispielhafte Figuren. Tor, Abenteurer und Einsiedler bei Grimmelshausen* (Graz and Köln: Hermann Böhlaus Nachf., 1963), pp. 170–175.

28 *Bird's-Nest I*, p. 74.

It frightens him that he nearly caused a shepherd to commit suicide. Moreover, he becomes aware of his own sins: his sloth, his petty thefts, and the seduction of the girl. No longer does to want to "conceal misdeeds, whoring and thievery through invisibility"[29] as do those who love darkness because they do evil. God alone "in his supreme wisdom has reserved for himself omniscience. . . ."[30] But it should be noted that by abandoning the nest, the young rascal also ceases to prevent evil and to right the wrongs that he had discovered with the help of his magical object.

The halberdier's exit is morally enigmatic. He finds the gold coins that an evil woman, the former owner of the nest, had stolen with its magical help. He considers how he can use his suddenly acquired fortune to bring joy and restore honor to "the friendly girl" whom he had "robbed and violated in her sleep, as it were."[31] The moral worth of this resolution is equivocal. A similar episode occurs in Grimmelshausen's main novel when neither Simplicissimus nor Heartsbrother, his pious friend, hesitates very much to spend the tainted money that Simplicissimus has taken from Olivier after the death of this villainous highwayman and murderer.[32] Perhaps the good ends to which the treasure is to be put are supposed in each case to nullify its immoral origin, in much the same manner in which King David was a great king despite his dissolute and immoral youth.[33] Perhaps the innocent way in which the halberdier acquired the gold coins implies that the money is no

[29] *Ibid.*, p. 142.
[30] *Ibid.*, p. 143.
[31] *Ibid.*, p. 147.
[32] *Simplicissimus*, V, Chs. 1 and 3.
[33] In his *Ratio Status*, Grimmelshausen points out that David was "reprehensible" because he lied, robbed, and murdered, for which he would not be praised among Christians even by clerics, but he was a legitimate king obliged to persecute the hereditary enemies of his nation; hence he could not be accused of any iniquity.

Was nun dieses vor ein Stück der Redlichkeit und eines Gottseeligen gewesen/ wurden auch unter uns Christen die Geistlichen kaum loben; Aber deme sey wie ihm wolle/ David war allbereit ein gesalbter König der Israeliten/ und dannenhero Ambtshalber verbunden seiner *Nation* Erb-feinde zuverfolgen/ und wie im Krieg erlaubt ist/

longer tainted; he found it knowing that its former owner, who had stolen it with the help of the Devil, suffered violent death in consequence of her sin. Perhaps Grimmelshausen agreed with some of his readers that finding something means owning it; the treasure no longer belongs to anyone. Finally, there is the remote possibility that Grimmelshausen wrote the concluding passage in the first part of *The Enchanted Bird's-Nest* with tongue in cheek, casting a last ironic glance at the young halberdier in his new role of a converted sinner proposing to make amends in a manner that entangles him anew in the evil he has just renounced.

The False Messiah: *The Plot*

The False Messiah casts further light on the folly of superstition. In the second part of *The Enchanted Bird's-Nest*, the owner of the magical object is not a Simplicius-like simpleton, but a merchant who is full of enterprise. Instead of merely observing life with the help of the nest and discovering the mainsprings of human action, which people so carefully conceal from public sight, he uses the bird's-nest for his own selfish ends. His projects are more ambitious than the mere theft of food and wine, which the halberdier, like any picaro, commits in order to get by without working. Nor does the merchant try to check the evildoers around him and help their victims. Instead, he does evil himself with perfect abandon. Since the nest gives him a measure of supernatural power denied to ordinary mortals he is capable of sinning in a grand manner. Comparing the halberdier with the merchant, we may say the novel passes from a reflective phase to one of reckless and fantastic action. The second part of *The Enchanted Bird's-Nest* contains two main adventures. The first involves an act

---

seine Feinde mit allerhand List/ Betrug/ Vortheln/ *Stratagematis* und was den anhängig zu schwächen; also ist diss Orts David keiner Unbillichkeit zu beschuldigen.
(Grimmelshausen, *Simplicianischer Zweyköpffiger Ratio Status* [Nüremberg: Felszecker, 1670], p. 58. Cited by courtesy of the Yale University Library.)

of brutal revenge that the merchant commits on his unfaithful wife and her helpers. The story can be traced to one of Bandello's novelle, but Grimmelshausen took it from the German translation of a later French version of the original tale. The second adventure is the story of *The False Messiah*.

The plot of this story is simple enough. In 1672, the merchant comes to Amsterdam, at that time a center of trade and wealth outranking even London in commercial importance. He hears rumors to the effect that war between France and the Low Countries is imminent, and in order to protect himself as best he can he decides to get hold of as much money as possible. While searching the house of Eliezer, the wealthiest Jew in the city, he unexpectedly sees Esther, Eliezer's beautiful daughter, but with the nest in his possession he is not observed by her. He falls passionately in love. Since she is closely guarded by her parents, he cannot satisfy his desire to possess her. Fortunately a man named Erasmus unwittingly comes to his assistance. Erasmus, a former Jew who has been baptized, tells the merchant a great deal about the beliefs of the Jews, including their faith in the coming of the Messiah and their expectation that this momentous event will be preceded by the return of the prophet Elijah.

The rest is easy for the merchant. He raises the religious fervor of the Jews to a fever pitch by elaborately faked messages from heaven which he scatters in the synagogue through a blow tube. Making use of the bird's-nest he plays Elijah among the gullible people. Next, he appears at night in Eliezer's bed chamber as the angel Uriel, announcing to the half-frightened, half-skeptical old man that his daughter Esther has been chosen to lie with Elijah and conceive the Messiah. Eliezer, his family, and all the Jews in Amsterdam rejoice, or as Grimmelshausen expresses it, they now have flutes in their hearts. Preparations are made to receive the angelic lover in Esther's bedroom with all the luxury and consideration owed him. The merchant gets what he wants. Nine months later Esther gives birth to a girl! The Jews, far from being dismayed, believe that God in his wisdom wants to protect the

child from Christian persecution and will turn the girl into a
boy at the appropriate age.

Under the impact of the miracle that has occurred in the
Jewish community, Erasmus begins to waver in his newly
acquired Christian faith. Furthermore, the merchant learns
that Esther, too, had been ready to become a convert, leave
her father's house, and marry none other than Erasmus. Now
as the Messiah's mother she has again become a firm believer
in her religion. In short, not only had the Christian merchant
sinned terribly by impersonating an angel and deflowering a
Jewish virgin, not only had he fortified the religious beliefs of
the Jews with his tricks, but he had also been directly responsible for three or four lost souls: those of Erasmus, Esther,
Josanna (her nursemaid), and the child.

The merchant decides to make amends. He tells Erasmus
almost the whole truth and induces him to disabuse Esther
of her religious delusion. This Erasmus does by means of
another lie, convincing her that it was not an angel but he,
Erasmus, who had visited her and that the child instead of
being a future Messiah is his own. Thereupon Esther and the
nursemaid secretly leave Eliezer's house and in hiding prepare themselves for baptism. In the meantime, the merchant
steals a fortune from Eliezer, making use of his precious nest
and of a mandrake root that opens any lock at will. When
Erasmus and Esther are joined in marriage according to
Christian rites, the merchant provides them with a handsome
dowry stolen from Esther's father. At the wedding, the merchant sees Esther again, and his passion flares up in renewed
fury. He nearly loses his mind, especially when he learns —
alas, too late! — that his own wife has just died; he could have
married the beautiful woman himself. Erasmus, sensing the
danger of being murdered by his benefactor, boards a ship
with Esther and the child and flees Amsterdam leaving the
merchant in great misery.

The story of the man who pretends to be a god or an angel
in order to possess a woman can be found in the literature of
many ages and many lands, including ancient Greece and

India, ancient Rome, medieval Europe, Renaissance Italy, France, and Germany.[34] Often, though not invariably, the deception is enlarged by a fraudulent promise that a demigod, hero, or savior will be born of the scandalous union. This theme is familiar from Boccaccio's tale of Frate Alberto in the *Decameron* and perhaps from a novella by Matteo Bandello or from the tale of the Weaver who loved a Princess in the Sanskrit *Panchatantra* stories, but there are many older and newer versions. Probably Grimmelshausen did not use the classical sources, but modern derivations in which a fraudulent promise to a Jewish maiden contributes to the success of the deception. Today Grimmelshausen's sources are familiar to only a few specialists. Grimmelshausen avidly studied compendia of learning and read many German translations and adaptations of Spanish, French, Italian, and English works. His literary debt was large, a statement that is true of almost all Baroque authors. For example, various details in *The False Messiah* may have been taken from a fifteenth-century Fastnachtsspiel by Hans Folz, *Von der Juden Messias*.[35]

Probably more important to Grimmelshausen as a writer and as an observer of human folly than any literary antecedent in the long history of the theme was some extraordinary news that spread over Europe in the years immediately before *The Enchanted Bird's-Nest, Part II* was written. This was the news of Sabbatai Zevi, a Sephardic Jew, born in 1626, who under the influence of the Lurian Cabbala and driven by self-delusion claimed to be the redeemer of the Jews. On his extensive travels he succeeded in gaining a large following of believers in his messianic mission. In the seventeenth century, apocalyptic fears and millenial frenzy were spurred by religious persecution — for example, the burning of witches in Germany, and the savage terror in Poland, which in 1648–1649 cost the lives of 300,000 Jews — by the long and destructive Thirty Years War, and by heavenly portents such as the

[34] Otto Weinreich, *Der Trug des Nektanebos* (Leipzig and Berlin: 1911).
[35] *Ibid.*, pp. 98–99.

appearance of the comets of 1618 and 1652. There were many learned calculations to determine the year in which the world would come to an end. Sixteen hundred and forty-eight, 1666, 1668, and 1673 were all miracle years in the belief of some Jewish or Christian messianists. A contemporary, Friedrich Brekling, enumerated "one hundred and eighty visionaries of that century, men and women, who were millenarian dreamers and eschatologists."[36]

Grimmelshausen may have read an account of the enthusiastic delusions which news and rumors about Sabbatai Zevi aroused in many Jewish communities in Europe. For example, the *Theatrum Europaeum,* which Grimmelshausen is known to have consulted on various occasions, reported the following happenings in 1666.

> In their blind zeal the Jews residing in Amsterdam wanted to excel all others and could not contain their jubilation. . . . They held joyous, public celebrations in their synagogue. Candles were burned and psalms about the redemption of Israel were chanted, all in the presence of several hundred, if not a thousand Christians. . . .[37]

Sabbatai Zevi discarded his messianic role by eventually choosing conversion to Islam in preference to martyrdom. He died ten years later, in 1676, but the faith he had inspired survived his conversion and death.

Man Playing God

In order to understand Grimmelshausen's intention in *The False Messiah,* it is useful to compare his treatment of the theme with its classical sources and with the use which three eminent postclassical authors made of them, even though Grimmelshausen may not have known either these sources or their later distinguished literary exploitation.

[36] Abba Hillel Silver, *A History of Messianic Speculation in Israel,* with a new preface by the author (Boston: Beacon Press, 1958), p. 162.

[37] Cited from *Theatrum Europaeum,* Vol. 10, by Arthur Bechthold, *J. J. Ch. v. Grimmelshausen und seine Zeit* (Munich: Musarion Verlag, 1919), p. 159.

In certain tales about the birth of Alexander, the great magician and astrologer Nectanebo, the last king of Egypt, falls in love with Olympias, the wife of King Philip of Macedonia. He persuades the queen, who is more beautiful than the moon, that a god loves her and will visit her first as a snake, then as the horned Ammon, next as Herakles, then as Dionysos, and finally in the human form of Nectanebo himself. The queen does not resist, and Nectanebo, before leaving her room, announces to her that she has conceived by him an invincible son who will rule the world.[38]

In a story by Josephus,[39] the Roman knight Mundus declares his love to Paulina, the young and beautiful wife of Saturninus and a woman of excellent character. He is rejected by her, but the priests of Isis intercede in the service of the lovesick Mundus, convincing Paulina that the god Anubis is enamored of her beauty and desires to lie with her in the temple. Mundus then enjoys her, pretending to be Anubis. After the adulterous act he humiliates the woman by disclosing to her how he deceived her in order to conquer her virtue. The story is supposed to be founded on fact and the ensuing scandal is said to have led to the destruction of the temple of Isis by Emperor Tiberius in the year 19 A.D. Only in the Latin translation of Josephus does Mundus-Anubis announce that Paulina will give birth to a divine child.

In the tenth letter of Aeschines, Cimon, an Athenian youth, observes a maiden named Callirrhoë bathing in the river Scamandros in observance of a local custom required of prospective brides. Cimon hides from the girl's sight in the bushes alongside the riverbank. When she addresses the river god with the words, "Scamandros, receive my virginity," Cimon emerges from his ambush with reeds in his hair saying like a god, "I accept it with pleasure,"[40] and disappears with her from sight. Later he is reproached by a companion who has

38 Otto Weinreich, loc. cit.
39 Flavius Josephus, Antiquitates Judaicae XVIII. 3.
40 Eshine, Discours, texte établi et traduit par Victor Martin et Guy de Budé (Paris: 1928), II, 134.

witnessed the incident and is in fact the narrator of the story. Cimon makes light of his frivolity, saying that many other maidens have been deceived in the same manner before.

These ancient stories reverberate with echoes of the mystery religions which promised man communion with a god through sacred orgies. In spiritualized form such beliefs appear later in the notion of mystics that there is a special way to communion of the human soul with God. The stories, however, suggest the most ruthless degradation of religion to a mere device for attaining the pleasures of love. Moreover, in the Aeshines letter, as well as in Josephus, the lover is not satisfied with sacrilege for the sake of sensual pleasure but offers a frivolous excuse for his crime or cruelly humiliates the victim of his passion by disclosing to her in the end the sacrilegious trick used in overcoming her reserve. The motif of the man who plays god in order to reach his aim in love, with its juxtaposition of the sacred and the sexual, the fraudulent, the cruel in the human heart must have fascinated Grimmelshausen, just as he was attracted by the closeness of madness to religious zeal.[41]

The three principal postclassical authors who should be briefly considered at this point are Boccaccio, Bandello, and Pierre Bayle. The story of Frate Alberto[42] is inspired, like all tales in the *Decameron,* by Boccaccio's desire to entertain educated Renaissance society with a basically anti-Christian view of love as man's natural right to pleasure. This view is implied rather than overtly stated. The direct attack is not on religious belief, but on the monk, an unreconstructed cheat, procurer, hypocrite, and murderer and, to a somewhat lesser extent, on Madonna Lisetta, his mistress, who is ludicrously stupid and vain and boasts of being "paradisiacally fair." Boccaccio's elegant story lacks the fierce sarcasm and vindictive scorn that is heaped on superstition in the story of *The*

---

[41] *Simplicissimus,* III, Chs. 2–6 (the story of the madman who thinks that he is Jove), and V, Ch. 2 (the first conversion of Simplicissimus following the outburst of a madman in a church).

[42] Boccaccio, *Decameron,* Fourth Day, Second Story.

False Messiah. In Boccaccio's story, Madonna Lisetta's superstitious credulity receives no special attention. More than on religious superstition, the plot relies for plausibility on the stupid vanity of the lady and the hypocrisy of the voluptuous monk. The story ends with a scene in which Frate Alberto is exposed to public ridicule and shame on the Piazza San Marco in Venice.[43]

Bandello chose the adventure of Mundus and Paulina for the theme of one of his polished novelle. Since he followed the Greek version of Josephus, he did not mention the fraudulent promise that a divine child would be born of the union. In introducing his tale, Bandello distinguished between religion and "good usances," but he refrained from any comparisons of Roman and Christian religious beliefs. He said, "Now how much weight religion had with the Romans at a time when all good usances were marred, you shall hear out of hand. . . ."[44] As in many other of his novelle, he told an old tale of the past rather than a story involving his contemporaries. A little further on, Bandello presented the ancient "superstition that the Gods got women with child" as an explanation of Paulina's credulity: the Romans did not suspect such "wickedness" as that possessed by Mundus and the priests of Isis "to be hidden under the colour of religion."[45] But Bandello made no comments in the novella on religion in general, and any possible inference concerning Christian beliefs is left to readers who are daring enough to disregard the difference between heathen superstition and Christian religion.

As we turn from the Renaissance novelists to Pierre Bayle, the picture changes. His comments on the theme appear in

[43] For a distinguished comment on the story of Frate Alberto, cf. Erich Auerbach, *Mimesis* (Garden City, New York: Doubleday Anchor Books, 1957), p. 177–202.

[44] *The Novels of Matteo Bandello, Bishop of Agen.* Now first done into English prose and verse by John Payne (London: 1890) (printed for the Villon Society for private circulation), Vol. 5, Part III, Story 15, p. 255.

[45] *Ibid.,* p. 257.

note "C" to the article "Scamander" in his *Dictionnaire*. "When we consider that wit and learning never appeared with so much lustre, as in the age that Aeschines lived in," Bayle remarked, "we may the better apprehend the fatal power of a false religion. It destroys good sense, it extinguishes the light of nature, and in some sort degrades a man to the condition of a brute beast."[46] He then attributed the downfall of Callirrhoë to "the impertinences of poets, canonized by the heathen priests,"[47] who succeeded in making the maiden believe, her noble education withstanding, that "rivers were deities who crowned themselves with reeds, and could enjoy a woman." Referring also to Josephus, Bayle said that in the age of Tiberius another illustrious lady became the victim of deception. Then Bayle contrasted these happenings among the ancients with Christian civilization. He denied that monks "who have played so many tricks chiefly to inveigle women" ever dared to tell them that a saint would want to lie with them. "The ideas of purity and immateriality have always been strictly joined in Christianity with those of beatification." Bayle stressed that unlike the ancient stories, Boccaccio's tale is merely fiction. To this praise of Christianity, however, Bayle added one sentence that makes it clear that he spared the Christian monks in his comments in order to obscure his contention that true Christian religion as well as "false religion" can "destroy good sense and extinguish the light of nature." Immediately following the sentence on beatification that has been quoted, Bayle said, "But I have no doubt, if they [i.e., the monks] would undertake such a thing, but they might bring such devout women, as there are to believe that, of which the Roman votary of Anubis suffered herself to be persuaded."[48]

[46] Pierre Bayle, "Scamander," in *Dictionnaire,* English trans. (London: 1734), Vol. 5, p. 77.

[47] *Loc. cit.* The French text reads, more simply, "les impertinences des Poëtes canonisées par les Prêtres" (Pierre Bayle, "Scamander," *Dictionnaire historique et critique* [5e édition; Amsterdam: 1734], Vol. 5, pp. 75–78).

[48] The original reads, ". . . mais je ne doute point que si on l'entreprenoit on ne vînt à bout de persuader à telles dévotes qu'il y a, ce que la Dame Romaine dévote d'Anubis laissa persuader" (*loc. cit.*).

Thus, Bayle contended that the Christian monks who have seduced so many women would never use the ruse of impersonating a saint or an angel in their amorous conquests. But were the monks to resort to such methods in the manner of the fictional Frate Alberto, the virtue of devout Christian women might falter because of their religion, just as Callirrhoë and Paulina succumbed for that reason. So Bayle suggested that as a source of delusion about love true religion does not differ from false religion.[49]

The False Messiah: *Irony*

It is possible that Grimmelshausen, in satirizing the superstitions of the Jews, took a position somewhat resembling that of Bayle when the latter pointed to certain deplorable consequences of false religion among the Greeks and Romans. That Esther is not the target of Grimmelshausen's derisive humor is evident from the treatment of her character in the story. She lacks the vices of vanity, lust, greed, and the other qualities that Grimmelshausen often attributed to women. There is no suggestion of her being the least amorous. Compare Esther with the princess in the story of *The Panchatantra*. When the beautiful princess is visited by the weaver in the guise of god Vishnu, she is "gazing at the moon, her mind idly dallying with the thoughts of love."[50] And when the queen, her mother, finally suspects her trespasses and hastens in great perturbation to the maiden's apartments, she finds "her daughter with lips sore from kissing and with tell-tale traces on her limbs."[51] Similar details suggesting the pleasures of love are included in Boccaccio's story of Frate Alberto. Grimmelshausen did not admit such erotic suggestions to his tale. The seduction in Esther's bedroom is told smilingly in dialect, as if Grimmels-

---

[49] The point is missed by Otto Weinreich, who wrote in his excellent monograph that "it is not worthwhile reporting Bayle's statements in detail; they are remarkably beside the point ['*schief*'] . . ." (*op. cit.*, p. 80).
[50] *The Panchatantra*, trans. from the Sanskrit by Arthur W. Ryder (Bombay and Calcutta: Jaico Publishing House, 1949), p. 82.
[51] *Ibid.*, p. 84.

hausen were talking about the aftermath of a country dance. Esther has only those traits which are necessary for the plot to be credible: beauty, reserve, and religious faith. While she is credulous, she is not more gullible than any other member of her family and community.

Grimmelshausen's tale is centered on a religious superstition, the expectation of a second Messiah. This belief is described in considerable detail as the main prerequisite of the extraordinary deception perpetrated in Esther's chamber. When Grimmelshausen described the seduction he smiled, but when he talked about the beliefs of the Jews his humor grew profoundly ambiguous, as is illustrated by the following instances.

The merchant learns from Erasmus that the words "I, the Lord, will hasten it in his time" are taken by the Jews "to mean that suddenly and in great haste God will send their Messiah, by postal coach, as it were, and put them into the Promised Land as into an earthly paradise."[52] Again, the Jews "doubt these tales about their future Messiah as little as a good Christian doubts that the true Messiah has already come."[53] Note that this observation (made by the merchant after he has allegedly repented his sins) can be read to mean that the gullibility of the Jews equals the gullibility of the Christians.

When the merchant, impersonating the angel Uriel, appears in front of Eliezer's bed at night, he addresses him as follows:

> Let your heart not be frightened and let your soul banish all needless fear! For lo, I am the angel Uriel, who stands in the presence of God. I have been sent by the King of Kings and His prophet Elijah, whom you have served all your life in the fear of God, in order to bring you the glad tidings for which the house of Jacob has prayed for so long a time: The chosen people of Israel shall be redeemed.[54]

This is close, even in language, to the way in which, according to Luke, the angel Gabriel speaks to Zacharias, promising him

[52] *Bird's-Nest II,* p. 398.
[53] *Ibid.,* p. 397.
[54] *Ibid.,* p. 402.

the miraculous birth of a son, John the Baptist: "Fear not, Zacharias: for thy prayer is heard. . . . I am Gabriel, that stand in the presence of God; and am sent to speak unto thee, and to shew thee these glad tidings."[55] In Grimmelshausen's tale, Eliezer at first doubts the angelic promise, since he thinks that God has chosen Sarah, his old wife, to become the mother of the Messiah: "True, everything is possible for the Lord, but how can this happen when my Sarah is old and unable to bear children?"[56] In the Scriptures as well, the advanced age of the woman divinely chosen for miraculous childbirth is twice the cause of all-too-human doubt in the possibility of the miracle. Genesis speaks of Sarah's faithless laughter when Abraham entertains the three angels and is promised that his wife would bear a child: "Now Abraham and Sarah were old and well stricken in age; and it ceased to be with Sarah after the manner of women. . . . And the Lord said unto Abraham, Wherefore did Sarah laugh, saying, Shall I of a surety bear a child, which am old? Is any thing too hard for the Lord?"[57] And according to Luke, Zacharias hearing that Elisabeth shall bear him a son replies to the angel Gabriel, "Whereby shall I know this? for I am an old man and my wife well stricken in years."[58]

The angel punishes Zacharias for his doubt with dumbness during Elisabeth's pregnancy. Five months later, when Gabriel announces to Mary, the virgin, in Nazareth, that she shall give birth to the son of God, Mary wonders how this shall be "seeing I know not a man,"[59] but the angel reminds her that Elisabeth conceived a son in her old age, adding "For with God nothing shall be impossible."[60] In Grimmelshausen's tale, Eliezer uses

---

[55] Luke 1:13–19.

[56] "Dem Herrn ist zwar alles möglich, aber wie wird dies geschehen können, dann meine Sara alt und zum Kinderzeugen untüchtig worden ist?" (*Bird's-Nest II*, p. 402).

[57] Genesis 18:11 and 18:13–14.

[58] Luke 1:18.

[59] Luke 1:34.

[60] Luke 1:36–37.

the same argument to reinforce his doubt rather than to silence it, when he says, "True, everything is possible for the Lord, but . . . my Sarah is old. . . ." In order to deal with this doubt the merchant, in the role of the pretending angel, merely needs to enlighten Eliezer that his young and beautiful daughter, and not his old wife, has been divinely chosen to become a mother. The humor in this passage is as subtle as it is daring. Nature prevails over religion quite naturally — or employs it persuasively — so that at the end of the conversation even skeptical old Eliezer need no longer qualify his belief that with God nothing is impossible by "it is true . . . but . . . ." The merchant, however, in his disguise might well have recited to himself at this juncture the passage from *The Praise of Folly*, where Stultitia says to her listeners, "But why not speak to you more openly, as I usually do? I ask whether the head, the face, the breast, the hand, or the ear — each an honorable part — creates gods and men? I think not, but instead the job is done by that foolish, even ridiculous part which cannot be named without laughter. This is the sacred fountain from which all things rise. . . ."[61]

Subsequently, Grimmelshausen dryly referred to Eliezer as "the grandfather of the Messiah."[62] Esther is promised a painless childbirth, but it is noted with a malicious chuckle that she suffers the same birth pangs as other women do. When the newborn Messiah is discovered to be a girl, the Jews firmly believe that God in his wisdom resolved to protect the child from Christian persecution, from "another Herodian play."[63] Grimmelshausen (through the mouth of Erasmus) ridiculed the expectation that the girl-child will be turned into a young man later, but added that if this expectation were really fulfilled it would be

---

[61] Erasmus, *The Praise of Folly*, Leonard F. Dean, translator (New York: University Classics, Hendricks House, Farrar, Straus, 1946), p. 49. It is not known whether or not Grimmelshausen read Erasmus' famous book. Nor is it easy to make a plausible conjecture regarding the use of his name in *The False Messiah*.

[62] *Bird's-Nest II*, p. 404.

[63] *Ibid.*, p. 410.

"nothing novel and hence no miracle."[64] In the meantime, he designated the child with outrageous scorn and daring, as "the slit Messiah."[65] Later, when the girl is baptized, she receives the name Eugenia, for a reason which, the narrator says, he cannot fathom; he does not mention that Eugenia means "the well-born child." Finally, Esther is given an additional Christian name at the time of her baptism, and this name is Mary; she becomes Mary Esther.

The Sugar-Coated Pill

Overtly, Grimmelshausen's tale is that of a Christian sinner, who is punished and reformed at the end of the novel, and of Jewish superstition, which is ridiculed. The merchant repeatedly scorns the folly of the Jews and in particular their belief in the coming of the Messiah. Does not every Christian know that God sent the Messiah a long time ago? In addition, there are lengthy passages in which Erasmus, the somewhat fickle convert to the Christian faith, admonishes the sinful merchant to reform. To be sure, this zealous and learned new Christian later lets himself be bought by the merchant and lies to his beloved that he is the father of her child. Then, in numerous other passages, the merchant as narrator interrupts his comic tale to remind the reader how terribly sinful he really used to be. Even these pious passages, however, contain certain phrases which suggest that the merchant's contrition is hardly more than a conventional act of hasty compliance with Christian rules. For example, when at the end of the story he is possessed by his renewed passion for Mary Esther, he feels his self-restraint to be so mortifying as to believe at once that he has made sufficient amends for his former indulgence "and become once more worthy of God's grace."[66] Similarly, when Erasmus senses the merchant's re-

[64] *Ibid.*, p. 423.
[65] *Ibid.*, p. 414.
[66] *Ibid.*, p. 430.

kindled passion for Mary Esther — "oh horrible ungodliness!"
— the merchant remarks, "Meanwhile, the good Lord who, as
I have said, watches his flock, opened Erasmus' eyes."[67] Does
the clause "as I have said" reinforce the statement that the
Lord watches his flock? Or does it rather resemble Eliezer's
equivocal addition, "It is true," to the Biblical quotation "with
God nothing shall be impossible"?

Grimmelshausen's Christian outlook has never been seriously
doubted by any literary critic of his work. In particular, *The
Enchanted Bird's-Nest* has uniformly been considered to depict
the world from the viewpoint of a Christian moralist. The
humorous aspect of the tales contained in this novel are considered to be the sugar-coating of the pill of Christian truth
that Grimmelshausen wanted his readers to swallow. The
ancient image of the sugar-coated pill is traditional among
satirists through the ages and is associated with two different
ideas, one concerning laughter as a medicine for unchristian
melancholy and the other concerning truth as being unpalatable
because of its bitterness. Grimmelshausen, too, often used the
image of the sugar-coated pill, among other places in the
Second Preface to *The Enchanted Bird's-Nest, Part II*. It is
necessary to take a closer look at the relevant passage. It reads:

> Since man shrinks from committing acts of shameful vice in
> somebody else's presence, (although the other is a sinner, too,
> and perhaps more godless than himself) how much more will he
> abstain from evil, nay from the smallest sin, if he heeds the
> teaching of *The Bird's-Nest*, which is that he be aware of being
> watched everywhere by the All-Holy, who hates sin, the All-Just
> who fails neither to reward goodness nor to punish evil, the All-
> Mighty from whose hand and divine power no one can escape.
>
> It is true, the author has treated this very serious matter in his
> usual comic style and included many jests in this work, just as
> he did in the biography of *The Adventurous Simplicissimus*.
> Perhaps only one in every seventeen readers will understand the
> author's teaching, while the others will think that he produced
> his writings to while away their time. But this will not make him
> stray from his old chosen path. He trusts that the kernel of truth

[67] *Ibid.*, p. 433.

will be discovered by sensible people who can use it and benefit from it. It is well known that patients do not like to swallow bitter, if salutary, pills, but readily take them sugar-coated. Thus, imitating a careful physician the author has coated and sweetened the galling bitterness of his censorious writings so that the unsophisticated reader may well fail to take them for helpful medicine and enjoy them instead like unhealthy dainties. . . .[68]

Thus Grimmelshausen explained that he did not write his novel for entertainment but for instruction and that it would be understood correctly only by very few readers. At the same time he explained what the novel is meant to teach the reader: that he is being watched by God and should not believe that his sins will go unpunished. A literal understanding of this message must ignore the difficulty that only the first, passive, part of the novel can be said to show how man dissembles and does evil in the belief that he is not being watched, while the second part, presenting a more active use of the bird's-nest, shows man doing great mischief and evil not because he believes that he is unobserved but because invisibility gives him added power to do so. And invisibility is a divine as well as a satanic property.

Let us disregard this difficulty, however, and assume that Grimmelshausen did intend to tell his readers to be mindful of God, who takes account of whatever man is doing and metes out rewards and punishments justly. Then the question arises how this can possibly be the kernel of truth that "perhaps only one in every seventeen readers will understand." Yet, precisely this interpretation of the Preface and, more generally, of Grimmelshausen's intention in all his Simplician writings, governs the critical literature.

"Seventeen" was one of Grimmelshausen's favorite numbers."[69] Grimmelshausen employed it often to mean "very

[68] *Ibid.*, p. 330.
[69] On number symbolism in Grimmelshausen, cf. Siegfried Streller, *Grimmelshausens Simplicianische Schriften. Neue Beiträge zur Literaturwissenschaft*, Vol. 7 ([East] Berlin: 1957); Horst Hartmann, "Bemerkungen zu Siegfried Strellers Theorie der Zahlenkomposition," *Zeitschrift für deutsche Literaturgeschichte*, Vol. 5 (1959), pp. 428–436; and

many." Today, we might colloquially say "one in a thousand" to convey the meaning of "hardly anyone," where Grimmelshausen said "only one in seventeen." Now Grimmelshausen saw to it that hardly anyone, in fact, no one, could miss the Christian teaching of *The False Messiah* and of his other Simplician tales, for the reader is lavishly treated to sermonizing in the Prefaces, at the end of the novels, and many times in between. By no stretch of the imagination can this Christian teaching be considered to be hidden or in the least difficult to grasp. The passage quoted from the Preface to *The Enchanted Bird's-Nest, Part II,* is therefore more puzzling than appears at first glance.

On the basis of a comprehensive inspection of the prefatory material appearing in old books, a critic has recently come to the conclusion that "the more daring the content [that an author offers in his writings to the reader] the more assiduously is the work morally fortified and buttressed in the Preface."[70] In licentious and sensational literature, pious tricks are sometimes played in the Preface in order "to bestow absolution and an honorable character even on the most ambiguous products."[71] The same critic called this phenomenon "the dialectic of the comic novel" and referred for illustration to *Moll Flanders,* the autobiography of a thief and prostitute, which Defoe presented in the Preface as an edifying book. These observations are sensible, but do they apply, as the critic believes, to *The Enchanted Bird's-Nest?* Recognizing that no other book in Grimmelshausen's work is morally and religiously justified in "such insistent, almost pleading manner" as is the second part of the *Bird's-Nest,* he exclaims, "No wonder, for nowhere is the 'style' so 'comic' as in the '*Bird's-Nest, II*' with its gross, erotic Messiahscenes in Amsterdam."[72] But this explanation is not convincing.

Siegfried Streller's reply to Hartmann's criticism, "Spiel oder Forschungsgegenstand," *op. cit.,* pp. 437–440. On "seventeen" see also Manfred Koschlig, "Der Bart-Krieg—Ein Werk Grimmelshausens," *Neophilologus,* Vol. 24 (1938), pp. 42 ff.

[70] Hans Ehrenzeller, *Studien zur Romanvorrede* (Bern: Francke Verlag, 1955), p. 78.

[71] *Ibid.,* p. 133.

[72] *Ibid.,* p. 78.

There are very many scenes in Grimmelshausen's works which are more comic and more erotic than is that of the seduction of Esther. The sexual activities overheard by the innocent young Simplicius in the goosebin, Simplicius in girls' clothing arousing homosexual desires in his mistress, the adventures of Simplicissimus as a male prostitute in Paris, the seduction of Courage as a young girl after she reveals her true sex to her master, the sadistic scene of the rape of Courage by many men in quick succession — all this is far more daringly erotic than anything to be found in *The False Messiah*. What is extraordinarily "comic" in this tale is the treatment of religious beliefs, and it is very likely indeed that it is the discussion of this topic, rather than the erotic passages, that needed moral support and buttressing in the Preface.

Unless we assume that Grimmelshausen grossly exaggerated, for rhetorical effect, the difficulty of understanding the plain, traditional, and frequent Christian pleas made in the Preface and many times elsewhere in the novel, we are thus obliged to consider the possibility that his treatment of religious belief itself may point to the answer. To put it differently, unless we make the absurd assumption that *The False Messiah* is written for readers of devotional tracts and sermons, we must put ourselves in the position of readers with different interests. Let us not forget that Leibniz admired *The Adventurous Simplicissimus*, while less intelligent readers in Grimmelshausen's time found the author a boring preacher of morality.[73] Grimmelshausen's treatment of Jewish beliefs is ambiguous enough to hoodwink those readers who attribute conventional anti-Jewish views to the author. Just as the joke in the story is not only on Esther, it does not seem to be exclusively on the Jews. In this connection it may be mentioned that at the very end of the novel, and thus at the end of the Simplician cycle of novels,

73 Leibniz' view of Grimmelshausen's *Simplicissimus* is stated in a letter to Duchess Sophie of Hannover, dated April 1688. The letter is quoted and discussed in Manfred Koschlig, "Das Lob des 'Francion' bei Grimmelshausen," *Jahrbuch der deutschen Schillergesellschaft*. Vol. 1 (Stuttgart: Alfred Kröner Verlag, 1957), pp. 30–73.

a Protestant parson and a Catholic priest try vainly to convert a Jew to Christianity. The latter replies that in so important a matter, where salvation hangs in the balance, he had better postpone his decision and remain a Jew until the two Christian shepherds and the representatives of other branches of Christianity have reached an understanding as to which of them has the key to salvation.

In the seventeenth century, no writer could dare to tell the story of the Divine Pretender in a Christian setting and ridicule Christian beliefs in the manner in which Grimmelshausen made fun of Jewish beliefs. Among the numerous works dealing with the ancient motif throughout the ages, there is only one in which the author, Morlini, had the poor taste to show the seducer in the assumed role of Christ, but this shocking adventure was turned into comedy in the last instant. Before the pretender reaches his goal, a companion of the villain, in the mask of Peter, beats the false Christ with clubs.[74] Thus Morlini brought the story to a tolerable ending, barely managing to turn blasphemy into farce.

Grimmelshausen wrote neither in the period of the Italian Renaissance nor in a literary climate of enlightenment. He was a man of the Baroque age formed by war, the Counter-Reformation, and religious conflict in Germany. He wrote for an audience from whose memory the extraordinary story of Sabbatai Zevi had not yet faded, so that he could safely and, as it were, naturally, put his tale of the divine pretender into a Jewish setting. Moreover, he was familiar with literary precedents which, though less distinguished in the world of letters than his own story, had done the same. But everything considered it is unlikely that *The False Messiah* is merely a humorous tale about Jewish beliefs. Perhaps a parallel to Grimmelshausen's prefatory remarks that "only one in seventeen readers" will understand him is to be found in Rabelais rather than in Defoe. Rabelais wished for himself a reader who like a dog

---

[74] Morlini, *Novellae* (Paris: 1855), No. 69 (1st ed.; Naples: 1520). Cf. Otto Weinreich, *op. cit.*, pp. 121–132.

would break open the bones of his book in order to suck its marrow.

To Laugh and To Weep

In one of the opening chapters of Grimmelshausen's novel *The Strange Skipinthefield,* three people are seated around a tavern table talking about the nature of man.[75] They are Simplicissimus, in some regards the author's fictional double; Skipinthefield, the happy-go-lucky comrade of Simplicissimus in his younger days during the Thirty Years War and now an old cripple with a wooden leg; and finally a Swiss clerk to whom Courage, the camp follower, dictated the story of her life. Simplicissimus is in an unusually solemn mood, moralizing more than in any other of Grimmelshausen's works and often rebuking Skipinthefield for his impatience and swearing. While the three men are talking, Simplicissimus overhears a misunderstanding that occurs between a customer and the tavern-keeper who has confused two similar-sounding words. This reminds Simplicissimus of an incident in his youth and suddenly he laughs out loud; but he refuses to tell his companions what it is that amuses him. Excessive laughter, he says, is foolish and sinful.

The Swiss tries to change his mind. Why not please an old comrade by telling him about the incident? Does not *The Adventurous Simplicissimus* contain many jests which the solemn man saw fit to include in the story of his life? In reply, Simplicissimus gives the usual justification of "the Simplician style of writing." The story of his life, he says, presents the truth, which almost no one likes to see or hear any more, in a pleasing garb so that it will be accepted, yet he might have erred in his autobiography by giving too free a rein to his sense of humor.

At this point, the Swiss mentions Seneca's preference for the laughing Democritus to the weeping Heraclitus and praises

---

[75] *Skipinthefield,* Ch. 3.

laughter as a gift of man with which he is born. Simplicissimus disagrees. "Both weeping and laughing belong to man, but it would be folly either to laugh all the time or to weep all the time . . . to everything there is a season."[76] This rebuttal with the help of Ecclesiastes[77] does not seem to satisfy Simplicissimus, for he adds that nevertheless man is born to weep rather than to laugh: Jesus Christ wept several times in his life, "but nowhere do the Holy Scriptures say that he ever laughed."[78] Seneca, a heathen, may have preferred laughing to weeping, but Christians have reason "to weep about the wickedness of man rather than to laugh about his foolishness."[79]

Skipinthefield is dumbfounded. He bursts out swearing that hearing all this he would wager that Simplicissimus had become a priest, but the Swiss behaves more graciously than the blustering old soldier. Since the writings of Simplicissimus (i.e., of Grimmelshausen), are full of moral teachings, he says, surely the incident that a moment ago came back to his mind and made him laugh must be "funny to hear and useful."[80] So, please, would he not tell it after all? Thereupon Simplicissimus yields. The story he tells is based on a misunderstanding involving the word "Sekret" (privy) and the name "Margreta." Sometime in the past when he was still a boy, a young officer in urgent need of relieving himself asked him for the way to the privy, but Simplicissimus, the boy, confusing "Sekret" with "Margreta," pointed to the wrong door. The officer rushed on and could not help passing water "in the sight and presence" of Margreta.[81]

The listeners around the tavern table laugh, evidently considering the story a good jest. What a pity, remarks the clerk, that Simplicissimus failed to mention this incident in the story of his life. The famous man replies that his book would have

[76] *Ibid.*, p. 17.

[77] Ecclesiastes 3:1.

[78] *Skipinthefield*, p. 17.

[79] *Loc. cit.* For the possible source of this observation in Thomas More's writings, cf. Chapter 14, note 43.

[80] *Skipinthefield*, p. 18.

[81] *Ibid.*, p. 19.

grown to unseemly size had he reported all the funny incidents that had ever happened to him. Besides, he regretted that he had told so many ludicrous tales in his book that now it was being read like *Til Eulenspiegel*, to waste time rather than to learn something useful. Then turning to the clerk, Simplicissimus asks what he thinks of *The Adventurous Simplicissimus*: has this book made him worse or better? To his question the young Swiss gives a remarkably modest reply, which might still serve as a warning to those critics who talk about the meaning of Grimmelshausen's Simplician writings too glibly. His judgment, says the clerk, is too feeble for scolding or praising the book.

This lively scene, including the conversation and the story Simplicissimus finally tells to his companions, contains many, if not all, the elements of Grimmelshausen's "sense of humor": the pun; stupidity (of the young Simplicius) leading to a misunderstanding and to unreasonable behavior (on the part of the young officer); an irrepressible physical need which gives nature a sudden, unexpected ascendency over nurture; coarseness; a misfortune — in this case only embarrassment — that may happen to anyone and causes others to laugh with a sense of relief because it did not happen to them. Finally, there is the thought-provoking sequence of events: immediately prior to his protest that religion is no joking matter and Christ had never laughed, Simplicissimus cannot suppress his own laughter, and immediately following his serious lecture in the "theological style," he does tell a coarse, funny story in the "Simplician style."

Grimmelshausen frequently distinguished between these two styles of writing. By theological style he meant a way of writing in which instruction and admonitions are given seriously and directly, as in a sermon, while the Simplician style is a way of comic writing, teaching those who need to learn by amusing them. In the second dedicatory poem of Grimmelshausen's conventional novel, *Dietwalt and Amelinde* (1670), it is said about the author of *The Adventurous Simplicissimus* that he "subtly hints at the truth through laughter," and this is as good a statement as any of the Simplician style and the general intention of Grimmelshausen's Simplician writings.

Telling the truth laughingly — *ridendo dicere verum* — is a form of writing with a long and venerable history. Jests were used for the purpose of serving serious moral purposes not only by medieval Christian preachers,[82] but also by ancient and modern satirists. As a satirist using "the Simplician style," Grimmelshausen was in the company of many other seventeenth-century moralists. Moscherosch, Grimmelshausen's predecessor as a satirist, pointed out at the end of his satire on the life of the soldier that it had been his main purpose to arouse hatred of vice and folly through humorous entertainment ("Schertz-vnd Lust-Reden"), since people neither liked nor tolerated a serious treatment of their faults.[83] Similarly, Logau said of truth that it was bitter but could be made sweet by laughter,[84] and the learned Christian moralist Johann Balthasar Schupp was "aware that the children of the world, as he called them, require another approach than the poor and the orphaned. The whores of Hamburg . . . the wealthy lechers, the self-willed great, will not listen to the serious preacher; they require the jest, the fable, and the truth told laughingly."[85]

Grimmelshausen's social satire is the most conventional aspect of his work; he began as a Christian moralist. His first book, *Der satyrische Pilgram* ("The Satirical Pilgrim"), published in 1666, criticizes the world in reference to the seven cardinal sins and the condemnation of these sins remains a major concern of Grimmelshausen's satire in the Simplician writings.[86] The literary devices for attacking the immorality of the world are satire,

---

[82] Ernst Robert Curtius, "Jest and Earnest in Medieval Literature," in *European Literature and the Latin Middle Ages* (New York: Pantheon Books, 1963), pp. 417 ff.

[83] Hans Michael Moscherosch, *Gesichte Philanders von Sittewald*, Felix Bobertag, editor (Berlin and Stuttgart: 1883), p. 398.

[84] Friedrich von Logau, *Sinngedichte* (Stuttgart: Bibliothek des Literarischen Vereins, 1872), Vol. 113, III. 4.84 and II. 6.83.

[85] Hildegarde Wiechert, *Johann Balthasar Schupp and the Baroque Satire in Germany* (New York: King's Crown Press, 1952), p. 106.

[86] Cf. Walter Ernst Schäfer, "Laster und Lastersystem bei Grimmelshausen," *Germanisch-Romanische Monatshefte,* Vol. 12 (July 1962, Neue Folge), pp. 233–243.

allegory, and serious preaching, i.e., stern warnings to the reader not to follow the example of the fools and sinners whose behavior the author has just described with gusto and in considerable detail.

Most famous is Grimmelshausen's parody of the stylish praise of a lady. The young fool Simplicius, asked to sing her praise, follows the traditional description of female beauty, but instead of comparing the eyes with the stars, the color of her skin with the whiteness of lilies, and thus paying conventional homage to her unearthly, divine beauty, the fool conjures up a series of grotesque images. He compares her hair to sausages and its yellow color to that of the excrement of young children; the whiteness of her brow reminds him of a skull "that has been exposed to the elements for many years," her black eyes are likened to the coal dust in front of his dad's stove, her firm breasts to a full udder of a she-goat, and her graceful figure makes him wonder whether she has had diarrhea for eight weeks. These "subhuman" comparisons[87] rely for comical effect in no small part on the violation of taboos observed in high society.

Grimmelshausen made fun also of the pretentious style of polite society. Some of these parodies, which appear in several of his works, may have lost their bite today; others are still singularly effective, particularly when, as in various scenes of *Courage, the Adventuress,* the author presents long-winded, stilted courtesies as mere preliminaries to sexual activity. Such activity then is the point at which the affectation of polite manners is pierced. For example, at one time, Courage describes the courteous advances of a young nobleman who has fallen in love with her and her way of meeting these advances with stylishly studied reserve; then she concludes, "In short, we behaved just like a couple of pigeons, locked up together by a pigeon-breeder for pairing; they wear themselves out until they finally get down to business. We did too."[88]

[87] Paul Gutzwiller, *Der Narr bei Grimmelshausen* (Bern: Francke Verlag, 1959), p. 99.
[88] *Grimmelshausens Courasche,* J. H. Scholte, editor (Halle: Max Niemeyer, 1923) (hereafter cited as *Courage*), Ch. 13. The quotation in

Like social or amorous pretensions, superstitious beliefs are treated very often as a laughing matter; laughter confronts these beliefs with the real, physical world. In one of Grimmelshausen's grotesque tales a village mob burns down a house because everyone believes that a young calf lying near the hearth has turned into a man-eating monster.[89] Often Grimmelshausen used puns in order to make a point. For example, early in *The Adventurous Simplicissimus* a hermit and a small boy, Simplicius, have a talk. To the hermit's consternation, the boy confuses "Kirche" (church) and "Kirsche" (cherry), "beten" (pray) and "Bett" (bed). Like Erasmus, Rabelais, and Shakespeare, Grimmelshausen knew that puns and plays on words are not only funny, but also that they lend themselves to saying by indirection something that could be said straightforwardly only in violation of moral or religious taboos. The great humorist, the child, and the court jester make people laugh by saying disarmingly what they want to say, so that neither zealots nor the powerful can silence them. Later in the conversation between the child and the hermit, Simplicius' version of the Paternoster includes the lines, "lead us not into no temptation, but deliver us from the kingdom and the power, and the glory, forever and ever." When the hermit then recites to him the correct text of the prayer and comes to the words, "and give us this day our daily bread," the boy interrupts him, "Oh, and cheese, too?"[90] It is difficult to unravel the various strands of humor woven into this dialogue. The foolishness of the child adds to the fun that mounts. So does the juxtaposition of religion and nature, of sacred and edible things with their faint suggestions of blasphemy innocently made by the boy to the pious old man.

Profoundly comical in a similar vein is the famous Jove episode in *The Adventurous Simplicissimus*, probably one of the

the text is from the English translation of this novel by Hans Speier, Grimmelshausen, *Courage, the Adventuress, and The False Messiah* (Princeton, N.J.: Princeton University Press, 1964).

[89] *Courage*, Ch. 26.
[90] *Simplicissimus*, p. 26.

stories by Grimmelshausen that has been studied more diligently than any other part of his work.[91] In none of the various interpretations has any significance been attached to the fact that the madman who believes that he is Jove, the Greek god, is the only figure in Grimmelshausen's works of whom it is explicitly said that he does not like to be laughed at. When Simplicissimus meets this strange man, he makes a deliberate effort to suppress laughing at him. Jove, on his part, is very serious. While he is capable of giving good practical advice to Simplicissimus on occasion, in moments of madness he fancies himself to be a divine being. As such he presents to his listeners an imposing and extraordinarily interesting vision of a world in which the Christian churches are reunited and peace on earth is established by a German hero. When his flight of fancy has taken Jove to sublime heights, Simplicissimus notices that the god lets his breeches down "and scratches himself because he is plagued by fleas." In view of this sobering detail alone, it is difficult to contend that Grimmelshausen believed in the possibility of unifying the Christian churches and of attaining German national grandeur. But precisely this interpretation has been advanced in all seriousness by at least one distinguished scholar.[92] In baroque art and literature, ancient gods often appear as allegories of Christian imagination; conversely, a hermit is often the symbol of a sage. In the light of this tradition, attention must be paid to the fact that Jove says that his power depends on the will of "the great numen."[93] Grimmels-

[91] On the meaning of "Jove" in *Simplicissimus* see J. H. Scholte, "Der 'Simplicissimus Teutsch' als verhüllte Religionssatire" in *Der Simplicissimus und sein Dichter* (Tübingen: Max Niemeyer, 1950), pp. 13 ff.; Julius Petersen, "Grimmelshausen's "Teutscher Held,' " *Euphorion*, Vol. 17 (1924), pp. 1–30; Günther Weydt, "Don Quijote Teutsch," *Euphorion*, Vol. 51 (1957), pp. 250–270; Manfred Koschlig, "Das Lob des 'Francion' bei Grimmelshausen," *Jahrbuch der deutschen Schillergesellschaft*, Vol. 1 (1957), pp. 30–73; and James Hyde, *The Religious Thought of Johann Jacob Christoffel von Grimmelshausen as Expressed in the Simplicianische Schriften* (Dissertation, Indiana University, 1960), [typewritten]).

[92] Julius Petersen, *loc. cit.*
[93] *Simplicissimus*, p. 208.

hausen presented this Jove as a fleabitten, half-mad son of
the godhead, who does not like to be laughed at, but believes
that he knows how the world can be saved (by the sword) and
how the churches can be reunited.

There are also a few stories in *Ewigwährender Kalender*
(*Everlasting Almanac*), which illustrate the skeptical function
of Grimmelshausen's humor.

> At a gay party the question came up as to what were the three
> best things on earth. When it was Simplicissimus's turn, he said,
> "Eating, drinking, and sleeping; for if we were deprived of any
> of these, we would be done for." He was contradicted by a
> clergyman who maintained that praying is better and more neces-
> sary, since it lifts the soul up to God and brings it closer to its
> origin. To this Simplicissimus replied, "Your words contradict
> me, it is true, but your deeds confirm that I am right, since you
> practice the three things I have mentioned more frequently and
> more gladly than praying, fasting, and waking."[94]

At first sight this anecdote seems to be a relatively harmless
joke at the expense of a clergyman, but the humor springs from
the contrast of manifestly solid animal needs with the lofty
commands of religion. More powerful, and indeed closer to
blasphemy, is the impact of the following story.

> A woman belonging to the reformed church, who knew her
> Bible by heart, participated in a disputation at L(ippstadt) held
> at the dinner table. She asked so many questions of those who
> were present that no one could answer her any more, or perhaps
> no one wanted to, lest he offend the rich, distinguished lady.
> Hence, she had the floor all to herself. This was tiresome to Sim-
> plicissimus and in order to shut her up, he asked her who had
> been the father of the Apostles James and John. When she re-
> plied, "Zebedee," he said, "That should be enough for you
> women, and don't try to get more."[95]

The point is that at that time "Zebedee" was an euphemism for
penis. To be sure, this anecdote expresses Grimmelshausen's
antifeminine views, which he shared with many moralists of his

---

[94] Grimmelshausen, *Ewigwährender Kalender*, Engelbert Hegaur,
editor (Munich: Albert Langen Verlag, 1925), p. 204.
[95] *Ibid.*, p. 202.

age, as well as his impatience with idle learning; but the sting of the story is the rejection of the woman's interest in the Holy Scriptures by an earthy allusion to sex. Similar in spirit, yet even more daring, is the following anecdote.

> In Phillipsburg, a soldier's wife sat together with a Jewess; she was sewing and at the same time talking about religion. The Christian woman wanted to draw in Simplicissimus to make her point, but he answered, "I think it would be best if you left disputations alone, because you are already agreed on the main article of faith: both of you regard highly the resurrection of the flesh."[96]

While the double meaning of "Zebedee" in the previous anecdote permits only a weak blasphemy, the second story is an outrage. It substitutes the sexual connotation of the phrase, "the resurrection of the flesh," for its sacred meaning. The pun is not Grimmelshausen's invention. It can be found in the *Decameron* and in Rabelais' *Gargantua and Pantagruel*. Donne, too, in one of his *Elegies*, made use of the sexual imagery that appeared in the pun.[97] The joke may well have reached Grimmelshausen by oral tradition through which jests of this kind presumably traveled from generation to generation and from upper to lower classes; the conflict between nature and religion is enduring.

Like the ambiguous treatment of omniscience and omnipotence in *The Enchanted Bird's-Nest* and of the birth of a Messiah, these stories and anecdotes — and the Simplician writings contain many more — throw doubt on the contention, made by almost all critics,[98] that Grimmelshausen was a deeply religious man. This contention must be regarded as controversial, whereas the author's rare gift as a story teller, his irony,

---

[96] *Ibid.*, p. 213.
[97]   "We easily know
         By this these Angels from an evil sprite,
         Those set our hairs, but these our flesh upright."
                    (Donne's nineteenth *Elegie*)
[98] An important exception is the book by Paul Gutzwiller, *op. cit.*

his delight in portraying human follies, his insistence on giving nature its due, his grim humor — all these are indisputable.

Close reading of *The Adventurous Simplicissimus*, including the accounts of the hero's three conversions, raises further questions about the depth of Grimmelshausen's religious faith; so does a careful perusal of *Courage, the Adventuress*.[99] At the very least, it seems certain that Grimmelshausen was deeply troubled by the government of God whom Simplicissimus addresses at one point as "a dark light."[100] It is for this dark light that the halberdier gives up the nest and renounces a career of thwarting or punishing evil and helping the needy; it is in this dark light that, converted, he decides to do penance for his sins and to use for this purpose tainted money magically stolen by an evil woman. It is in this dark light that the merchant makes amends for having used the nest in playing God and enjoying love. He bribes Erasmus to marry the girl who has been defrauded of her virginity, and Erasmus, the pious Christian who, shocked by the impiety of the merchant, preached repentance to him, and wins his bride by a lie that is as convenient as it is big. This lie also serves to bring about Esther's conversion. And Esther's new Christian name is Mary.

Grimmelshausen said in respect to his main novel that he

---

[99] Cf. Chs. 14 and 15 above.

[100] "Ach allerhöchstes Gut! du wohnest so im Finstern Liecht! Dass man vor Klarheit gross/ den grossen Glantz kan sehen nicht." (*Continuatio des abentheurlichen Simplicissimi*, J. H. Scholte, editor [Halle: Max Niemeyer, 1939, p. 107]). J. H. Scholte, "Das finstere Licht," in his *Der Simplicissimus und sein Dichter* (Tübingen: Max Niemeyer, 1950), pp. 81–106, has shown that this verse was taken from a poem by Vittorio Colonna. Grimmelshausen found it in the German translation (1619) by Aegidius Albertinus of Tomaso Garzoni's *Piazza Universale*, a compendium from which he often borrowed material for his writings. Scholte has pointed out that Grimmelshausen changed the words in Albertinus "unerforschliches Licht" (*inaccessibil luce*) in the original to "finsteres Licht." Scholte regards this interesting change as proof of Grimmelshausen's closeness to medieval Christian doctrines, Neo-Platonism and Cusanus (*op. cit.*, p. 103). More convincingly, Gutzwiller has interpreted this stanza as "Schauer vor der Unerreichbarkeit Gottes," and as a substitute for true love of God (Gutzwiller, *op. cit.*, p. 69).

gave nature its due in his description of the world.[101] He described it laughingly but with defiant insistence on the horrors of natural life, its inconstancy, its filth, and its violence.[102] Perhaps Grimmelshausen's clear perception of human folly and evil made it possible for him to accept God as a dark light. Perhaps his grim laughter at the victory of nature over "good usances" and religious dogmas gave meaning to his work and some comfort to him as it gave pleasure to his readers and something more to "one out of every seventeen" of them.

[101] The reference to Simplicissimus as "a natural man" occurs in his talk with Jove (*Simplicissimus*, p. 210). Grimmelshausen's claim that he gave nature its due in *The Adventurous Simplicissimus* appears in the dedicatory poem he wrote to *Dietwalt und Amelinde:* "Er beschreibt so Naturäl diese Welt sammt ihren Sachen" (Grimmelshausen, *Dietwalts und Amelinden anmuthige Lieb- und Leids-beschreibung*, Rolf Tarot, editor [Tübingen: Max Niemeyer, 1967], p. 100.)

[102] "Die Gottferne des menschlichen Daseins lässt sich in jedem seiner Werke nachweisen." (Paul Gutzwiller, *op. cit.*, p. 89.)

Index

325